DIGITAL CHARACTER DEVELOPMENT

THEORY AND PRACTICE

SECOND EDITION

DIGITAL CHARACTER DEVELOPMENT

THEORY AND PRACTICE

SECOND EDITION

ROB O'NEILL

CRC Press
Taylor & Francis Group
Boca Raton London New York

CRC Press is an imprint of the
Taylor & Francis Group, an **informa** business

AN A K PETERS BOOK

CRC Press
Taylor & Francis Group
6000 Broken Sound Parkway NW, Suite 300
Boca Raton, FL 33487-2742

© 2016 by Taylor & Francis Group, LLC
CRC Press is an imprint of Taylor & Francis Group, an Informa business

No claim to original U.S. Government works

Printed on acid-free paper
Version Date: 20150707

International Standard Book Number-13: 978-1-4822-5077-0 (Hardback)

Visit the Taylor & Francis Web site at
http://www.taylorandfrancis.com

and the CRC Press Web site at
http://www.crcpress.com

This book is dedicated to every artist who ever had the honor and pleasure of working at Pacific Data Images (PDI), 1980–2015

Contents

List of Figures

List of Tables

Acknowledgments

THE SECOND EDITION OF THIS BOOK would not have been possible without all the hard work, innovation, and creative engineering by those who developed the ideas summarized within. The thoughtful reviews by Terran Boylan and Adán Peña added valuable insights and critical thoughts that made this a better book. I cannot thank them enough for the time they invested in reviewing versions of the manuscript.

I owe a huge debt to all the members, past and present, of the Character Technical Direction crew at DreamWorks Animation (PDI and Glendale) for their friendship, camaraderie, and ever-present desire to educate at every level. Special thanks to modeler/rigger extraordinaire Lee Wolland for the use of his immaculate human model for the creation of model screenshots and to Mark Snoswell, president of the Computer Graphics Society, for his generous donation of the cgHuman for the creation of muscle images in this book. His model set is an amazing resource for study and use in production.

I owe a huge debt to Dr. Bonnie Gustav of Brooklyn College (retired) for getting me hooked on biological anthropology and the evolutionary anatomy that goes with it, and to Anezka Sebek of Parsons School of Design for helping me harness that into a career in animation. The first edition of this book still owes a huge thanks for the support of my colleagues and students in the Department of Digital Arts at Pratt Institute who provided much of the inspiration to write this text. Extra special thanks still go to my former graduate research assistants at the Pratt Digital Arts Research Lab, Paris Mavroidis and George Smaragdis, whose hard work is still reflected in many of the images in this book. Those guys have gone on to have continuously amazing careers.

The book was made so much better by the inclusion of interviews with the talented and generous Terran Boylan, Stephen Candell, Josh Carey, Brad Clark, Daniel Dawson, Robert Helms, David Hunt-Bosch, Cara Malek, Stephen Mann, Tim McLaughlin, Ken Perlin, Wade Ryer, Nico Scapel, Javier Solsona, and Lee Wolland. Their views are their own and they in no way endorse any of the other material in the book, but I hope they like it.

Thanks to my parents, grandparents, brother, and sister for fostering my sense of imagination and humor, two critical skills for working in animation production. Extra special and most important thanks go to Jane and Hayden, who supported me writing this second edition even when it meant long nights and weekend days away.

Introduction to the First Edition

Digital characters are a driving force in the entertainment industry today. Every animated film and video game production spends a large percentage of its resources and time on advancing the quality of the digital characters inhabiting the world being created. We have entered an era when digital characters have reached a level of sophistication that has prompted some critics to question if a digital actor can win an Academy Award for acting. As artificial intelligence and behavioral animation become more integrated with hand-animated entities, we will see a dramatic increase in the realism and interactivity of these characters. Practitioners of the subject will also require a deeper understanding of the underlying conceptual foundation as the complexity of the technology increases. The field of character technology has matured into a topic that spans the realms of anatomy, animation, computer science, performance, and behavioral psychology. The contemporary uses of digital characters are varied and range from entertainment to biomedical, industrial simulation, and beyond. This book is an overview of the history, theory, and methods for creating digital characters. Many books cover the step-by-step creation of digital characters using a particular piece of software. This book forgoes existing software and deals with the concepts from a software-agnostic point-of-view.

Recently, characters such as Gollum from *The Lord of the Rings* series (2001–2004) and Davy Jones from the *Pirates of the Caribbean* series (2006–2007) have both been discussed with regard to earning awards for achievement in acting. Almost more compelling, a recent panel entitled The Biology of King Kong, part of the 2006 Tribeca Film Festival, included a discussion on how the titular character in *King Kong* (2005) was incredibly true to life and believable as a real gorilla. Panel member Roger Fouts, codirector of the Chimpanzee and Human Communication Institute, discussed how pleased he was that the rise in technology and artistry has allowed for digital doubles and replacements for roles that were usually reserved for trained animals. While most critics are waiting for a believable human replacement, there is no better compliment for the team that created this photoreal digital character and no better indicator of the potential of character technology.

Rob O'Neill
Brooklyn, NY, 2008

Introduction to the Second Edition

AS WITH THE FIRST EDITION, this book is an overview of the history, theory, and methods for creating digital characters from a software-agnostic point-of-view. Since writing the first edition of *Digital Character Development*, published in 2008, much has changed for digital characters in games and films. Not only have they become ubiquitous and appear in more films and games than can be counted, but the quality has become outstanding. I gave a lecture on digital actors at the Art Center in Pasadena in 2013, and it dawned on me (during the lecture) that the notion of "high resolution" was a moving target and what we were starting to talk about was "full resolution," which is us. Research has dug deeper into capturing the microscopic motion of the human eye and the elastic principles of skin to give us better approximations as we try to navigate around the creepiness that sometimes emerges from seeing digital characters into characters that surprise and delight us. At this point, we are closer to capturing and representing the magic that is life through digital characters, and the challenge of making a single compelling character has expanded to making an entire cast of believable characters. Digital characters walk seamlessly next to human actors in films on a regular basis without anyone noticing, and these characters are also expanding their roles in entertainment beyond films and games. We are also using them to capture a moment in time and to bring back someone no longer with us. A perfect example of this was the 2012 performance of Virtual 2Pac at Cochella Music Festival when a ghostly (hologram-like) digital double of the late rapper Tupac Shakur created the illusion of him performing alongside Snoop Dogg. This surprised spectators at the shows and later online and continues to be a watershed moment when digital characters challenged ethics and expectations by providing an audience with a performance by an artist they thought they would never see in person. I imagine this is only the tip of the iceberg for this idea.

Rob O'Neill
Los Angeles, California

I

An Introduction to Digital Characters

CHAPTER 1

Overview

1.1 OVERVIEW OF THIS BOOK

This book is about *character technology*. Character technology is the merging of animation principles, requirements, and three-dimensional (3D) computer graphics technology into a set of concepts and methodologies resulting in an animatable character.

This book is intended to provide an introductory overview of the theory and practice of digital character development, often called character rigging, from a software agnostic point of view. As a starting-off point for more complicated mathematical discussions and more artistic exploration, this text straddles the line between the arts and sciences that are required for the creation of compelling digital characters. In the course of this discussion, digital characters created for both games and films are addressed. As this subject is a moving target, updates, errata, and additional resources are compiled at http://www.charactertechnology.com.

We start with the evolution and history of digital characters. This is critical to the understanding of how characters are developed, alongside the techniques and technologies for creating them. We then begin the process of building characters from the inside out. Character setup (often referred to as character rigging) starts by defining the anatomical considerations required and how they relate to the structure of the character motion system (Figure 1.1) or the mechanical architecture that drives the model. At this point, we will deal with the control structure for the motion system. The motion system defines the motion architecture for the character and provides the interface to animation. From there, the look of the character in motion is defined by the deformation system—the planning and implementation of techniques that sculpt the character's shape—as the motion system drives the transformation of the points on the model. Much of the life and emotion of a digital character is read through the face, and while facial setup is a mix of motion and deformation systems, the issues intrinsic to this aspect

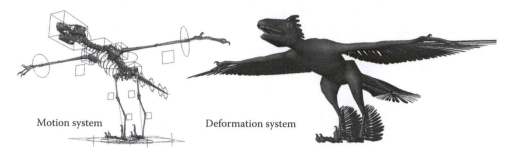

FIGURE 1.1 Screen capture of a character motion and deformation system. Character by George Smaragdis and Rob O'Neill.

of character development requires specific attention. In the areas of motion systems, deformation systems, and facial setup, we cover techniques currently in use by mixing descriptive text with algorithms and graphical representations of code for potential implementation.

Digital characters would be nothing without the means of moving them. Section III covers keyframe strategies and curve interpolation, with an emphasis on performance through traditional techniques. This is followed-up by motion capture and how human performers are stepping into the shoes of digital characters. In addition, code often also drives motion, so procedural animation, artificial intelligence, and multicharacter systems used for crowd simulations are a common component of modern character development. Finally, interactive characters—characters that are controlled in real-time by a user—are considered with a focus on the setup and limitations for characters created for game and nongame-related interactive media.

We conclude with the future of digital characters in which we look into research questions that remain outstanding and some challenges for work beyond them.

1.2 DEFINING DIGITAL CHARACTERS

The word "animation" basically means "physically or graphically moving," derived from latin *anima* which refers to living beings, spirit, and feeling, and the Greek *anemos* for wind and breath. An animated character could be said to have had the divine wind (animus) breathed into it. A digital character can be defined as an animated entity that has been brought to life using a computer. These characters are often found in films, television, interactive media projects, and in almost all contemporary video games. The creation of these entities can employ off-the-shelf software or custom programming to attain the desired results. Nomenclature for this digital species is diverse and continually evolving. "Digital actors," "virtual actors," "vactors," and "synthespians" have all been used, but all these imply a connection to acting, and thus humans. The term "avatar" has also been used as a catchall phrase, but this term has evolved into a representation of a player or human inhabitant in an interactive system. The film *Avatar* (2009) took the term avatar and extended it to someone interacting with the world as another person. Not surprisingly, in that film, a human took on the avatar of a fantastic digital character.

For the purposes of this book, we will refer to computer-generated entities as *digital characters* to encompass all imaginable forms and acting abilities, with an emphasis on 3D animation media.

An interesting distinction has been made in the film industry between digital characters and digital creatures [1], the main differentiation being that of performance. A digital beast attacking a group of tourists would be described as a digital creature, whereas a compelling gorilla who falls in love with the film's starlet would be described as a digital character. This distinction comes from the amount of work required in creating the character, the amount of screen time, and the viewer's connection with the character on screen. This distinction actually raises the idea of scalable design or classes of digital characters where there is a wide range of requirements for characters in the film. However, this book ignores the distinction between digital characters and digital creatures, as the underlying functionality and setup is the same.

Creating a digital character with the ability to produce a rich performance requires the interaction of a number of subjects. In a digital space, this process walks the line between aspects of art and science, using technology as a bridge. This book covers all facets of digital character development, but focuses primarily on the realm of what has been traditionally called "character rigging" or "character setup." This is the process of creating the architecture, called the "rig" (Figure 1.2), and methodologies required for animating the motion of the character, by means of user-set keyframes or procedural control. This is a crucial role that requires knowledge of both anatomy and animation. With increasing complexity of characters needed for various forms of media, a knowledge of programming to reinvent or extend the available tools is crucial.

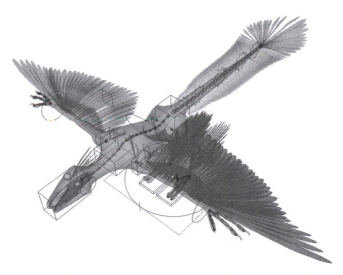

FIGURE 1.2 Character rig and model. Character by George Smaragdis and Rob O'Neill.

1.3 ROLES IN THE CREATION OF DIGITAL CHARACTERS

There are many tasks when it comes to digital character development. While job titles are constantly evolving and technological growth empowers individuals to accomplish more on their own, it is worthwhile to discuss some of the roles associated with the creation of digital characters. At the start of production, the art team comprised of concept artists and character designers who describe the overall look of the characters. Character modelers then take the character designs developed by the art team and build a set of digital sculptures, or "models," based on production specifications for size, proportion, style, and geometric surface type. Once approved, this model is handed off to the position most benefiting from this book, the character technical director. Often called a "rigger," "character setup artist," or "creature developer," the character technical director's title at some studios may even be condensed down to something as nondescript as technical director, but the role remains the same. Character technical directors are responsible for taking the 3D model and adding all of the "bones" and "muscles" that allow an animator to move the character in a predictable manner and deform those surfaces in a manner consistent with the aesthetics of the production. They are charged with designing and installing the motion system, which provides the architecture and control structures for how the rig is animated, as well as the deformation system, which defines how the model is affected by the motion system and the animation that drives it. Other components such as dynamic cloth, hair, and accessories (jewelry, weapons, etc.) associated with the characters are often also the domain of this role.

Once rigging is completed, that character is handed off to animators and the technicians responsible for attaching motion to the rig, but the character technical director will continue to oversee the maintenance of the rig until the end of production. In the early stages of a production, character technical directors may spend time researching and developing new techniques for improving their character pipeline and the workflows and methods by which they create and deliver character rigs, with an eye toward specific challenges of future productions.

1.4 CONCLUSION

Digital characters are developed using various techniques, collectively called character technology. This technology is developed in partnership with a studio's research and development (R&D) department or harnessed from third-party software and implemented by the character technical director based on the needs of the production. This book serves as an overview of the concepts and the technology behind digital characters to foster the development of innovative techniques and compelling performances.

FURTHER READING

McLaughlin, T. Taxonomy of Digital Creatures: Interpreting Character Designs as Computer Graphics Techniques. *SIGGRAPH'05: ACM SIGGRAPH 2005 Courses*, 2005.

CHAPTER 2

Contemporary Issues Related to Digital Characters

T HE CHALLENGE OF CREATING a compelling digital character that looks and behaves in an appealing manner is a tremendous undertaking. Digital characters share the same difficulties inherent in traditional (hand-drawn) animation, but the trend toward realism presents many additional challenges. In this section, we will examine the design decisions that must be acknowledged in the development of a digital character and the pitfalls that can arise along the way. Characters created for live action integration and those for fully animated productions share the same challenges, and some of the best lessons come from the worlds of illustration and robotics. Also, in this section, we will look at how digital characters are being used in important areas such as education and user surveys, where the delicate connection between the character and the user makes all the difference between a successful exchange and an off-putting experience.

2.1 VIEWER PERCEPTION AND THE UNCANNY VALLEY

It's all in the eyes ...

The perception of digital characters is determined by the reaction of the viewer to the look and performance of the character on screen. While a poor performance by a human actor may result in laughter or snickering by the audience, the unconvincing performance by a digital character in a live action film has a much more jarring effect, particularly when that character is supposed to be realistic. Conversely, animated characters with a high degree of abstraction or a cartoon-like appearance are generally more accepted by the audience, as the demands of reality are diminished. That being said, the stakes are higher for characters which must be

FIGURE 2.1 Abstraction of the human face by Scott McCloud. (Reprinted from McCloud, S., *Understanding Comics: The Invisible Art*, copyright 1993, 1994 by Scott McCloud. With permission of HarperCollins Publishers.)

integrated with live human actors in real-life situations, as they must rely on complex subtlety and nuanced expressions to match their living counterparts.

Writer and comic book theorist Scott McCloud [2] has distilled the distinction between character realism and abstraction. An abstract character with a simplified face has the ability to emote more clearly via the process of amplification through simplification. By reducing details, we are allowed to focus on the specific features required to create a performance and thus the expression is amplified (Figure 2.1). We have seen this in the incredible popularity of animated characters, such as Mickey Mouse and Bugs Bunny, where their simplified designs have the ability to captivate a wide range of audiences.

When it comes to digital characters, much of the discussion with regard to believability and the ability to forge a connection with the human observer is rooted in the study of robotics. Long before digital characters were at a level of sophistication to even address this subject, engineers were experimenting with the visual representation of emotion in real-world robots. Humanoid robots and even animatronics share many similarities with digital characters, from the computational aspects of kinematics to their perception by viewers. The connection between them can be encapsulated by the observations of Japanese roboticist Masahiro Mori, who in 1970 raised the idea of the "Uncanny Valley" [3].

Mori's concept states that as we approach a realistic visage of a human, the familiarity level plummets. The drop generally takes place at around the 75% point towards realism and we experience a drop-off into a familiarity valley where the connection to the entity becomes more akin to how we perceive zombies and prosthetics (Figure 2.2). This is a common issue that, for the most part, cannot be expressed by the viewer, but is endemic to digital characters. We as humans are naturally accustomed to the nuances and idiosyncrasies of a living person. What the "Uncanny Valley" describes is how we perceive the small percentage of "nonhumanness" in

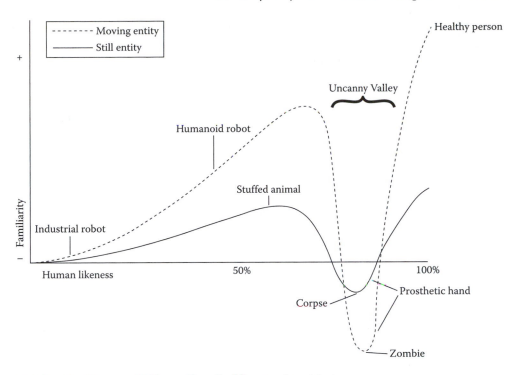

FIGURE 2.2 The Uncanny Valley as described by Masahiro Mori.

a character and fixate on that. The other details become irrelevant to us and our senses tell us something is unnatural about what we are seeing. We focus on the lack of skin translucency, the stillness of the eyes, or the slightly robotic motion. The character that was once appealing has given way to an animated corpse and our sense of familiarity plunges. It is interesting to note that animated and still objects adhere to a similar pattern, but animated entities come much closer to tricking the viewer.

This small percentage that defines the Uncanny Valley is what animators and roboticists are charged with overcoming when they are in the process of creating something that is supposed to be "alive." This is not a simple feat. At some point, most of us have experienced an "uneasy" feeling when watching a digital character. Perhaps in watching a film with a character that you were supposed to connect with, you felt as if that character was lifeless, not in a stiff, poorly animated way, but in a manner that can only be described as "creepy." The most cited examples of this phenomenon are the films *Final Fantasy* (2001), *Polar Express* (2004), and *Beowulf* (2007). All of the films incorporated motion capture, and each stand as a production achievement in many ways, but it was discrepancies in the character's faces that created the most unease, the so-called "dead-eye syndrome." The real/unreal notion was even discussed by the late film critic Roger Ebert in his review of *Final Fantasy* (2001) [4]:

> Not for an instant do we believe that Dr. Aki Ross, the heroine, is a real human. But we concede she is lifelike, which is the whole point. She has an eerie presence that is at once subtly unreal and yet convincing.

The question then remains, how do we combat the lack of subtlety in these characters that causes viewers to have such an unsettled reaction to them? Part of the answer lies in the design of the character and the style of the film. As we have seen, when possible, a more stylized character will communicate easier to its audience. It is not as simple as replicating what we look like that makes a character convincing. If we are the full resolution version of what we are trying to create, what are the elements that we need to nail in the lower resolution versions of ourselves in order to have them read convincingly?

The essence of a photoreal character generally comes across most easily when stylistic choices are made that accentuate character attributes, such as the eyes. In real life, the eyes are one of the main conduits of communication to the viewer. A character's expressions should read as well in a still pose as they do in motion. Motion, however, adds a level of complexity as this is where you get into behavior and the psychology of the character. The animator is responsible for what is going on inside the character's head. This is accomplished through a combination of the broad and subtle actions of the character. Behavioral cues that trigger a negative response come about from behavior that is categorized as abnormal. In the following sections, we raise questions about how the style and use of a character inform its setup in addition to taking a brief look at how we perceive people in day-to-day interactions and the notion of abnormal psychology. To help look at this from another perspective, we discuss how psychologists use digital characters in their own research as "interview avatars."

2.2 HOW DO STYLE AND USE DICTATE SETUP?

When planning the character setup for a project, the overall style must be analyzed and the manner of motion planned out. Although most character setups tend to be complex, the requirements of the setup are predicated on the style of motion required of that character for the project. This is especially true for characters expected to behave in a more stylized, cartoon-derived manner. Often the difference comes down to the deformation stage, which dictates the shape and profile of the character in a pose. Such decisions could result in the character deforming in either a realistic manner (adhering to a realistic anatomy) or a cartoon "rubber hose" style. The "rubber hose" style of animation was initiated with Oswald the Lucky Rabbit, created by Ub Iwerks and Walt Disney in the 1920s, and exemplified by the Olive Oyl character in the *Popeye* cartoon series created by Fleischer Brothers. Other examples of this style of animation include early Mickey Mouse and Bugs Bunny cartoons. The difference between cartoon "rubber hose" animation and that of more realistic motion is the presence or lack of definable visible anatomical structures, such as bones. Complex digital characters created for integration with live action feature films often contain an underlying structure that mimics the skeletal and musculature needed if that character actually existed, no matter how fantastic. For the readers with knowledge of character setup, this discussion of "bones," versus the lack thereof, is referring to the visual anatomical and kinematic representation and not the underlying methodology used to setup the character. Although it is assumed that a realistic character with bones and muscles is more complicated than the malleability of a "rubber hose" digital character, they both have their own challenges. The notion of volume preservation in both scenarios is one of the major concerns for a character rigger. Anatomical characters typically represent volume changes through the bulging and relaxation of muscles. Cartoon-styled characters have their volume managed in terms of squash and stretch, a basic animation principle that dictates that no matter how extreme the deformation, the volume of the character should be maintained.

When starting a new project, these basic questions need to be addressed during pre-production:

1. What is the overall visual style or genre of the project?

2. Is this a realistic character whose underlying anatomy visually reacts to motion?

3. Do the character's body and limbs need to squash and stretch with motion?

4. What are the key elements of the project's design language that need to be realized for all of the characters?

Hopefully, these questions are asked and answered before character rigging begins. Many of these questions can be answered by developing or consulting concept illustrations of the character.

The intended use of a digital character also has a tremendous impact on the design and architecture of how it is built. The difference between characters built for games and film animation is very different (yet becoming more similar every year), but there are levels and distinctions within these two uses that will also influence setup. The distinction between lead, secondary, and tertiary characters plays a part, as does whether a character in a game is going to be controlled by the player or not. There are limitations to real-time game engines that will influence how the character is developed. Because film characters are not interacted with their final form, there can be a complexity distinction between what the animator interacts with and what is rendered. Thus, with careful construction, there is no limitation to what can be built into a film character, budget notwithstanding. Some basic questions can be asked of the production to determine how character usage will impact setup.

1. In what software will the character be animated?

2. Is the character intended for rendered animation or a game engine?

3. If the character is to be used within a game engine, what types of deformations does it support and what are the limitations with regard to number of joints?

The challenges that result in answering all of these questions are the topic of this book. Beyond form and function, we also need to consider acting and the psychology of digital characters to understand how we relate to them based on how they relate to us.

2.3 CASE STUDIES IN THE PSYCHOLOGY OF DIGITAL CHARACTERS

A number of psychologists have begun to study digital characters with research topics ranging from how they interact with humans to how effective digital characters are as interviewers for survey use. This research offers additional insights into how artists can transcend the "Uncanny Valley" in the creation of digital characters. The psychology of a digital character allows us to think objectively about our own behavior and let that inform how we perceive our digital counterparts. The full depth of this subject is outside the scope of this book to go into detail, but worth a brief discussion as it is increasingly informing the way digital characters are designed and animated.

We are arguably wired from before birth to instinctively recognize how a human acts, down to the smallest details. Any clue that something is not behaving as expected makes us assume there is something out of the ordinary about that thing. This is a steep challenge for digital characters and falls into the category of abnormal psychology, the discipline that studies people consistently unable to adapt and function effectively in a variety of conditions. Digital characters are inherently abnormal. It takes tremendous nuance to overcome the smallest pathology to create a character whose actions do not deviate from what would be considered "normal." Character pathology is often discussed with regard to pure character motion, where popping knees or an unnatural stance can make something appear injured, when in fact it is purely just poorly animated motion or flawed rigging. Pathology at a character's performance level can have a much more damaging effect on the viewer's experience, as noted above. Viewers often describe the motion and expressions of digital characters as "too perfect." The implication here is that a little bit of idiosyncrasy is actually part of the recipe that makes us human. Striking the balance between character traits and character flaws is a delicate line.

A deeper, sustained connection to digital characters is required when it comes to interactive media that strives to teach or collect important information. With this in mind, we can look at situations where digital characters are being tested in the realms of education and automated interview situations.

Educational software strives to teach lessons through new forms of interaction and connection with their users. The idea that a digital character in the role of a teacher, adviser, or guide could be compelling enough to create a strong connection with a student is an exciting and active subject of research. Preliminary systems are already in place in children's software, agent-based teachers for medical situations, military training, and even at the simple level as help agents for commercial software. Research demonstrates that the use of digital characters has many benefits, as discussed by James C. Lester and his group at North Carolina State University [5]. This group works to capitalize on the emotional connection we, particularly children, feel toward digital characters.

> Because of the immediate and deep affinity that children seem to develop for these characters, the potential pedagogical benefits they provide are perhaps even exceeded by their motivational benefits. By creating the illusion of life, lifelike computer characters may

significantly increase the time that children seek to spend with educational software, and recent advances in affordable graphic hardware are beginning to make the widespread distribution of realtime animation technology a reality. (p. 269)

Lester [6] has demonstrated in other experiments a phenomenon he has termed the "persona effect," the positive response and sense of engagement shown by users when interacting with an animated agent. The conjecture is that, particularly for children, animated pedagogical agents will have a higher success rate than similar software without animated agents. It can be hypothesized that children are more accustomed to seeing animated characters than adults. It is also possible that their ability to recognize nuanced behavior is not as tuned as an adult's, making them more forgiving of the shortcomings of current digital characters and therefore able to have more meaningful interaction with them.

Winslow Burleson [7], during his work at MIT, used sensors and input devices to look at the subtle nonverbal cues that can make digital characters more adept at social situations. He found that in interactions with pedagogical agents, as in human–human interaction, responsiveness can be enhanced by nonverbal social mirroring, the imitation of another's nonverbal cues. By using a 4-second delay, the character's mirroring behavior is not consciously detected by users, yet this is a short enough time for the mirroring to have a social effect. The use of animated agents in education is an ongoing research topic. Similarly, digital characters in the role of interview agents is another application helping us probe deeper into the nuanced relationship between digital characters and humans.

Collecting information via human-to-human interviews is a time-consuming and costly endeavor. The process is also ripe with sources of error and can generally be viewed as inconvenient for the respondent (the person answering the questions). However, human interviewers have been shown to result in higher response rates and improved respondent comprehension over questionnaires. Questionnaires, on the other hand, incur lower costs, increased privacy, and convenience and control for respondents. The hope of using a digital character as an interviewer is that they will actually reap the benefits of both the human interviewer and a questionnaire. The nonjudgemental, anonymous aspect of digital characters may also have some benefit. But what are the drawbacks of this forward thinking technology? Frederick G. Conrad and his group at the University of Michigan are developing digital conversation agents for use in interviewing scenarios. Conrad and Michael Schober [8], of New School University, held workshops, entitled, "Envisioning the Survey Interview of the Future," intended to expose survey methodologists to upcoming technologies that might be applicable to survey data collection. One of these technologies is video game characters and the associated game engine as a vehicle for survey data collection. To test the hypothesis that animated agents are more successful than live humans, Conrad and his group are conducting exploratory laboratory experiments [9]. Rather than developing the actual agent software, they simulate animated agents using, what they term, a "Wizard of Oz" technique where respondents believe they are interacting with a computer-generated agent when, in fact, they are interacting with an actual human interviewer whose image has been rendered graphically in the user interface as if it were computer-generated. The overall goal of the proposed work is to determine when animated agents might help and when they might hurt the quality of responses.

A very thorough overview of a psychological approach to designing game characters is collected by Katherine Isbister [10]. In it, Isbister covers the principles required for game characters to create powerful social and emotional connections with users interacting with current and next-generation gaming environments. By tackling issues of culture and gender alongside the tools we use to communicate such as the body, face, and voice, Isbister's text challenges us to make conscious decisions about every aspect of designing and animating a digital character and the impact these decisions have on a character's effectiveness.

The research steps outlined in the case studies above may seem small, but their results can make our interactions with digital characters more effective, seamless, and "natural." All of this research is relevant to characters in the entertainment industry. As we put people face-to-face with digital characters and break down our understanding of human behavior into pieces that can be analyzed and recreated individually, it is only a matter of time before this knowledge will make its way into video game and films. The critical topic of behavior will be readdressed later when we discuss facial animation, procedural motion, and artificial intelligence. The historical and evolutionary steps that have occurred are outlined next and will help to inform the technical practice of building digital characters.

2.4 EXERCISE

Start designing a character you would like to use throughout this book. If it is a human, then think about Mori's "Uncanny Valley." What level of stylization will give you the right place on that continuum so as to not present you with the challenge of creating something almost real, but not quite. In what medium will this character exist? What aspects of the character's design can you accentuate to make it appealing?

1. Create a character bible which includes descriptions and sketches of your character. It should also include references for details of the character that you collect over time. These references can be images, quotes, or pieces of fabric that define a texture. Whether these elements make their way into your character formally or strictly remain as inspiration is something that only time will tell; so do not hesitate to collect anything that strikes a chord.

2. Get feedback from others about the character bible. Does the design of the character tell part of its story through the use of details, such as period clothing or elements?

3. Incorporate the feedback you receive to refine the character bible.

FURTHER READING

For a solid overview of the psychology behind character design, refer to

Isbister, K. *Better Game Characters by Design: A Psychological Approach (The Morgan Kaufmann Series in Interactive 3D Technology)*. Morgan Kaufmann Publishers Inc., San Francisco, CA, 2006.

An interesting panel conversation about Mori's Uncanny Valley took place at Siggraph 2007 in San Diego California. The citation to the abstract is below, but video transcripts are also available.

Chaminade, T., Hodgins, J. K., Letteri, J., and MacDorman, K. F. *The Uncanny Valley of Eeriness*. In SIGGRAPH'07: ACM SIGGRAPH 2007 panels, p. 1, ACM Press, New York, NY, 2007.

Scott McCloud's *Understanding Comics* is required reading:

McCloud, S. *Understanding Comics: The Invisible Art*, HarperCollins Publishers, New York, NY, 1994.

CHAPTER 3

Interview: Josh Carey, Rigging Supervisor, Reel FX Creative Studio

3.1 BIO

Josh Carey is the Rigging Supervisor at Reel FX Creative Studios in Dallas, Texas. While at Reel FX, he has rigged and supervised the rigging on projects such as *The Book of Life*, *Free Birds*, the *Looney Tunes* 3D shorts, *Open Season 2* and *3*, *Kung Fu Panda* consumer products and DVD work (including the *Secrets of the Furious Five*), *Madagascar 2* consumer products work, *Escape from Planet Earth*, and countless other feature and commercial projects. Of the *Looney Tunes* shorts, *Coyote Falls* got a VES award nomination as well as an Oscar shortlist nomination.

Josh Carey, Rigging Supervisor, Reel FX Creative Studio

The Tweety and Sylvester *I Tawt I Taw a Puddy Tat* was nominated for an Annie as well as the shortlist for the Oscars in 2012. Most recently, Josh was part of the team that tackled the rigging and technical challenges for Reel FX's *Book of Life* movie. In addition to mentoring and supervising at work, he is also a cofounder of RiggingDojo.com, an online school for technical artists and riggers for both the film and game industry.

3.2 Q&A

Q: *The components of character technology are diverse and span the artistic and technical spectrum. How did you get your start in the industry? Based on where you see the field heading what experience/training do you recommend people have?*

A: My first start in the industry was while I was still in school at the Art Institute of Ft. Lauderdale. A friend of a friend needed some rigging help and I was known as the guy that did "that tech stuff." It pretty much just exploded from there through freelance and knowing people that needed tech help with pipeline, scripts, and rigs. I made my way to Austin, TX, to help out a small startup company called The Animation Farm, and it was definitely an awesome experience to help build up a studio from the ground up. I learned a lot along the way.

I recommend that students try it all—modeling, animation, surfacing, sculpting, rigging, and lighting. They won't know what their calling is until they get a taste of everything. And of course, their desires may change. As far as training goes, dedicated schools are there for a base introduction, but typically they have all left students unprepared to go into the field. Companies expect a lot more these days, even as I look at reels I am blown away at what students can do these days compared to when I was a student. Online schools are a good filler for the specialized skills that people need to be successful. For the most part, the students we get at Rigging Dojo have it figured out that they want to do something technical, whether it is coding, development, rigging, pipeline, etc.

Training also shouldn't stop at the student level. Everyone should always be learning and improving their skills, which is why it's awesome that there are online schools where industry professionals can take courses to level up.

Q: *Creating compelling digital characters is part art and part science. What is the greatest challenge you encounter on a daily basis? What aspect of character technology keeps you up thinking at night?*

A: In my position, the greatest challenge daily is making all the animators happy. There are a lot of ways to rig a character, but to do it in a way that makes sense to all (or at least the majority) of animators can be difficult. More control with less controls is always the challenge.

We're always looking for ways to create great rigs with less and less time. Efficiency and workflow are super important things that I stress on daily. I also think about rig speed a lot. Animators can get more done if they can work with a fast rig, so I'm always looking forward to future software/technology that can make a feature film character rig move in real-time.

Q: *What are the ingredients for a successful digital character?*

A: A successful character has a very strong team behind it. You need a great design, of course, and a model that is executed appropriately to meet that design. It has to work in 3D, too; not all designs come across properly in 3D, so designs can change at the modeling stage. You need a good front end team that works together—modeling, animation, rigging—so they can really figure out how the character needs to work, move, deform, act. That's the performance side. The other half is getting the character to look good visually—surfacing, cloth, hair. Everyone's job affects the other departments, and a great team can collaborate appropriately to meet each others needs. I think the really successful digital characters have every department bringing their "A" game.

Q: *While the industry is competitive, it is ultimately respectful of great work. Outside of the work you have been personally involved in the production of, what animated characters have you been impressed or inspired by? What is the historical high-bar?*

A: I'm always in awe of complex characters from other films. There's a lot of cool stuff in *The Lego Movie* that I'd like to dig through. The characters in *Cloudy With a Chance of Meatballs* looked fun and cartoony, really pushing the style similar to what we did with the Looney shorts. The dragons in *How to Train Your Dragon* look great, and the octopus in the trailers for the *Penguins of Madagascar* looks like a really fun character to rig too. I really enjoy seeing those unique characters and wonder how others tackled the issues that I know always come up during a production.

The historical high-bar is hard to say—it's a moving target that gets higher and higher each year. Hopefully others will think that our segmented wooden puppet arms in *Book of Life* have set a bar of some sort—they're one of the most complex rig problems that our team has been tasked.

Q: *Where do you see digital characters in 10 years? Where are animated characters for film and games heading?*

A: In 10 years, I hope we see a lot more styles emerging from studios. The standard CG look is tough for studios to get away from since it's so established and it works, but I think (hope) we will see more and more productions trying to push that boundary. As far as the tech goes, I hope it gets easier, but I know that as tools get easier to use, more and more requirements and desires will be needed. I can see that more out-of-the-box tools will become the norm. Perhaps going as far as personal motion capture at an animator's desk to get quick blocking. Maybe tactical feedback for manipulating a rig with your hands. Think about how the tablet turned everyone's expectations for using apps into something that you do with your fingers—can that be translated into our field? Will animators be able to use rigs with their own fingers?

CHAPTER 4

History of Digital Characters

4.1 INTRODUCTION

This chapter deals with the evolution and history of digital characters. Digital characters have developed in response to the needs of the projects in which they were employed and have largely been driven by story requirements. By using an evolutionary model to frame the historical development of digital characters, we group innovations into five stages, leading us to contemporary projects and hints at what is ahead. The history of digital characters follows and paves the way for the primary concepts in this book.

4.2 THE EVOLUTION OF DIGITAL CHARACTERS

The scale of history for digital characters is not a large one. Digital characters found their start, and some might argue greatest success, in the realm of interactive video games. The act of arranging pixels into images in the form of characters of some variety goes back to the first days of computer imaging. Moving these pixels in two dimensions over time (also known as animation) was not far behind. Alongside developments into character motion came character interactivity, complex imagery, and eventually three-dimensional graphics. The artistry and the technology tended to advance together, each pushing the other, and they continue to do so today. As graphics hardware provides systems with more power for real-time graphic processing, the level of interactivity and visual complexity available increases. Advances in technology are the ecosystem for developments in character complexity and in many ways sets the pace for digital character technology development. Before we look at the historical path of digital characters in various forms of media, it is worth taking a look at the changing technology and methods that have brought digital characters to where they are today and which may give us insights into where they will go in the future.

If we were to frame the development of digital characters, a general framework for our discussion on the history of digital characters may be to look at this history from an evolutionary perspective. Let us use as a theoretical model the path proposed by artist and animator Matt

Elson [11] in 1999. Elson's five stages of digital character evolution deal with the technology and methods with which 3D character animation is carried out. Each stage is characterized by a technical advancement interrelated with a paradigm shift regarding motion.

Stage 1 in Elson's schema is typified by "keyframe animation" or the process of positioning a character every few frames, then letting the system interpolate the in-between frames. Animation at this stage is modeled on the workflow of twentieth-century cel animation which included a master animator who drew the keyframes and a more junior "in-betweener" who did what was expected of their title. A primary technical innovation of this phase is programmable expressions, in which technical directors define interactive relationships between objects in the 3D environment. These expressions provide the opportunity for complicated, nonhierarchical relationships within the character to add, for example, automatic secondary motion. Another example of a programmable expression is the flexing of associated skin or muscles when a joint is bent. Other noteworthy developments of the keyframe animation era include restructured hierarchical objects, 3D paint of textures, and skinning (the process of attaching the model to joints). Critically, keyframe animation is said by Elson to be cumbersome and requiring large crews and complex infrastructures with a high ratio of technical-to-creative talent. Control of the characters generally being achieved at the expense of production efficiency.

Stage 2 in Elson's schema is "layered animation and single skins." Although largely a technical stage, it involves the creation of a rearchitected workflow that enables animators, programmers, developers, artists, and technical directors to work on individual modules that address their respective areas of production. These modules are contained and encapsulated from the larger production until they can be plugged in with the other components. These parallel workflows make it possible for large teams of artists to work simultaneously on a project. This restructuring of pipelines and processes happens in part due to improved application programming interfaces (APIs), which allow third-party developers to write object-oriented system extensions and plugins for animation sofware. There is also a move away from straight-forward animation production to layerable animation, allowing different motion types to be combined on the same character.

The third stage described by Elson is one he terms "scripted memory and behavior." This stage is characterized by the dynamic animation of crowds via scripted actions. Crowd dynamics such as these are already being implemented and available in commercial packages like Stephen Regelous's MASSIVE™. Complex animation and the creation of realistic natural phenomenon using tools such as procedural systems for creating hair, fur, cloth, clouds, smoke, and grass are implemented in this stage as are dynamics and physics tools for simulating gravity, motion damping, and wind. On the character technology side, anatomical systems for simulating muscle, bone, fat, and other underlying structures of the body in the form of layered deformations are included. Motion capture becomes merely another animation method rather than a last resort. Skeletons become smarter, with built-in functions for pose-mirroring, and position and motion memories. Animation clips, or as Elson calls them, "performance blocks," are kept in a library and reused as needed, for example, in crowds.

It is safe to say that we have achieved stage 3 of Elson's schema. Stages 4 and 5 are where Elson's predictions turn toward the slightly more fantastic and futuristic. Keep in mind, as we will find later, the notions encapsulated by these stages are current topics in character technology research and development both in academia and industry.

Elson's fourth stage, "character autonomy," is where true character independence begins. In this particular stage, embedded physics systems in the character will enable it to move about an environment with weight, mass, and improvisational behaviors giving the appearance, though not yet the reality, of intelligence. He provides a note for the fearful animator here, "Animators will still be in great demand to craft all of a character's behaviors, actions, and responses" [11].

The fifth and final stage of Elson's evolution of digital characters is "personality." Here Elson departs from the realm of procedural animation to true artificial intelligence. Elson describes this stage as characters that have developed emotional and cognitive interior lives. He argues they will begin to "think" and interact with their environment, each other, the animator, and the end user, employing knowledge structures for their basic decision-making. Characters will understand and respond to human speech, so they will be able to translate, perform menial tasks, and sift and sort the digital expanses of data for us.

Elson concludes by pointing out that his stages represent an ideal world and that future developments will likely be more mundane. There is no company or facility systematically proceeding from one neat and tidy level to the next because software companies are busy responding to market demands and production studios are busy responding to both their own and their client's visions. All of the elements mentioned are in development in various places, though most are in limited use, lacking systematic integration and a compelling economic reason to be pulled together. This book attempts to bring all of these stages together, but with an emphasis on the performance imbued by the animator or performer, with a lesser emphasis on the application of artificial intelligence (AI).

This framework is helpful in understanding the scope of technologies under the umbrella of digital character technology. However, without historical insights into previous efforts, we are likely to not move forward at the pace that hardware and software is progressing. Our understanding of digital characters in the context of film and interactive media is crucial.

4.3 HISTORY OF DIGITAL CHARACTERS IN FILMS

For our discussion of digital characters in films, a differentiation should be made between characters that have been created for full computer graphics (CG) films, such as *Toy Story* (1995) or *Shrek* (2001), and those that have been created in service of visual effects for a live action production such as *The Lord of the Rings* (2001) or *Guardians of the Galaxy* (2014). The difference is mainly stylistic. For characters to be integrated into the environment surrounding them, the design, construction, animation, shading, and texturing of that character must match the rules of the world that they inhabit. Characters for a CG world are inherently easier to integrate, as they will share the modeling, shading, and lighting process with their environments as opposed to those created for integration into filmed environments, which need to be composed with the real world in mind. Much of this integration lies in the realm of texturing, lighting, and image compositing, as even the most stylized character can be integrated with the reality of the scene. Architecturally, in a contemporary production setting, these characters are built and animated in an identical manner using some variety of off-the-shelf or proprietary 3D animation software. It is worth walking through the history of digital characters in film—both animation and live action film—to get a sense of the breadth, scope, and explosion of these characters in recent years. This historical overview also serves to illuminate the great strides that have been made in such a short amount of time.

In 1976, *Futureworld* was the first feature film to use 3D computer-generated images (CGIs) for an animated hand and face, created by Information International Incorporated (III). While it was supposed to be the actor Peter Fonda, the animated hand was actually a digitized version of Edwin Catmull's (eventual cofounder of Pixar) left hand.

Looker (1981) featured the first full CGI human character, Cindy, who was made from simulated body scans of actress Susan Dey [12] and was also created by Information International Incorporated. This was also the first use of surface shading as we know it today.

The following year, a major achievement in both the film industry and the world of computer graphics, in general, came with the release of *Tron* (1982), which included the polyhedron character, "Bit" (Figure 4.1), built and animated by Digital Effects, Incorporated. This is arguably the first animated digital character in films, though its basic design and limited animation did not allow for much complexity. The character had three states, one for its neutral state, one for "yes," and one for "no."

In the mid-1980s, we start to see digital characters begin to take more compelling forms. The Lucasfilm Computer Graphics short film *The Adventures of Andre and Wally B.* (1985) introduced the idea of incorporating traditional character animation techniques to basic geometric 3D shapes in support of a fully realized short film. Frank Thomas and Ollie Johnston, two of Walt Disney's *Nine Old Men*, upon visiting the production of the short, saw a convincing demonstration by John Lasseter that animation principles such as squash and stretch, anticipation, overlap, and follow through were not alien to computer animation [13].

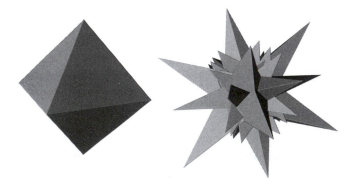

FIGURE 4.1 "Bit" from *Tron* (1982), recreated here as a morphing polyhedron shape with states for "yes" and "no."

Created in a similar manner, the Dire Straits *Money for Nothing* music video (1985) featured low-detail, but highly engaging animated characters, animated by Ian Pearson, Gavin Blair, and David Throssell at the London-based studio, Rushes. The same year, however, the first fully animated, photorealistic digital character in a feature film was a medieval knight that sprang to life from a stained glass window in *Young Sherlock Holmes* (1985). The 30-second sequence took 6 months to accomplish, but was a stunning achievement by the team at the Computer Graphics Division of LucasFilm, now Pixar, and a huge technical achievement, planting the seed for the potential of using computer-generated characters in films as a viable practice.

Since then, a few small appearances by digital characters emerged including the CG owl created by Digital Productions from the opening title sequence in *Labyrinth* (1986), the formidable animation on multiple characters in Pixar's *Luxo Jr.* (1986) short, and its follow-up, *Tin Toy* (1988), which featured an Uncanny Valley inhabiting, albeit complex, crawling human baby. On the more abstract and procedural animation front, *Stanley and Stella in 'Breaking the Ice'* (1987) featured an implementation of a flocking algorithm by Craig Reynolds [14] along with Symbolics Graphics Division and Whitney/Demos Productions. This flocking algorithm paved the way for the crowd scenes which are so prevalent in films today.

With the sale of the LucasFilm Computer Graphics Group to Steve Jobs and the subsequent creation of Pixar (which focused entirely on CG productions and software), the creation of Industrial Light and Magic (ILM) by George Lucas, and the growing presence of Pacific Data Images (PDI), there started to develop a center of gravity for computer graphics and digital characters in northern California. The confluence of talent and resources led directly to ILM's creation of the amorphic pseudopod in *The Abyss* (1989). The use of realistic lighting algorithms and actor interaction in *The Abyss* took the art of digital character creation and ray-traced rendering to a new level by creating a seamless digital character that was perfectly matched to its live action environment. The pseudopod replicated actor Mary Elizabeth Mastrantonio's face with its watery tentacle and appeared to communicate by movements that resembled facial expressions. See Table 4.1 for more projects employing digital characters before 1990.

Continuing in this tradition, *Terminator 2: Judgment Day* (1991), also with effects by ILM, introduced both Hollywood and the public to the large-scale use of CG in feature films. The liquid-metal T-1000 Terminator, the first computer graphic-generated main character to be used in a film, "morphed" into any person or object and was animated naturally based on human motion. Although not a formal digital character, the ILM effects in *Death Becomes Her* (1992) featured photorealistic skin and the first complex human skin replication which linked Meryl Streep's body and head together with a digital neck during a shockingly magical head-twisting incident. In the same year, *Batman Returns* (1992) featured a flock of digital bats produced by VIFX. The year 1992 also featured hypothesized virtual reality (VR) avatars in *The Lawnmower Man* (1992) with animation by Angel Studios.

ILM's 1993 hallmark, *Jurassic Park* (1993) pushed the limits of photo-realism with their digital dinosaurs. This film raised, if not created the bar, for digital characters both in terms of

TABLE 4.1   Notable Projects Featuring Digital Characters (Pre-1990)

Year	Title	Format	Company
1976	*Futureworld*	Feature	Information International Inc. (III)
1979	*Pacman*	Video Game	Namco
1981	*Donkey Kong*	Video Game	Nintendo
1981	*Looker*	Feature	III
1982	*Tron*	Feature	III, MAGI/Synthavision, Robert Abel & Associates, Digital Effects
1984	*The Adventures of Andre and Wally B.*	Short	Lucasfilm
1985	Dire Straits *Money for Nothing* Music Video	TV	Rushes
1985	*Tony de Peltrie*	Short	Philippe Bergeron, Pierre Lachapelle, Daniel Langlois, Pierre Robiboux
1985	*Young Sherlock Holmes*	Feature	Pixar
1986	*Labyrinth*	Feature	Digital Productions
1986	*Luxo Jr.*	Short	Pixar
1987	*Captain Power & the Soldiers of the Future*	TV	ARCCA Animation
1987	*Stanley and Stella in Breaking the Ice*	Short	Symbolics Graphics Division
1988	*Nestor Sextone for President*	Short	Kleiser–Walczak Construction Company
1988	*Tin Toy*	Short	Pixar
1989	*Knick Knack*	Short	Pixar
1989	*Prince of Persia*	Video Game	Brōderbund
1989	*The Abyss*	Feature	ILM

realism, number of characters, and quality of motion. These were the first fully digital characters seen with daytime natural lighting interacting with each other, human actors, and the environment, with about 8 minutes of total screen time. Most importantly, *Jurassic Park* broke down the barrier for film-makers who previously thought it was unfeasible or too expensive to create large-scale digital character animation by proving that it was possible, cost-effective, and capable of producing high-quality results. See Table 4.2 for more projects employing digital character from 1990 to 1994.

At this point in the mid-1990s, much attention was focused on creating realistic humans for film effects. In 1995, two examples of the early use of creating digital human stunt people included *Judge Dredd* (1995), and *Batman Forever* (1995). Both films featured digital replacements for human actors, the first being Sylvester Stallone, during action sequences. The idea of digital replacement was not new, but stemmed directly from synthespians created by Kleiser–Walczak Construction Company (KWCC) in the late 1980s. The term "synthespian" can be attributed to Jeff Kleiser of KWCC, a portmanteau of the words "synthetic," meaning not of natural origin, and "thespian," meaning dramatic actor. Kleiser created the first digital actor for his 1988 short film *Nestor Sextone for President* (1988) which premiered at SIGGRAPH alongside a course on "synthetic actors." One year later, Kleiser and Diana Walczak presented their first female synthespian, Dozo, in the music video *Don't Touch Me*. KWCC actually produced the

TABLE 4.2   Notable Projects Featuring Digital Characters (Early 1990s)

Year	Title	Format	Company
1990	*Robocop 2*	Feature	Kevin Bjorke
1990	*Total Recall*	Feature	Metrolight Studios
1991	*Another World*	Video Game	Eric Chahi
1991	*Terminator 2: Judgment Day*	Feature	ILM
1992	*Alone in the Dark*	Video Game	Infogrames
1992	*Batman Returns*	Feature	Video Image
1992	*Death Becomes Her*	Feature	ILM
1992	*Lawnmower Man*	Feature	Angel Studios
1992	*Wolfenstein 3D*	Video Game	id Software
1993	*Doom*	Video Game	id Software
1993	*Flashback*	Video Game	Delphine Software
1993	*Insektors*	TV	Studio Fantome
1993	*Jurassic Park*	Feature	ILM
1993	*VeggieTales*	Video	Big Idea Productions
1993	*Virtua Fighter*	Video Game	Sega-AM2
1994	*ReBoot*	TV	Mainframe Entertainment
1994	*The Mask*	Feature	ILM

digital stunt person in *Judge Dredd* and, as we will see, went on to create a number of big screen digital actors.

The year 1995 also marked a watershed moment when Pixar released *Toy Story*, their feature-length animated film filled with a cast of digital characters both human and toys. This film established the benchmark for all-computer animated feature productions, much like *Jurassic Park* (1993) did for live action visual effects. Yet, in the case of *Toy Story*, the quality of character acting, personality, and performance became the hallmark that all digital characters were expected to achieve.

From this point until the late 1990s, digital characters in films, while not commonplace, were becoming more prevalent with films such as *Casper* (1995), *Jumanji* (1995), *Dragonheart* (1996), *Starship Troopers* (1997), *Men in Black* (1997), and *Godzilla* (1998), all of which featured digital characters in key roles. Even James Cameron's *Titanic* (1997) included huge crowds of simulated people. During this time, CG animated films such as PDI's *Antz* (1998) and Blue Sky's short *Bunny* (1998) were giving Pixar and its second film, *A Bug's Life* (1998), some competition.

In 1999, we see the use of digital characters taking an increasingly important role in live-action feature films. In *Star Wars Episode 1: The Phantom Menace* (1999), a number of highly photorealistic digital characters were created. One, in particular, Jar Jar Binks, had as much screen time as the human actors. The authenticity of Jar Jar Binks' appearance was in fact so realistic that when the first pictures of him appeared in Vanity Fair [15] many took him to be a human in makeup. These pictures were, of course, composited images created by ILM. ILM also flexed their muscles, quite literally, with their work on *The Mummy* (1999), which featured an animated anatomical reconstruction of the title character, while in motion, integrating effects and character technology. Taking this anatomical animation a step further, was Sony Pictures Imageworks who created the visceral deconstruction and reconstruction of Kevin Bacon's character in *Hollow Man* (2000). Character technology had evolved into a set of techniques capable of reconstructing characters from the inside out, with anatomically accurate models and rigs. See Table 4.3 for more projects employing digital character from 1995 to 1999.

TABLE 4.3   Notable Projects Featuring Digital Characters (Late 1990s)

Year	Title	Format	Company
1995	*Babe*	Feature	Rhythm & Hues
1995	*Batman Forever*	Feature	Warner Digital
1995	*Casper*	Feature	ILM
1995	*Fade to Black*	Video Game	Delphine Software
1995	*Judge Dredd*	Feature	Kleiser–Walczak Construction Company
1995	*Jumanji*	Feature	ILM
1995	*La Cite des Enfants Perdus* (City of Lost Children)	Feature	BUF
1995	*Toy Story*	Feature	Pixar
1996	*Dragonheart*	Feature	ILM
1996	*Duke Nukem 3D*	Video Game	3D Realms
1996	*Tomb Raider*	Video Game	Core Deisgn
1997	*Alien: Resurrection*	Feature	Blue Sky—VIFX
1997	*Batman & Robin*	Feature	Warner Digital
1997	*Geri's Game*	Short	Pixar
1997	*Mars Attacks!*	Feature	ILM
1997	*Men in Black*	Feature	ILM
1997	*Spawn*	Feature	ILM
1997	*Starship Troopers*	Feature	Sony Pictures Imageworks
1997	*The Lost World: Jurassic Park 2*	Feature	ILM
1997	*Titanic*	Feature	Digital Domain
1998	*A Bug's Life*	Feature	Pixar
1998	*Antz*	Feature	DreamWorks Animation
1998	*Bunny*	Short	Blue Sky
1998	*Godzilla*	Feature	Centropolis
1998	*Grim Fandango*	Video Game	LucasArts
1998	*Mighty Joe Young*	Feature	Dream Quest, ILM
1998	*Small Soldiers*	Feature	DreamWorks
1998	*Thief: The Dark Project*	Video Game	Looking Glass Studios
1999	*Outcast*	Video Game	Infogrames
1999	*Star Wars: Episode I: The Phantom Menace*	Feature	ILM
1999	*Stuart Little*	Feature	Sony Pictures Imageworks
1999	*The Matrix*	Feature	Manex
1999	*The Mummy*	Feature	ILM
1999	*Toy Story 2*	Feature	Pixar

The first lead role for a computer-generated character occurred in 1999 with *Stuart Little* (1999). This film set a new benchmark for computer-generated characters, like the pseudo-pod from *The Abyss* (1989) before it, by increasing the amount of actor interaction and adding complex elements, such as fur, to the carefully crafted rendering. In the year 2000, Disney created the film *Dinosaur* (2000) which had the first entirely photorealistic computer-generated cast. This film, unlike others, with all animated casts, for example, Pixar's *Toy Story* (1995), utilized film shot backgrounds instead of an entirely CG environment. This required that digital characters matched the lighting and visual complexity of the rich natural settings used in the film.

Entering the twenty-first century, we encounter a deluge of digital characters. Human and humanoid characters began to take center stage with the release of *Final Fantasy: The Spirits Within* (2001) (Table 4.4), *Shrek* (2001), and *The Lord of the Rings: The Fellowship of the Ring* (2001). While *Final Fantasy* received poor critical response due to the characters lack familiarity, *The Lord of the Rings* series brought the role of digital characters to a new level. A major step, *The Lord of the Rings: Fellowship of the Ring* (2001), the first film in the subsequent trilogy, had digital characters surrounding the main characters with seamless integration. They even went so far as to create a character, Gollum, that because of its performance in the later films posed the question, could a digital character receive an acting award for its performance? Gollum's

TABLE 4.4 Notable Projects Featuring Digital Characters (2000–2001)

Year	Title	Format	Company
2000	*Deus Ex*	Video Game	Ion Storm
2000	*Dinosaur*	Feature	Disney
2000	*For the Birds*	Short	Pixar
2000	*Hitman: Codename 47*	Video Game	IO Interactive
2000	*Hollow Man*	Feature	Tippett Studio
2000	*The Operative: No One Lives Forever*	Video Game	Monolith Productions
2001	*A.I.: Artificial Intelligence*	Feature	PDI, ILM
2001	*Black & White*	Video Game	Lionhead
2001	*Evolution*	Feature	PDI, Tippett Studio
2001	*Final Fantasy: The Spirits Within*	Feature	Harmonix
2001	*Grand Theft Auto III*	Video Game	Mainframe Entertainment
2001	*Half-Life*	Video Game	Valve Software
2001	*Halo*	Video Game	Bungie Studios
2001	*Harry Potter and the Sorcerer's Stone*	Feature	MPC, CFC, The Mill, Cinesite, ILM, Sony Pictures Imageworks
2001	*Jimmy Neutron: Boy Genius*	Feature	Nickelodeon
2001	*Jurassic Park III*	Feature	ILM
2001	*Monsters Inc.*	Feature	Pixar
2001	*Shrek*	Feature	PDI/DreamWorks
2001	*The Lord of the Rings: Fellowship of the Ring*	Feature	WETA
2001	*The Mummy Returns*	Feature	ILM

animation was informed by the motion capture of actor Andy Serkis' performance, but because of the great attention to detail for every aspect of this character, Gollum took on a life greater than any single contributor. See Table 4.4 for more projects employing digital character from 2000 and 2001.

The Lord of the Rings series also advanced the role of the digital stunt person, with these "digital doubles" replacing live actors midshot. In general, the digital double has evolved into a commonplace role with increasing screen time as evidenced in films based on comic books where superheros such as Spider-Man (*Spider-Man* series [2002–2007]) and Superman (*Superman Returns* [2006]) are nearly indistinguishable from the actors portraying them. An often cited example of a well-integrated digital character is Davy Jones from the *Pirates of the Caribbean: Dead Man's Chest* (2006) and *Pirates of the Caribbean: At World's End* (2007). This character, while informed by the performance of actor Bill Nighy, can be argued as one of the most compelling digital characters in films. Capturing the subtle movement of the eyes and face, this character tricked many viewers into thinking that it was created by an elaborate make-up job.

Some highlights from feature films in the recent past include *Beowulf* (2007), where motion capture and advances in rendering skin were employed by Sony Imageworks to create a rich full CG animated feature that set a new bar for animated feature films; *Transformers* (2007), where ILM created the incredibly complex mechanical rigs for the battling robots that still needed to be emotionally expressive; *The Curious Case of Benjamin Button* (2008), where Digital Domain utilized their expertise and refined processes for creating digital doubles and face replacement to age actor Brad Pitt in reverse; *Avatar* (2009), where Weta Digital used performance capture extensively to create digital characters that were indistinguishable from reality and to feature them in a fully CG 3D photorealistic world; *Tron Legacy* (2010), where Digital Domain, once again used their expertise to allow Jeff Bridges to do the performance capture necessary to bring a digital version of his younger self (the age he was in the original *Tron*) back to the screen; *Gravity* (2013), employed long, continuous, uninterrupted shots to give viewers a flawless look at their cast of digital doubles. Digital characters are in a huge number of films every year. They have become the characters that studios build tentpole movies around but they have also, at times, been added as a quick fix digital double for a shot that could not be achieved. They are no less complicated but the processes for creating them have become more widely known and the methods for realistic rendering and seamless compositing have lowered the barrier to putting a digital character on screen.

Outside films, digital doubles of performers no longer alive has become recent trend as part of music concerts. In 2012, Digital Domain created the *Virtual 2Pac* to bring an original performance of the late rap star 2Pac Shakur to life by way of an on-stage projection at Coachella music festival. The performance went viral online and started future-looking conversations on music, entertainment, ethics, technology, and intellectual property. This was clearly not the last time we would see such an event and it gave the viewer the sense of a character walking off the screen and into our lives.

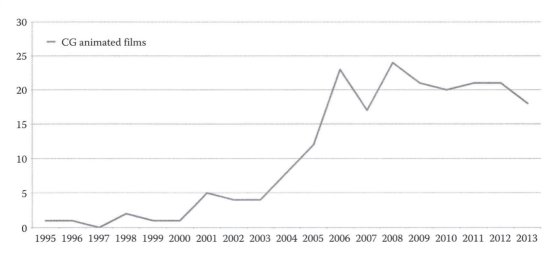

FIGURE 4.2   The number of computer-generated films from 1995 to 2013.

It has been more than 30 years since Bit appeared in *Tron*. With the rate at which digital characters appear in their own features, as creatures in live-action film, and as students and professionals create short films, the growth of animated character has exploded. In looking at Figure 4.2, it is clear that between 2003 and 2006, the number of CG animated films went from 5 or less a year to around 20 a year. Many of these are produced internationally and represent the growing knowledge of the process and tools to create a feature film. The art of creating digital characters has grown tremendously and with this pace it is likely to continue to incorporate new technologies for some startling results in the future.

4.4 OVERVIEW OF DIGITAL CHARACTERS IN INTERACTIVE MEDIA

As was mentioned previously, the process of creating digital characters for films and video games derives from the same root. The imitations of real-time rendering and the impact of interactivity account for the differences. One difference is perception, whereby many video games have the advantage of letting the viewer step into the shoes of that character and interact with its world. This provides a connection that passive media struggles to achieve. As opposed to films, outlined in the previous section, digital characters in games are too voluminous to list, as the majority of games have allowed the user to look through the eyes of a digital character. The first characters in commercially created and publicly accessible games were the famous *Pac-Man* (1979) character and the simple humanoid stick figure in *Berzerk* (1980). Developers realized early on that by attaching an image that we could relate to onto a character, the user would invest themselves into it. A simply designed character such as Pac-Man composed of only a few pixels, takes on the personality, or at least game-play tactics, of its user. Despite the simplicity, the ability to control digital characters in video games allows for a connection impossible in film. Tables 4.5 through 4.7 include highlights of more game projects employing digital characters in the late 2000s.

TABLE 4.5   Notable Projects Featuring Digital Characters (2002–2004)

Year	Title	Format	Company
2002	*Harry Potter and the Chamber of Secrets*	Feature	Cinesite, CFC, ILM, MPC, Thousand Monkeys
2002	*Ice Age*	Feature	Blue Sky
2002	*Men in Black II*	Feature	PDI, Sony Pictures Imageworks, ILM, Rhythm & Hues
2002	*Mike's New Car*	Short	Pixar
2002	*Minority Report*	Feature	ILM
2002	*Scooby-Doo*	Feature	Rhythm & Hues, Giant Killer Robots
2002	*Spider-Man*	Feature	Sony Pictures Imageworks
2002	*Star Wars: Episode II: Attack of the Clones*	Feature	ILM
2002	*Stuart Little 2*	Feature	Sony Pictures Imageworks
2002	*The ChubbChubbs!*	Short	Sony Pictures Imageworks
2002	*The Lord of the Rings: The Two Towers*	Feature	WETA
2002	*The Sims*	Video Game	Maxis
2003	*Boundin*	Short	Pixar
2003	*Elder Scrolls: Morrowind*	Video Game	Bethesda Software
2003	*Finding Nemo*	Feature	Pixar
2003	*Star Wars: Knights of the Old Republic*	Video Game	Bioware
2003	*The Animatrix: Final Flight of the Osiris*	Short	Square
2003	*The Hulk*	Feature	ILM
2003	*The Lord of the Rings: Return of the King*	Feature	WETA
2003	*The Matrix Reloaded*	Feature	ESC, Amalgamated Pixels, Animal Logic, BUF, Sony Pictures Imageworks
2003	*The Matrix Revolutions*	Feature	Tippett Studio, Sony Pictures Imageworks, ESC, CIS, BUF
2004	*Garfield: The Movie*	Feature	Rhythm & Hues
2004	*Gone Nutty*	Short	Blue Sky
2004	*Grand Theft Auto III: San Andreas*	Video Game	Rockstar North
2004	*Half-Life 2*	Video Game	Valve Software
2004	*Harry Potter and the Prisoner of Azkaban*	Feature	ILM, Cinesite, CFC, Double Negative
2004	*Hellboy*	Feature	Tippett Studios
2004	*Ninja Gaiden*	Video Game	Team Ninja
2004	*Shark Tale*	Feature	DreamWorks Animation
2004	*Shrek 2*	Feature	DreamWorks Animation
2004	*Spider-Man 2*	Feature	Sony Pictures Imageworks
2004	*The Incredibles*	Feature	Pixar
2004	*The Polar Express*	Feature	Sony Pictures Imageworks
2004	*Van Helsing*	Feature	ILM

Although we find that digital characters in films followed a steady trajectory, characters in games took off in a broad and faster manner. These early characters, such as Pac-Man, were digital cartoons. Other notable video game characters include Mario from the original *Donkey Kong* (1981) and the enduring *Mario Bros* series, Sonic The Hedgehog, Link from the *Legend*

TABLE 4.6 Notable Projects Featuring Digital Characters (2005–2006)

Year	Title	Format	Company
2005	*Chicken Little*	Feature	Walt Disney Feature Animation
2005	*Harry Potter and the Goblet of Fire*	Feature	Cinesite, ILM, BUF, MPC, Double Negative, The Orphanage, Animal Logic, Rising Sun
2005	*Hoodwinked*	Feature	Blue Yonder Films with Kanbar Entertainment
2005	*Jack-Jack Attack*	Short	Pixar
2005	*King Kong*	Feature	WETA
2005	*Madagascar*	Feature	DreamWorks Animation
2005	*One Man Band*	Short	Pixar
2005	*Psychonauts*	Video Game	Double Fine Productions
2005	*Shadow of the Colossus*	Video Game	Sony Computer Entertainment
2005	*Star Wars: Episode III: Revenge of the Sith*	Feature	ILM
2005	*The Chronicles of Narnia: The Lion, the Witch and the Wardrobe*	Feature	Rhythm & Hues, ILM, and Sony Pictures Imageworks
2005	*The Madagascar Penguins in a Christmas Caper*	Short	DreamWorks
2005	*Valiant*	Feature	Vanguard Animatino
2006	*Barnyard*	Feature	Nickelodeon Movies
2006	*Cars*	Feature	Pixar
2006	*Charlotte's Web*	Feature	Iloura, Rising Sun, Fuel
2006	*Everyone's Hero*	Feature	Dan Krech Productions
2006	*First Flight*	Short	DreamWorks
2006	*Flushed Away*	Feature	DreamWorks/Aardman
2006	*Happy Feet*	Feature	Animal Logic
2006	*Lifted*	Short	Pixar
2006	*Mater and the Ghostlight*	Short	Pixar
2006	*Monster House*	Feature	Sony Pictures Imageworks
2006	*Open Season*	Feature	Sony Pictures Imageworks
2006	*Over the Hedge*	Feature	DreamWorks Animation
2006	*Pan's Labyrinth*	Feature	Cafe FX
2006	*Pirates of the Caribbean: Dead Man's Chest*	Feature	ILM
2006	*Superman Returns*	Feature	Sony Pictures Imageworks, Rising Sun, The Orphanage, Rhythm & Hues
2006	*The Ant Bully*	Feature	DNA Productions

of Zelda series, Ratchet and Clank, Pitfall Harry, and Jak and Daxter all of whom have become household names and the stars of their own series of video games. Most digital characters in films have appeared in one, or at most four films, whereas our interactions with game characters can take many different paths. It is no surprise that games based on animated film characters

TABLE 4.7   Notable Projects Featuring Digital Characters (2007–2008)

Year	Title	Format	Company
2007	*Alvin and the Chipmunks*	Feature	Rhythm & Hues
2007	*Assassin's Creed*	Video Game	Ubisoft Montreal
2007	*Bee Movie*	Feature	DreamWorks Animation
2007	*Beowulf*	Feature	Sony Pictures Imageworks
2007	*Bioshock*	Video Game	2K Boston/ 2K Australia
2007	*Crysis*	Video Game	Crytek
2007	*Elder Scrolls: Oblivion*	Video Game	Bethesda Software
2007	*Fantastic 4: Rise of the Silver Surfer*	Feature	WETA
2007	*Ghost Rider*	Feature	Sony Imageworks
2007	*Golden Compass*	Feature	Rhythm & Hues
2007	*Harry Potter and the Order of the Phoenix*	Feature	ILM, Cinesite, CFC, BUF, Rising Sun, Baseblack, Machine, Double Negative
2007	*Mass Effect*	Video Game	BioWare
2007	*Meet the Robinsons*	Feature	Disney
2007	*No Time for Nuts*	Short	Blue Sky
2007	*Pirates of the Caribbean: At World's End*	Feature	ILM
2007	*Ratatouille*	Feature	Pixar
2007	*Rock Band*	Video Game	Harmonix
2007	*Shrek the Third*	Feature	DreamWorks Animation
2007	*Spider-Man 3*	Feature	Sony Pictures Imageworks
2007	*Surf's Up*	Feature	Sony Pictures Imageworks
2007	*TMNT*	Feature	Imagi Animation Studios
2007	*Transformers*	Feature	ILM
2007	*Your Friend the Rat*	Short	Pixar
2008	*10,000 BC*	Feature	MPC, DNeg
2008	*Cloverfield*	Feature	Tippett Studio, Double Negative, Fugitive Studios
2008	*Grand Theft Auto IV*	Video Game	Rockstar North
2008	*Hellboy II: The Golden Army*	Feature	Double Negative
2008	*Horton Hears a Who*	Feature	Blue Sky
2008	*Iron Man*	Feature	ILM
2008	*Kung-Fu Panda*	Feature	DreamWorks Animation
2008	*Madagascar 2*	Feature	DreamWorks Animation
2008	*The Chronicles of Narnia: Prince Caspian*	Feature	Rhythm & Hues
2008	*The Incredible Hulk*	Feature	ILM
2008	*Wall-E*	Feature	Pixar

are valued properties as the audience gets a chance to be the character they have been watching in films. Many game characters have changed from 2D bitmapped images into 3D geometry-based characters (such as Link from the *Zelda* series) as those found in films and covered by this book. In addition, digital characters in first-person shooters such as those in *Doom*, *Quake*, *Unreal*, *Halo*, and the *Half-Life* series were some of the first 3D digital characters and continue

FIGURE 4.3 Characters from *Gears of War 3*. (© 2014 Microsoft Corporation. All Rights Reserved. Microsoft, Xbox, the Xbox logo, *Gears of War*, Black Tusk Studios, and the Crimson Omen logo are trademarks of the Microsoft group of companies.)

to be a genre within gaming where much character technology development is done. Games such as the *Gears of War* series by Epic Games (Figure 4.3), *The Last of Us* (2013) (Figure 4.4) by Naughty Dog, *Ryse: Son of Rome* (2013) by Crytek (Figure 4.5), and the *Grand Theft Auto* series by Rockstar Games have advanced the acting of digital character in games to the point where they rival film-based characters.

The motion of characters in games is typically limited to precomposed animations that are triggered by user controls or in relation to the environment. Games have become increasingly complex, adding character physics and AI into the mix and triggering animation created

FIGURE 4.4 Sarah from *The Last of Us*. (The Last of Us © 2013/™ SCEA. Created and developed by Naughty Dog.)

FIGURE 4.5 Characters from *Ryse: Son of Rome*. (Courtesy of Crytek GmbH © 2014. All rights reserved.)

through a mix of hand-animated motion and motion capture. Cut scenes and cinematic interludes where the player is no longer in control are where characters often lose their believability and sense of familiarity. To a further degree, it is useful to distinguish player-controlled "player characters" and computer-controlled "nonplayer characters." As the names dictate, player characters are those controlled by the player via the controls supplied, like Pac-Man himself, while nonplayer characters are those driven by the system via a level of AI, like Blinky, Pinky, Inky, and Clyde, the ghosts from the *Pac-Man* game. Much research goes into making those nonplayer characters more life-like and indistinguishable from player characters. The embodiment of the player character by the user has been a key factor in the success of massively multiplayer online role-playing games (MMORPGs). These games such as *World of Warcraft* allow users to customize a character and play with other users spread across the world through centralized servers. The idea that you are playing with other humans adds to the realism of the experience and has opened the door for other collaborative virtual environments.

Notions of embodiment and telepresence are no better represented than in the online virtual world of *Second Life* [16] (Figure 4.6). Like an MMORPG, the *Second Life* world is inhabited by users from all over the world via 3D avatars. This has become a functioning community with notions of real estate, commerce, romance, and politics. *Second Life* has also transcended typical user groups by opening the door to inhabitable digital characters to users who might not typically play games but would be inclined to investigate the social networking and virtual exploration aspects of this environment.

Digital characters in games are also able to be modified or repurposed because with user control, characters can do things outside of the tasks related to the completion of the game. In this vein, a side branch of gaming is the use of game engines for the purpose of filmmaking, usually termed "machinima." In this situation, film-makers use and extend the functionality of the selected game engine to compose and produce real-time films. These films usually employ multiple people in a networked environment, controlling characters and playing the

FIGURE 4.6 Characters from *Second Life* by Linden Lab.

roles required. Machinima is also dependent on character customization and ground-up creation so that unique characters can mix with existing game characters. This process is a great leap for game technology, as putting the power of a game engine in the hands of anyone interested in making films opens the doors for low-budget productions in a completely synthetic space with infinite possibilities (Figure 4.7). Users build custom animations to create their performances and in a puppeteering fashion, trigger these animations when needed.

The evolution, history, and current state of digital characters leave us in an excellent place to start building our own. There are few limitations to developing what can be imagined by the artist. Through the use of code and new and established techniques, the characters discussed in both games and films will be only the starting point for what comes next.

FIGURE 4.7 Commercial machinima software, *The Movies* (2006). (© Lionhead Studios.)

FURTHER READING

Elson, M. 1999. The evolution of digital characters. *Computer Graphics World*, September 1999.

For a good overview of the industry and the art of animation, have a look at

Kerlow, I. V. 2004. *The Art of 3D Computer Animation and Effects*, 3rd edition. John Wiley & Sons Inc., Hoboken, NJ.

Masson, T. 2007. *CG 101: A Computer Graphics Industry Reference*, 2nd edition. Digital Fauxtography, Williamstown, MA.

CHAPTER 5

Interview: Tim McLaughlin, Associate Professor and Department Head, Department of Visualization, College of Architecture, Texas A&M University

5.1 BIO

Tim McLaughlin graduated from Pine Tree High School in Longview, Texas, in 1985. He earned his Associate of Arts degree from Kilgore College and then went on to earn both the Bachelor of Environmental Design (1990) and the Master of Science in Visualization Sciences (1994) degrees from Texas A&M University.

He joined the faculty of Texas A&M's Department of Architecture as an Associate Professor in September 2007 and became Head of the new Department of Visualization in January 2008. He continues to hold that position.

Prior to joining the faculty at Texas A&M, Tim worked in the visual effects industry at Industrial Light & Magic, a division of Lucasfilm Ltd. in San Francisco, California, where he led teams of artists and research scientists developing processes and producing groundbreaking award winning visual effects for films. His credit list includes 15 theatrically released feature film projects including *Mars Attacks!* (1996), *Star Wars: Episode I* (1999), *Van Helsing* (2004), and

Tim McLaughlin, Associate Professor and Department Head,
Department of Visualization, College of Architecture, Texas A&M University

War of the Worlds (2005). The work of Tim's technical artists contributed directly to Science and Technology Awards from the Academy of Motion Picture Sciences being given to teams of ILM researchers in 1998, 2001, and 2013.

At Texas A&M, Tim's undergraduate teaching area involves collaborative student projects that include computer animation production techniques and visual storytelling. His graduate teaching and research work focuses on developing animation systems for character articulation and deformation.

As Head of the Department of Visualization, he has overseen the creation of the Bachelor of Science and the Master of Fine Arts in Visualization degree programs. He is active in a variety of research and outreach activities that involve blending art and science in STEM education.

5.2 Q&A

Q: *The components of character technology are diverse and span the artistic and technical spectrum. How did you get your start in the industry? Based on where you see the field heading what experience/training do you recommend people have?*

A: I started my industry career working on *Jumanji* in 1994. On the heels of the success of *Jurassic Park* movie scripts requiring complex full body performances by animals and fantasy creatures were suddenly viable. At that time the biggest challenge I faced was control over the behavior of skin. We called this process enveloping at ILM. To do this job well I needed to understand anatomy and rigging, or chaining as we called it then. Coming out of Texas A&M University's Master of Science in Visualization program I had a solid foundation in both the art side and the technical side of computer graphics. In addition, I had done much of my school work, including the project side of my thesis, using Softimage in a Unix environment on SGI workstations. This matched the off-the-shelf side of ILM's pipeline. Additionally my demo reel featured projects focused on digital creatures. I'm sure that the kind of projects I was pursuing and the environment in which I worked made ILM more comfortable with my preparation.

I think this remains the key today for people trying to land their first job in the industry. The problem set has changed a bit, however. The significant differences are fidelity and scale. Visual effects, in particular, are striving to achieve incredibly high visual fidelity across projects that are enormous in scale. The only way to do so economically is through smarter systems. Knowledge of and experience with generative and procedural systems is key. Can you code a solution to a recurring problem? Great. Can you code a system that will provide a wide variety of viable solutions to a recurring problem? Even better. Can you create a system that will monitor itself to utilize the most appropriate resources to solve a problem? Now we're looking at the horizon of development for where the tools we use and how we need to use them are headed.

Q: *Creating compelling digital characters is part art and part science. What is the greatest challenge you encounter on a daily basis? What aspect of character technology keeps you up thinking at night?*

A: The work that currently keeps me most engaged is called the Perception Based Animation project. It involves the procedural generation of locomotion that expresses character. I'm working on this project using quadrupeds. The way an animal walks, trots, and runs tells us much about how heavy it is, how old it is, and whether it's a predator or not. Talented animators know how to include these characteristics in their animation. Unfortunately, the tools that talented and novice animators alike must use are nearly all based upon describing motion as transforms in space. The system I'm working on describes animation as characteristic features of motion. A direct solution to the problem gets complicated, however, because footfall rate and footfall pattern can be closely associated with size, age, and species. Providing control over the expressed qualities (size, age, and predator or not), and full control over gait type and speed is a problem that keeps me thinking.

Q: *What are the ingredients for a successful digital character?*

A: I love highly realistic synthetic animals and creatures. Successful realistic digital creatures exhibit the changing shape of muscle and fat through movement along with the rigidity of a skeletal structure appearing and disappearing under the skin. They also move as if the body is a connected system. This feature is primarily in the hands of animation to achieve, but successful setup of motion and control systems enables this sort of hierarchically-driven coordinated movement to be managed by the animator as a byproduct of the workflow of creating a performance rather than as an additional effort.

Q: *While the industry is competitive, it is ultimately respectful of great work. Outside of the work you have been personally involved in the production of, what animated characters have you been impressed or inspired by? What is the historical high-bar?*

A: Though I'm most intrigued by synthetic animals, my all-time highest achievement awards go to Digital Domain's work on *Curious Case of Benjamin Button* and ILM's work on Davey Jones in *Pirates of the Caribbean: Dead Man's Chest*. I worked on the latter project, but only during the final push to complete it and therefore can't claim much responsibility for the success of the character. These two characters completely fooled the audience into believing they were real actors in makeup or prosthetics. Digital creature-wise, the Rhythm & Hues' tiger in *Life of Pi* achieved the same believability. These are incredible pieces of movie magic made possible by really talented technical animators.

Q: *Where do you see digital characters in 10 years? Where are animated characters for film and games heading?*

A: I believe the most significant work for digital characters over the next 10 years lies not in their use for entertainment but in their use for medicine. The real-time capture and representation of macro and micro-scale behaviors of the human body coupled with sophisticated deformation and articulation systems will be key in being able to perform less invasive surgical procedures performing predictive analysis of the results of medical decisions. Many of the same techniques used for the setup and control of characters for entertainment in film and games are directly applicable to medical simulation and medical augmented reality.

That said, the use of character technology in film and games is going to increase. One key area is what I'll call "adaptive rigging." Think of a motion and control system as an on demand system that is responsive to the performance requirements of the shot or environment. Currently, we setup characters with performance expectations in mind. Our goal is to ensure that the character can meet the highest goals necessary for the project. Occasionally, but rarely, a special setup is used for performances that are more or less intense than the standard. Now imagine that we, instead, setup the system to be able to pull from a library of possible solutions based upon the need of a particular shot or an environment at the time that the performance is required. I believe this kind of adaptive setup will make projects more efficient and increase the capacity of the characters to meet unexpected or spontaneous motion, control, and deformation requirements.

CHAPTER 6

Character Technology
and Code

6.1 COMMONALITIES BETWEEN SOFTWARE

When it comes to character setup and animation technology, software has come and gone. This book is not about software, but it may be worthwhile to discuss some of the commonalities between contemporary applications with regard to character technology. Most animation packages have a common set of functionalities, which is presented slightly differently in each application. By making clear the fact that there are underlying principles behind this common functionality, this book will teach a crucial lesson to readers who will almost certainly need to adopt several different software packages or other technological tools over the course of their career. All animation software have some notion of the topics covered in this book. Although the names may be different, there is an overall trend across software platforms to use the same or similar names for nodes and techniques. Terms such as joints, constraints, deformers, nulls, and groups exist in some form or another but the real difference is interface. Interface knowledge comes with experience and coming to a new system with a firm understanding of the end goal desired and a road map for the steps needed to get there will ease the transition. This is especially important when learning a system that is specific to a studio and not available commercially.

Many studios invest a lot of time and money into developing proprietary software. This gives them a fully understood framework in which to develop tools as opposed to trying to build extensions onto existing third-party platforms where operations are occurring in a "black box." Many studios are in development on films for many years. Because of this, it is sometimes a safer bet to have full control over their proprietary software than to rely on the ebb and flow of a third-party developer that could stop supporting its software at any time. For character technology, this is particularly important, as much of the pipeline for developing a project will be based around the needs of the digital characters. Similarly, the ability to extend existing software is critical and this will usually require the development of custom code and plug ins for the existing system. Being able to do this on-the-fly allows for a system to evolve in response to the needs of production.

6.2 PROGRAMMING AND SCRIPTING

Character technology is a quickly evolving subject and one where no solution is a catchall for every situation. Therefore, it is imperative to have access to the underlying framework of your animation system. This is usually accomplished via a scripting interface or for more complicated development work, an API, which allows one to access the low-level functionality of the system via a programming language of some flavor.

Programming is the creation and maintenance of code. Whether that code is compiled into a binary executable file or not is one distinction between programming languages and scripting languages but the real difference lies in the desired access to the infrastructure that you are developing in. Programming languages are compiled and are typically used for speed-intensive extensions of the core software, whereas scripting languages remain in their original written form and are interpreted each time they are executed, mostly accessing the surface functionality of the core software. The differences between programming and scripting languages are diminishing, and languages such as Python [17] are bridging the gap by being a scripting language that can be executed as-is or compiled. In fact, Python is becoming a commonly used language across commercial and proprietary animation systems.

Programming languages such as C++ are typically used to build new applications or compiled plugins for existing software. Scripting is used internally to automate and combine small tasks into macros within the software and externally to interface with the operating system and the data stored on disk. No matter what the situation is, coding (or at least the ability to think algorithmically) is critical to the creation of digital characters. In fact, a general understanding of the concepts behind programming will always complement the other skills required for character setup. Consequently, we can address the software and language-agnostic manner with which we will describe code in the context of this text.

6.3 PRESENTATION OF ALGORITHMS IN THIS BOOK

This book is designed to cover the algorithmic thinking behind character technology and to be software-agnostic. Because of this, algorithmic concepts will be presented through graphical flowcharts as opposed to pseudo-code or the isolation of one particular language. The concepts can be implemented in any system, and the reader need not be fluent in a specific language or programming, in general. The code is represented using a simplified object-oriented programming (OOP) paradigm. OOP represents the code as "objects," with attributes that describe them and associated procedures, known as methods, which act on the data. For example, an algorithm for a simple joint rotation constraint that applies weighted rotation values to a series of

Class	
jointsToRotate:	string array
rotateWeight:	float array
inputValue:	vector
weight:	float

Instance	
jointsToRotate:	neck01
jointsToRotate:	neck02
jointsToRotate:	neck03
jointsToRotate:	neck04
jointsToRotate:	neck05
rotateWeight:	0.2
rotateWeight:	0.3
rotateWeight:	0.4
rotateWeight:	0.5
rotateWeight:	0.6
inputValue:	head.neckRot
weight:	head.neckRot.weight

FIGURE 6.1   Class and data diagram for a joint rotate constraint.

joints would be illustrated by an object class as shown in Figure 6.1 and a method as shown in Figure 6.2.

These figures represent the class and an object instance of that class (Figure 6.1), along with the method (Figure 6.2) for a joint rotation constraint. This constraint defines a special control by which a chain of joints have cumulative rotations applied via the control curve offset by a per-joint weight. A class defines the characteristics of an object, including its attributes, fields, and properties. An instance of this class is called an object. Objects provide specific data to the fields defined in the class. In our case, each class has a constraint associated with it. In programming parlance, this constraint would be called a "method." Methods are the algorithms associated with classes that give them their ability to manipulate the data stored in the object instances. In our example above, the class rotate constraint defines a list (array) of joints

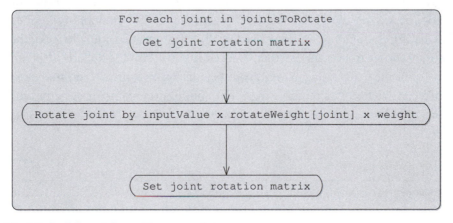

FIGURE 6.2   Method for a joint rotate constraint.

(`jointsToRotate`), the weight associated with each of those joints (`rotateWeight`), the value of the incoming animation control (`inputValue`), and the overall effect of this instance of the constraint (`weight`). The input object called `neckRot` provides the necessary data to create an instantiation of this class. When classes are built, they can become the generic building blocks of more complex systems. The actual constraint associated with this class is depicted in the flowchart found in Figure 6.2. All of the data defined in the class are utilized and manipulated in the process of curling the joint chain in a user-defined, weighted manner. The method cycles through all of the joints in `jointsToRotate` and stores the rotation matrix for each one of them, and then it multiplies the `inputValue` by the `rotateWeight` for each joint, and then multiples all of that by the `weight`. Although the `jointsToRotate` and `rotateWeight` attributes are fixed values which define the properties of the constraint's, `inputValue` and `weight` are animatable attributes which can be changed over the course of the animation, with `inputValue` being the main interface for the control.

Most methods in an animation system have some concept of a `weight` which allows the character setup artists to minimize, turn off, or bypass a constraint's execution to help with debugging. This ability to debug a rig allows an artist to get to the root of any problem or unexpected behaviors quickly.

The sections of code throughout the book are intended to represent simplified versions of what can be complicated tools. Some methods are represented in more verbose terms, and others utilize generic method calls for getting and setting vector and matrix values as needed. Complex operations, like dynamic simulation, are internally left as "black box" operations where it would be expected that the character setup artist or animator would turn control over to an established dynamics engine. In general, the code presented is intended to be more representational of the thought process behind constructing a constraint or deformer and not an exact blueprint for developing such tools.

The changing nature of character and animation technology is dependent and predicated in new software tools and techniques developed within those tools. Knowledge of the algorithms underlying currently existing tools also helps a character rigger know the right tool for specific situations by having an intimate familiarity with that tool's functionality. While those who work with existing character technology need not be programmers, knowledge of the subject is becoming increasingly important. Further, object-oriented thinking outside of generating code can be a useful mindset. Creating generic objects (such as regions of a rig) that can be used as modules and constructed in a reusable manner to build more complex systems will eliminate the redundancy of building these same blocks again. A library of reusable objects is invaluable to any project.

FURTHER READING

For a good overview of Python, start with the website:

http://www.python.org/

Some good introductory Python resources include

Lutz, M. 2007. *Learning Python*, 3rd edition. O'Reilly & Associates, Inc., Sebastopol, CA.

Zelle, J. M. 2003. *Python Programming: An Introduction to Computer Science.* Franklin Beedle & Associates.

For good practical books that are specific to programming and scripting related to animation production, and Autodesk Maya specifically:

Gould, D. 2003. *Complete Maya Programming: An Extensive Guide to MEL and the C++ API (Morgan Kaufmann Series in Computer Graphics and Geometric Modeling).* Morgan Kaufmann Publishers Inc., San Francisco, CA.

Gould, D. 2005. *Complete Maya Programming, Vol. II: An In-depth Guide to 3D Fundamentals, Geometry, and Modeling (Morgan Kaufmann Series in Computer Graphics and Geometric Modeling).* Morgan Kaufmann Publishers Inc., San Francisco, CA.

Wilkins, M. R. and Kazmier, C. 2005. *MEL Scripting for Maya Animators*, 2nd edition *(The Morgan Kaufmann Series in Computer Graphics).* Morgan Kaufmann Publishers Inc., San Francisco, CA.

For very hands-on tutorials for advanced rigging in Autodesk Maya, the "The Art of Rigging" series from CG Toolkit are quite thorough, but no longer in print: [18–20].

CHAPTER 7

Interview: Daniel Dawson, Lead Character Technical Director, DreamWorks Animation

7.1 BIO

Daniel Dawson studied computer science at the University of Washington and Washington State University before taking a job at a start-up animation studio in Florida. From there, Daniel went to Visual Concepts as a modeler and rigger working on the NBA 2K and NFL 2K series of video games. In 2002, Daniel started at DreamWorks and has worked on many films including *Shrek 2*, *Shrek 3*, *Shrek 4*, *Monsters vs. Aliens*, *Madagascar 3*, and *How to Train Your Dragon 2*. Daniel cofounded a company called Kickstand with Rob O'Neill, Greg Elshoff, and Phil McNagny. Kickstand produced computer-generated content, consulted on pipeline architecture, and sold software related to the computer graphics industry.

7.2 Q&A

Q: *The components of character technology are diverse and span the artistic and technical spectrum. How did you get your start in the industry? Based on where you see the field heading what experience/training do you recommend people have?*

A: When I was in school, there weren't many courses dedicated to computer graphics. I knew that a lot of people in the industry had computer science backgrounds, so that is what I chose to study. I also had an informal art background. That combination of technical and artistic skills has served me well in my career. That mix of artistic and technical challenges is what

Daniel Dawson, Lead Character Technical Director,
DreamWorks Animation

appeals to me most about my job. For character artists today, I think it's still valuable to have a range of skills. It's not uncommon to be writing code one day, and evaluating the aesthetics of a character the next day. In addition to traditional education, students today have access to excellent resources on the web. From YouTube videos to full courses taught by industry professionals, the options available online are better than ever before. I was able to quickly get up to speed on a game development engine by watching a comprehensive series of video tutorials online. I would encourage students to take advantage of these resources.

Q: *Creating compelling digital characters is part art and part science. What is the greatest challenge you encounter on a daily basis? What aspect of character technology keeps you up thinking at night?*

A: I find it challenging and enjoyable to strike a balance between anatomical realism versus more stylized and cartoony characters. Even cartoony characters can benefit from having a basis in anatomical realism. But it's also important to know where to push things and exaggerate proportions and physical limitations. Squash and stretch is an example of something that is not at all realistic, but provides a way for animators to really emphasize certain actions and emotions.

Also, it's important not to get stuck in a rut. I always try to look at problems with fresh eyes. I try to stay informed about what is happening in the rest of the industry, and be aware of emerging trends. This industry is a rapidly changing and evolving one, so it is important to stay flexible, and be open to new ideas and approaches.

Another challenge I find interesting is thinking about digital characters in terms of the "user experience" (UX). Digital characters are not often thought of in these terms, but a good user experience can make the process of animating more streamlined and enjoyable. At Dream-Works, we try to provide a very minimalist user experience by keeping the number of icons and handles to a minimum. There should be as few distracting elements as possible. Ideally, the animator should only see the character, and just be able to click and drag to move the character around, as if it was a stop-motion character armature. Icons and handles distract from the visual impact of the scene.

Q: *What are the ingredients for a successful digital character?*

A: At DreamWorks, we talk about "believability," which is different than realism. Characters can be very stylized, and unrealistic, while still being believable. On the rigging side, a believable character needs to have a sense of volume and mass. Preservation of volume gives characters a feeling of solidity. Grounding characters with credible anatomical underpinnings also helps provide believability.

Ultimately, what matters for the audience is that the character is able to emote. This requires a character that can convey subtle emotions through body language and facial expressions. Providing this subtlety in a character rig is challenging, and at the same time, rewarding. I find it incredibly gratifying to see a character I worked on in the hands of a talented animator, acting and evoking an emotional response from the audience.

Q: *While the industry is competitive, it is ultimately respectful of great work. Outside of the work you have been personally involved in the production of, what animated characters have you been impressed or inspired by? What is the historical high-bar?*

A: I am always amazed at the work done by visual effect studios, particularly Rhythm and Hues. Their work on *Life of Pi* was incredible. I used to pride myself on being able to identify CG effects in movies, but these days, I often find myself unable to distinguish real from digital. That's a testament to the incredible talent of the artists involved in these films. Disney has also been putting out some really amazing stuff lately, I particularly enjoyed *Tangled*. Also, Animal Logic's work on *The Lego Movie* was great. I appreciate the fact that they embraced the limitations of the Lego minifigures, and incorporated them into the animation style. It just goes to show that you can have compelling digital characters that aren't photorealistic recreations of humans.

Q: *Where do you see digital characters in 10 years? Where are animated characters for film and games heading?*

A: That is a difficult question, 10 years ago, I could not have foreseen where the industry is today. However, one thing on the horizon that will have a significant impact on digital character creation is virtual reality. It's clear that character interactions in virtual reality are much more compelling than those on a flat screen. Full head tracking allows digital characters to look you in the eye, and track you as you move around the scene. This will open up many opportunities in the areas of artificial intelligence, realistic digital character creation, and storytelling.

The obvious initial applications will be video games, but the potential for new forms of narrative storytelling is significant. This is a completely new medium and filmmakers and video game designers will need to figure out best practices and a new storytelling language. As Michael

Abrash of Oculus VR said, "I do not want to be in *Call of Duty*, it is terrifying." Many traditional video game genres will not be enjoyable in virtual reality; the immersive nature of virtual reality makes certain game genres too intense. In virtual reality, just exploring an environment can be extremely compelling; as a result, I expect exploration games such as *Myst* to make a comeback.

In addition, games where the player avatar matches what you are actually doing in real life (namely, sitting) are a good fit for virtual reality. For example, flight simulators, space dog fighting games, and car racing games are a perfect fit for virtual reality. Matching your avatar to what your body is doing in the real world is very important in VR. When your avatar doesn't match your movements, it is disconcerting and breaks immersion. This will push the fields of real-time motion capture and face capture. I'm extremely excited about the field of virtual reality, and I can't wait to see what implications it has for digital characters.

II

Character Technology

CHAPTER 8

Introduction to Character Technology

CONSTRUCTING THE ARCHITECTURE of a digital character is one of the most complicated aspects of animation production. Considerations must be made for the mechanical structure, as well as the deformation of the character model. In addition, an interface either for the animator, motion capture system, or a procedural system or a procedural system to control the character is required. All of these decisions are based on the type and nature of the production. Requirements for film animation and video games are different, so the limitations and concerns for each medium will be highlighted. This work requires the eye of an artist and the thought process of an engineer.

8.1 NOMENCLATURE

Character technology, and more generally animation technology, is full of terminology, and each software package uses its own terms to describe similar concepts. In the pantheon of computer graphics phrases, the realm of character technology is one of the least standardized with regard to nomenclature. For the purposes of clarity and to propose a uniform language for the discussion of character technology, the following terms are defined:

Motion system: The collection of joints, constraints, and controls which provide the kinematic basis for the rig.

Joint: The transformable hierarchical matrix which forms the atomic unit for the motion system.

Parenting: A hierarchical relationship between objects.

Constraint: A method that defines a nonhierarchical relationship between joints. This may include solvers to procedurally place joints.

Solver: A constraint that procedurally determines the relationship of joints through calculation and/or simulation.

Control system: The collection of controls that provide an interface for the animator to manipulate the character and drive the motion system.

Control: The object, attribute, or interface through which an animator manipulates the character motion system.

Deformation system: The collection of methods used to attach and modify the character model via the changing motion system.

Surface: An element of the overall geometric character model which is deformed by the deformation system.

Deformer: A method for modifying the position of vertices of a surface.

Different studios also use different terminology for these elements but the above should provide a baseline to carry us through the concepts covered in this book.

8.2 THE PIPELINE FOR DIGITAL CHARACTER CREATION AND MAINTENANCE

In the creation of games and films, the production pipeline is the path data travels through the production process. This includes asset management, access to assets by multiple artists, and the workflow from one stage to the next. As can be seen in Figure 8.1, the character technology pipeline starts with the development of the character model. Once the model is completed, it is handed off to the character setup artist who builds the motion and deformation systems.

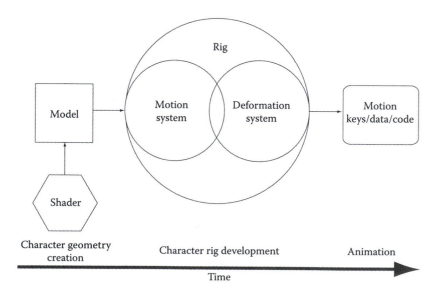

FIGURE 8.1 Character technology pipeline.

The shading and texturing of the character comes into play at around the same time as the animation (at the end of the pipeline), but ideally happens as early as the model is completed.

Modularity and efficiency are keys to character pipelines, and characters need to be standardized in terms of their functionality and element naming. This is essential not only for artists setting up characters and those maintaining characters they did not setup, but also for animators who need a consistent and reliable control set. Standardization also allows for the ability to craft "smarter" production tools. Standards lead to safer assumptions which can lead to the automation of common tasks. The structure of the production pipeline revolves around the idea of *references* to assets which have been "published" or "mastered," as opposed to each scene having a *static* inclusion of the character rig. Similarly, the ability for artists to work on versions of the rig insulated from the live rig that is in animators' shots is important. This can be accomplished as easily as artists working in a workshop directory and as complicated as working in "production trees," which are local versions of the main production directory structure. Production trees are parallel versions of the production assets that reference the main master production tree. By having access to a personal copy, or shadow, of the latest production assets, a character setup artist can test solutions without affecting the rest of production. Once the solution is implemented in a manner that has no unforeseen circumstances down the line, that asset can be "checked in" to the main tree and all other parallel trees can get access to it. Checking a file out through this notion of *revision control* gives that artist the ability to exclusively edit it. Other artists needing to edit that file will have to wait until the owner checks it back in. They then will get the latest version of the file and make their edits from there. Often times multiple files need to be edited to facilitate a change, so associations are made through revision control for grouping files together to define an asset. Similarly, every production has its own standard for managing collections of files which define the version state of an asset at any time. In the same way that software applications have version numbers, asset states are also numbered for tracking. By integrating production trees with revision-controlled assets, defined by a collection of files, characters and assets can always be rolled back to a previous working state.

The evolving state of an asset on the main production tree is ideally seamlessly handled thanks to referencing. Referencing is a means of establishing a symbolic link to an asset stored on the production tree as opposed to storing that asset within each scene. Referencing then allows an artist to have a file "virtually open" in a scene by accessing the reference to it. By including a reference to the asset, the animator, for example, cannot modify the original asset. This leaves it open for other artists to continue to work on it. Having assets referenced allows for a simultaneous workflow among artists and the flexibility to change the design, look, and functionality of an asset across production. Most animation systems include a method for referencing assets and for managing the shot inventory via a referencing system. In proprietary systems, it is possible to handle the shot population and asset referencing via a production database. In this case, scenes can be a description of assets in the scene with data about their position over time, likely stored as animation curves. When the shot is edited, the database is queried for the latest assets and then connected to the stored animation curves for proper placement and motion. Thus, the shot is built at runtime via scripts which query the database and make the proper connections instead of being stored as a static collection of assets. This runtime build step is a powerful process where code can be run on the assets and the construction of the shot to implement edits or updates procedurally, on a shot-specific or production-wide basis. Once automated by the production pipeline interface, the shot-building process is transparent to the user and provides a high level of control in the technical administration of the project.

Maintenance is a critical concern for the character pipeline. Setup artists need to have access to the character in an insulated environment while animation is taking place so that changes can be made and tested before that character is once again "published" into production. More specifically, setup artists need to be able to make changes to the character rig while maintaining whatever animation has been applied. Once fixed or modified, these changes should automatically propagate into the production pipeline so that animators have access to the latest rig. Referencing makes this possible. Fixes often require adding a new attribute that is a modified version of an existing control. This maintains any current animation, but provides the new control if needed, as opposed to changing the functionality of an existing control in a nonbackwards compatible manner and running the risk of changing in-process animation. As animation is produced, it goes through a process of reviews and revisions until it is considered finished and "approved" by the animation supervisor and project director(s). As such, it is important to have approved final animation remain unchanged by rig updates. Thus, it is sometimes necessary, in extreme cases, to be able to lock a version of a rig and tie that version to the approved animation, leaving them bound together and in a read-only state. It is becoming increasingly common that the geometry deformed by the rig per-frame is written out as a geometry cache. As opposed to locking the rig for this shot, the visible output of the rig is stored on disk in the form of a series of models. This "bakes" the animation as geometry and effectively frees the animation from changes to the rig. These models are then read by the renderer at render time and the rig is never evaluated again for that shot. While managing these per-frame models is a storage issue, the costs are often outweighed by the ability to control the model disconnected from the rig.

Shot-specific deformations are often produced by editing the character models after the animation is finalized. Details, such as finger contact compression when a character touches something, for example, sell the idea of the character realistically interacting with the environment and other characters in the shot. These shot-specific deformations are rarely included in the rig and are dependent on animation, so they are enacted on the geometry cache for the scene. While baking character geometry is a method for locking animation from rig changes, it has an increasingly important role in production and has become quite common.

8.3 SURFACE TYPES OF GEOMETRIC MESHES

Modern digital characters are created by sculpting a 3D surface or model. This model is then deformed by the character rig. The surface type of this model is dependent on the strategy and

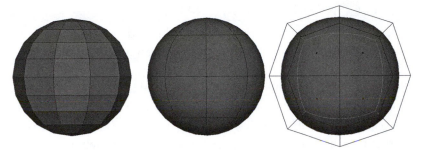

FIGURE 8.2 Surface type sphere primitives (polygon, NURBS, subdivision surface).

pipeline of the production, but at this point, we typically breakdown surface types into three categories, polygonal, Bézier-spline-based, and subdivision surfaces (Figure 8.2).

Polygon: Polygons are the most simple surfaces, composed of vertices connected by edges to form polygons which are connected to form polygonal meshes. These are often the only option for video games based on the architecture of most real-time engines. Polygon configurations for production are usually limited to triangles (three sides) and quadrilaterals (four sides), with the ideal being quadrilateral polygons as they usually result in better deformations on character models. In the past, some game engines required polygons to be triangular but this is not a requirement anymore.

Nonuniform rational Bézier-spline (NURBS): A NURBS curve is defined by its order, a set of weighted control points, and a knot vector. NURBS curves and surfaces are generalizations of both B-splines and Bézier curves and surfaces, the primary difference being the weighting of the control points which makes NURBS curves rational (nonrational B-splines are a special case of rational B-splines). One-dimensional NURBS curves evolve into only one parametric direction, usually called "s" or "u," whereas two-dimensional NURBS surfaces evolve into two parametric directions, called "s" and "t" or "u" and "v." These NURBS surfaces are often called patches and are then stitched together to create a model.

Subdivision: Subdivision surfaces are a method of representing a smooth surface via the specification of a coarser piecewise linear polygon mesh. The smooth surface can then be calculated from the coarse mesh as the limit of an iterative process of subdividing each polygonal face into smaller faces that better approximate the smooth surface. As NURBS have to be created in patches and stitched together to create a seamless surface, subdivision surfaces can achieve the organic qualities of NURBS as a single surface and thus avoiding stitching. Because of this, subdivision surfaces are the preferred method of modeling character and scene geometry.

Much of the acceptance of these surfaces is based on their access in commercial applications. Studios can write the necessary tools to implement a custom surface type and integrate it into their production pipeline. The independent user does not usually have such a luxury and is subject to the availability in their tool set. Irrespective of the surface type, there are similar guidelines that should be followed for the development of a digital character.

8.4 MODELING CONCERNS FOR ANIMATION

When a character is going to fill a theater screen, it is subjected to viewer scrutiny at an unparalleled level. A clean model with a well thought out flow of edges and layout of points (topology) is critical for character deformations. Areas that require extreme deformations require more resolution than areas that have limited motion. The general idea with character modeling is to lay out the topology in such a way that the areas of articulation have the necessary resolution to bend effectively while maintaining the desired shape. The default pose of the character should be arranged so that the different body parts are far enough from each other to make deformations easier in a relaxed muscular state and ideally at the midpoint of their deformation range. The midpoint of a deformation range for arms usually leaves the arms straight out to the side in a "T-Pose," which is directly in-between raising the arm above the head and resting it at its side. Because characters are rarely called to raise their arms over their heads, modelers will often model characters with arms halfway down at the character's side in an "A-Pose" (Figure 8.3). Elbow and knees are also often modeled slightly bent so that the deformation process starts with a shape that is closer to the extremes that the rig is responsible for producing while deforming the model. The point of all of these is to make the deformation setup as efficient as possible and a well-planned starting point is essential. It should be pointed out, however, that some motion and deformation systems work best given a straight orientation for elbows and knees. Because of this, be sure you are familiar with the features in the software in which you are working.

The humanoid knee and shoulder are examples of where this can be quite straightforward and where it can be the most complex. The human knee (Figure 8.4) is essentially a hinge joint that rotates around one axis and for the most part in one direction around the axis. To preserve the volume of the knee area, two joints are placed, one at the top part of the articulation area and another at the bottom of the articulation area, to give the impression of large confluence of bone

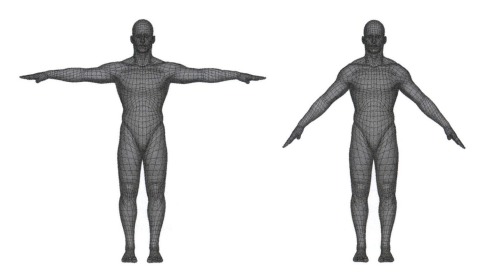

FIGURE 8.3 Character model in T-Pose and A-Pose. (Model by Lee Wolland.)

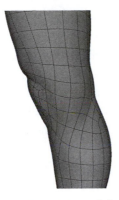
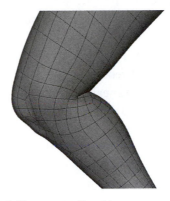

FIGURE 8.4   Knee model, straight and flexed. (Model by Lee Wolland.)

and muscle that fold when the knee is bent. The topology of the model's surface should reflect an understanding of how this region articulates. This relationship means that communication between the character modeler and the character setup artist should start early and iterate to reach the optimum result.

Contrary to the relative simplicity of the human knee, the human shoulder is a complex relationship between a ball and socket (in the aptly named "ball and socket" joint). This allows the upper-arm and shoulder region to (1) rotate in many combinations of all three rotation axes and (2) translate thanks to the shoulder's loose attachment to the axial body via its attachment to the scapula and clavicle (Figure 8.5). This complex region requires well laid out points to aid in the deformation of the model, as it will be affected by a number of joints and is one of the more mobile regions of the body.

Typically, for each production, the topology for characters is defined early and then used to shape the rest of the characters, when possible, using the original as a template. Sharing topology across characters allows rigging solutions and other pipeline concerns to be propagated across characters. This provides a much-needed speed up in rigging time and efficiency.

With regard to the geometric resolution of a film character, there is almost no limitation. Animators require fast feedback with limited processing lag on the execution of a character

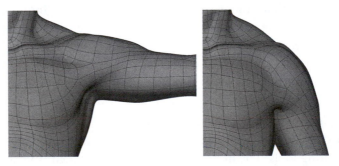

FIGURE 8.5   Shoulder model, straight and bent down. (Model by Lee Wolland.)

while they are interacting with it. In many cases, the high-resolution details generated through sculpting tools like Z-Brush or Autodesk Mudbox require a much higher resolution mesh than can be run interactively. This high-resolution mesh used for final display needs only be processed at the moment of rendering which is a noninteractive event and expected in films to run offline. This does not mean that the character setup artist should not be thinking about optimization at every step of the way, but there are certain speed allowances that are made in film production that are compensated for with processing power. Character interactivity in an animation system is a sensitive threshold affected by many factors but true interactivity requires that character response be instantaneous. When an animator moves a control, the affected element should move in real-time. Sometimes even the deformation of a low polygon mesh is enough to slow down a system, particularly when many characters are in a single scene. As a result, it is sometimes optimal (but not ideal) for an animator to work with a proxy representation of the final geometry. This proxy might be a low-resolution version of the character or rigid, nondeforming, replacements for the high-resolution skin. These are typically simple polygonal shapes that match the initial volume of the character elements and are parented to the appropriate rig elements. They then form a quick-responding approximation of the character. Any lag is a distraction and a time sink, so effort must go into making sure that deforming models, or even proxy geometry if needed, are fast enough for real-time feedback.

8.5 MODELING CONCERNS FOR VIDEO GAMES AND REAL-TIME ENGINES

There are almost no limitations for model resolution in film production, however this is a huge concern for real-time graphics engines. Before we delve into this, it is worth mentioning that commercials and television series are generally somewhere between the game scenario and the film one, although constraints for these projects are usually purely based on schedule and budgets. For games, polygons are exclusively used within most of today's game engines and polygon count, commonly referred to as polycount, is closely monitored. Modelers working in video games must go to great lengths to optimize polycount, and techniques are employed using textures and various other map-based techniques to add details to the model that transcend the surface topology. Bump and normal maps are created to add the appearance of surface details and complexity without increasing the polycount. Although graphics hardware constantly pushes up the possible polygon volume, the general contemporary consensus is that polycount for game characters in character-based games (such as first-person shooters, role-playing, or adventure games) should be between 10,000 and 20,000 polygons. This range will likely be humorous in a few years as in the time of the first edition of this book the general thinking was between 4,000 and 10,000 polygons.

Take, for example, this character from *Gears of War* (Figure 8.6). The designed character is created at a very high polygon count (in this case, 2 million polygons) using a mix of modeling and sculpting tools. The high-resolution detail is "baked" into a collection of maps, most notably a normal map, which replaces the surface normal on a low polygon mesh with

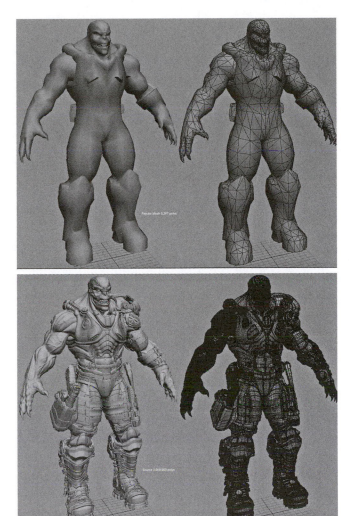

FIGURE 8.6 Low- and high-resolution polygon meshes for characters from *Gears of War*. (© 2014, Microsoft Corporation. All rights reserved. Microsoft, Xbox, the Xbox logo, *Gears of War*, Black Tusk Studios, and the Crimson Omen logo are trademarks of the Microsoft group of companies.)

a multichannel value derived from the high-resolution mesh. This allows the low-resolution mesh to be easily deformed by the engine, but the application of the complexity maps provides all of the detail that was modeled into the high-resolution mesh. Not all map technologies can be utilized by game engines. For example, deformation maps, such as displacement or vector maps (where the surface is changed by the values of the map), are heavily used in animated films and visual effects but have just recently started to be a viable option in game engines. As a point of reference, it is also enlightening to compare the models from the first *Gears of Wars* (2006) (Figure 8.6) with ones from *Gears of Wars 3* (2011) (Figure 8.7).

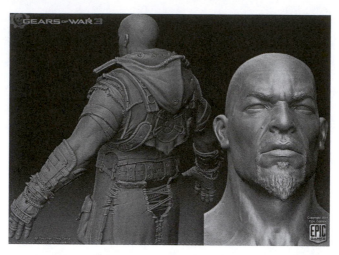

FIGURE 8.7 Characters from *Gears of War 3*. (© 2014, Microsoft Corporation. All rights reserved. Microsoft, Xbox, the Xbox logo, *Gears of War*, Black Tusk Studios, and the Crimson Omen logo are trademarks of the Microsoft group of companies.)

In addition, games often also require characters to be modeled with separate collision geometry—a very low polygon surface that rides along with the character rig and is used in the processing of collisions in the dynamics engine.

There are a number of limitations on the process of character setup for game engines. Due to the real-time constraint imposed by game engines, only a small subset of methods available to characters developed for animated films are applicable. Shortcuts and simplifications must be sought wherever possible, leading to a different set of problems and, in their own right, cutting-edge solutions. Every tool used in character setup would have to be interpreted and recreated to run in the real-time engine. For example, default tools such as joints that come in animation software packages have an easily mapped equivalent in most game engines, but other tools used to build a character's motion or deformation system either have to be recreated by the software engineers on the game team or ignored and not used in the setup by the character setup team.

Throughout this book, we will be comparing techniques and discussing the limitations and possibilities of game character development as opposed to those for film. As we live in an age of convergence, where films, games, and interactive media intermix and become less and less distinct, we will continue to see fewer differences between characters produced for different media.

8.6 EXERCISE

In preparation for taking a character design from 2D sketches and model sheets (concept designs that illustrate the character from many angles and poses), to a 3D model, it is important to take a step back and attempt to bring the 3D form into the real world. One way to do this is in the form of a posed maquette that harnesses the personality and attitude of the character.

This process will give you a better sense of the character proportions and volume and will help immensely as you move onto character modeling in your 3D package of choice.

1. Begin with making a metal armature. Not only will this help support your clay or plasticine model, but it will get you thinking about internal structure and point of articulation. Tip: To create volume while keeping the weight down, artists often use tightly bound aluminum foil to build up regions of the model.

2. Once the volumes are right, start covering the armature with the material of your choice to flesh it out.

3. Sculpt in minor features with as much detail as possible. The more decisions you can make that this point, the better off you will be when you digitally model your character.

4. Step back and think about the form. Does it work? Does it read from multiple angles? Get feedback and critique from others. Challenge the design to be better through iterations.

5. Maintain this feedback loop until satisfied.

6. Harden your maquette in the method associated with the materials you are using.

FURTHER READING

There are many software-specific books and training videos that cover low- and high-polygon modeling techniques.

Patnode, J. 2008. *Character Modeling With Maya And ZBrush*. Focal Press, Oxford, United Kingdom.

Russo, M. 2005. *Polygonal Modeling: Basic and Advanced Techniques (Worldwide Game and Graphics Library)*. Wordware Publishing Inc., Plano, TX.

For a more technical procedural overview of models and modeling, refer to

Ebert, D. S., Musgrave, F. K., Peachey, D., Perlin, K., and Worley, S. 2002. *Texturing and Modeling: A Procedural Approach*. Morgan Kaufmann Publishers Inc., San Francisco, CA.

CHAPTER 9

Interview: Wade Ryer, Character Technical Director

9.1 BIO

Wade Ryer has more than 10 years of experience in animated feature films. His credits include *How To Train Your Dragon 2*, *Rise of the Guardians*, *Kung Fu Panda 2*, *The Tale of Desperaux*, and *The Ant Bully*. He has worked for studios such as DreamWorks Animation, Method Studios, Framestore, Electronic Arts, DNA Productions, and ReelFX Creative Studios.

Born and raised in Binghamton New York, Wade attended Syracuse University and majored in Computer Graphics as well as a focus on illustration and sculpture. When he is not at a computer he enjoys boxing and spending time with his family. Wade resides in Los Angeles, California.

Wade Ryer, Character Technical Director

9.2 Q&A

Q: *The components of character technology are diverse and span the artistic and technical spectrum. How did you get your start in the industry? Based on where you see the field heading what experience/training do you recommend people have?*

A: I was very artistic from a very young age. I originally went to college at Syracuse University for Illustration, but I caught the CG bug once *Toy Story* came out. I ended up majoring in Computer Graphics. It wasn't easy to break into the industry. I spent several years doing graphic design and multimedia work before getting into 3D animation full time. I got in the habit early on of working on my own personal projects during off hours. I have found that to be key in keeping up with new technology and satisfying my creative itch. When you're working on a project of a film, you are fulfilling another person's vision. Your personal work is where you are in complete control and are free to create anything.

I recommend artists and students always work on the foundations. Foundations such as anatomy, design and form as well as basics of technical programming. There is always going to be new software, features and plugins, but a solid knowledge of the fundamentals will always be in need. The computer is just a tool, like a canvas and brush. Digital sculpture is great, but don't forget to study the greats like Bernini and Michelangelo.

Q: *Creating compelling digital characters is part art and part science. What is the greatest challenge you encounter on a daily basis? What aspect of character technology keeps you up thinking at night?*

A: I feel the greatest challenge about digital character is no longer their visuals, but how they fit into a story. We've been able to achieve incredibly photo real characters that believably interact with live action characters. Making a CG character that an audience can relate with, now that's a challenge. We are less and less limited by technology. I run into much more aesthetic challenges than technical challenges on a daily basis.

Q: *What are the ingredients for a successful digital character?*

A: It all depends on the direction that you're looking to take that digital character. A digital character from *The Lego Movie* will have completely different ingredients than a Hulk character from *The Avengers*. Both characters are successful in their own right. I do believe it comes down to character design and appeal.

Q: *While the industry is competitive, it is ultimately respectful of great work. Outside of the work you have been personally involved in the production of, what animated characters have you been impressed or inspired by? What is the historical high-bar?*

A: I have loved the characters that Disney has produced from *Tangled* though their most recent *Big Hero Six*. As far as animated feature films go, they are the setting the bar. The style, design and appeal of their characters is incredible. As far as creature work is concerned, it's tough to do any better than Weta. Their attention to detail and anatomy is second to none.

Q: *Where do you see digital characters in 10 years? Where are animated characters for film and games heading?*

A: Before looking into the future, you need to look into the past. In 2005, *King Kong* won the Oscar for best visual effects and *The Incredibles* won best animated film. Both still hold up today. I feel the biggest difference has been the ease of use of the tools and technology. It used to be only someone with an advanced computer science degree could figure out how to use the pricey expensive tools, but as time goes on, it's becoming easier and more artistic friendly. The industry is globalizing, the information on how to use the tools is out there. All you really need[is] a laptop and an idea and you can create it. As the tools become easier for artists to use, I do believe we'll see an evolution of more compelling, appealing characters that tell great stories.

CHAPTER 10

Anatomy for Character Setup

10.1 CHARACTER MOTION SYSTEMS AND ANATOMY

No matter how realistic, fantastic, or stylized a character is, the underlying skeletal structure must be considered, planned, and implemented in order to achieve the motion and esthetic required of that character. In this chapter, we look at the relationship between anatomy and the design and architecture of a character motion system. While digital characters do not need to precisely recreate the anatomical structure of the entity, it represents an informed understanding of the underlying structure and the motion for which it is designed and is crucial for capturing the essence of that character. Once understood, a decision can be made to stray from it, as dictated by the style of the production. For example, both a human neck and a giraffe neck have seven vertebrae, but in an animation system, it may be important to represent many more joints in a giraffe for both more animation control and smoother deformations. Building a basic understanding of comparative anatomy requires some familiarity with the terminology of biology, so an overview of terms and concepts precedes our overview of anatomical structures and their mechanical properties. Recreating these structures in 3D using matrices and hierarchical transformations follows this discussion and is similarly developed. Starting with a single joint matrix and methods of rotating it, we begin building hierarchies of joints and controlling them with constraints built on relationships between them or custom procedures. We conclude with the integration of dynamic simulation and user interface, which provide our initial methods of attaching motion to these systems.

10.2 ANATOMICAL DIRECTION

A *lingua franca* among anatomists is the language of anatomical direction. This is a common and standardized collection of terms that describe anatomical elements based on their position relative to each other. It also happens to be relevant in describing the position of rig elements in relation to each other. Anatomical position is the default pose that anatomical direction is based on. For the human body, anatomical position is described as standing erect, the eyes

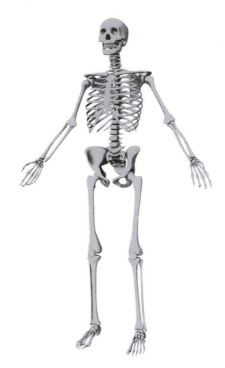

FIGURE 10.1   Anatomical position. (Model by cgHuman.)

looking forward at the horizon, the arms by the sides, and the palms of the hands and the toes directed forward (Figure 10.1). Keep in mind that this is anatomical position and not the "T-pose" that is so often seen in digital characters at their default state. Using the placement of the hands as an example, we can define descriptive terms for the position and direction of elements in relation to each other. If hands were to rest palms-down on a table, they would be said to face *inferiorly*. Turn them around and they face upward, or *superiorly*. Hanging to the sides, naturally they face each other, or *medially*; rotated 180° and they face out, or *laterally*; backwards, or *posteriorly*; forwards, or *anteriorly*. Essentially, three pairs of terms are defined to express the relationship of one structure to another (Table 10.1).

As most biological structures are generally symmetrical along one dividing plane, these terms are highly effective and often additional terms such as "left" and "right" are not used

TABLE 10.1   Anatomical Direction

Anterior (in front): Nearer to the front of the body
Posterior (behind): Nearer to the back of the body
Superior (above): Nearer to the top of the head
Inferior (below): Nearer to the bottom of the feet
Medial: Nearer to the median plane of the body
Lateral: Away from the median plane of the body

except for describing asymmetric details. This symmetry is helpful for the character modeler and the setup artist as it allows geometry and rig structures to be mirrored across planes to reduce work and to ensure symmetric functionality. Although in a 3D space, these planes are defined by the *xyz*-axis that they parallel, biologists have more descriptive terms for them. Once we have an agreed upon natural stance, we can define planes that transect the body, splitting it up into regions. The body is divided into two equal halves, a left and a right by the midsagittal plane, passing through the body at the midline. Splitting the body into anterior and posterior halves is the coronal plane which passes through the body perpendicular to the midsagittal plane. Passing through at right angles to the other planes described and dividing the body into upper and lower halves is the transverse plane. For humans, the transverse plane is located around the hips, splitting the body into equal top and bottom halves.

When it comes to describing structures that are local to a limb or relative to an appendage, the part that is closer to the midsagittal plane is the proximal end, whereas the part that is further away is the distal end. So a feature that lies closer to the hand on the forearm is considered distal to the elbow and proximal to the wrist. Combining terms is where the power of this descriptive syntax comes into play.

When we discuss comparative anatomy, we compare the relationship and differences of structures between species and it is necessary to use a different set of terms which are not related to relative space but to elements of the body. In humans, an orthograde animal, the shoulders lie above the hips, whereas in a dog, a pronograde animal, they lie in front of the hips (Figure 10.2). With this in mind, their position relative to other parts of the body is the same, thus speaking from a comparative point of view, it can be said that the shoulders are toward the

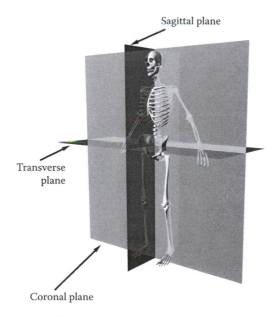

FIGURE 10.2 Body planes. (Model by cgHuman.)

head, or cranial end of the body, while the hips are toward the tail, or caudal end of the body. These terms are applicable to any vertebrate body regardless of its habitual position; bipedal, on two legs, or quadrupedal, on four legs.

- *Ventral:* The belly side of the body

- *Dorsal:* The backside of the body (think of a dorsal fin on a dolphin)

- *Cranial* or *cephalic:* Toward the head end of the body

- *Caudal:* Toward the tail end of the body

10.3 ANATOMICAL TERMS OF MOTION

Body structures are moved by the contraction of muscles. Muscles move parts of the skeleton that are relative to each other. All such movements are classified by the directions in which the affected structures are moved. In human anatomy, all descriptions of position and movement are based on the assumption that the body is in anatomical position (Figure 10.3).

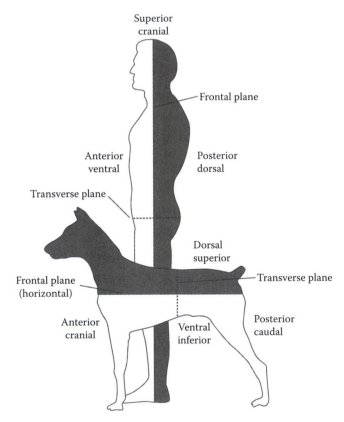

FIGURE 10.3 Human–dog comparison of anatomical direction.

- *Flexion:* A movement in which the angle between two articulating bones is decreased. Flexing the arm brings the hand closer to the shoulder.

- *Extension:* The opposite of flexion—the angle between two articulation bones is increased.

- *Abduction:* The movement of an extremity away from the midline of the body.

- *Adduction:* The opposite of abduction—movement of an extremity toward the body.

- *Rotation:* The movement of a bone around its own axis, such as rotating your arm at the shoulder.

- *Circumduction:* Where the distal end of an extremity moves in a circle while the proximal end remains stable, such as twisting the hand along the axis of the arm.

- *Supination:* Rotating the hand so that the palm is superior, facing forward.

- *Pronation:* Rotating the hand so that the palm is inferior, facing behind.

- *Inversion:* Movement at the ankle resulting in the sole of the foot being turned inward, toward the coronal plane.

- *Eversion:* Movement at the ankle resulting in the sole of the foot being turned outward, away from the coronal plane.

- *Elevation:* Raising a body part such as closing the jaw.

- *Depression:* Lowering a body part such as opening the jaw.

- *Protraction:* Translating a body part forward such as jutting the jaw out.

- *Retraction:* Translating a body part backward such as "clenching" the jaw backward.

- *Hyperextension:* When a body part is extended beyond the straight line formed by normal extension.

- *Plantar-flexion:* Normal extension of the foot (rotating downward on humans).

- *Dorsiflexion:* Opposite extension of the foot (tilting upward in humans).

While these terms have little meaning to animators, they provide an unequivocal vocabulary between character setup artists to describe motion. In most cases, a description such as "when I raise the character's left arm and twist the forearm, I encounter this problem" will suffice, but having access to a common vocabulary has its advantages. As with an understanding of anatomical direction, the terminology for anatomical motion provides a species-independent set of terms to describe character motion.

10.4 JOINT MECHANICS

While skeletal articulations in the natural world are constrained by their function, joints in 3D are, by default, built for articulation within three axes of rotational freedom. With this in mind, it is useful to understand the different types of joints common in nature, as the implementation of these as constraints allows for a sense of realism in the structure. There are four principal types of joints based on the kind of movement possible at each location.

Angular joints, in which there is an increase or decrease in the angle between two bones, are broken down into a series of subtypes. A *hinge* (monoaxial) joint provides rotation of one bone at the point of articulation with another in one degree of rotational freedom. The concave shape of the proximal portion of the human ulna (which is one of the two bones that makes up the human forearm) and the convex shape of the distal portion of the human humerus (the upper-arm) provide a perfect example of a hinge joint in this case represented by the human elbow. This type of joint provides the possibility for flexion-extension movements. *Ellipsoidal* (biaxial) joints allow for motion in two distinct planes of rotation, thus providing more flexibility to the articulating surfaces. The articulation between the carpal bones in the wrist and the distal end of the radius is indicative of a biaxial joint. Biaxial joints are often called universal joints. Flexion-extension and abduction-adduction are possible at this joint type. A *saddle* (multiaxial) joint, like the ellipsoidal joint, is an angular joint that results in flexion-extension and abduction-adduction motion but allows for three-degrees-of-rotation freedom. The human thumb, or more specifically, the first meta carpal of the thumb and its articulation with the carpals, is a saddle joint.

Gliding, or arthrodial, joints manage the simplest motion by which two relatively flat articulating surfaces move in a simple sliding action against each other with two degrees of translational freedom. This motion is created by the translation of one or two surfaces on a single plane. The motion of the articular processes of the vertebrae and between the vertebrae and the ribs is indicative of these surfaces. This gliding motion can be described as flexion-extension and abduction-adduction.

The third type of joint is a *pivot* (uniaxial) joint which provides a point of multidirectional rotation around a pivot point. The proximal heads of the radius and ulna in the human forearm at the elbow articulate via a pivot joint as do the atlas and axis vertebrae that are responsible for much of the rotation of the head.

The fourth and final articulation type is the *ball-and-socket*, ball, or spheroidal (multiaxial) joint, which is most notably located at the human hip and shoulder, and allows for complex rotations. Technically, this joint is capable of flexion-extension, abduction-adduction, and three-degrees-of-rotational freedom.

10.5 COMPARATIVE ANATOMY

Comparative anatomy is the study of similarities and differences in the anatomy of organisms. It is closely related to evolutionary biology and phylogeny (the evolution of species) and helps to

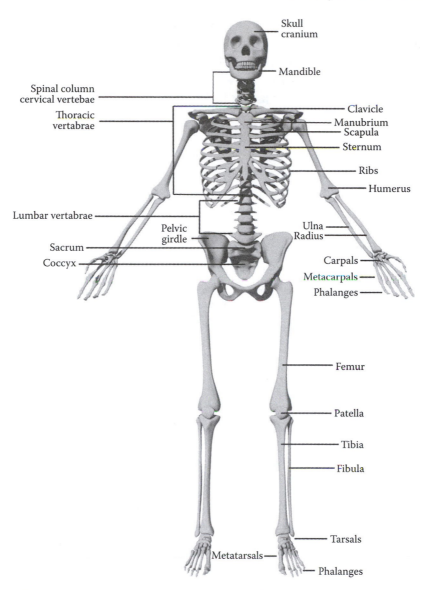

FIGURE 10.4 Basic human skeleton element names. (Model by cgHuman.)

inform character setup in that it provides a starting point based on what is known about existing organisms and ourselves (Figure 10.4). Two major concepts of comparative anatomy are

- *Homologous structures:* Structures which are similar in different species because the species have common descent (they evolved from a common ancestor). They may or may not perform the same function. An example is the forelimb structure shared by cats and whales.

- *Analogous structures:* Structures which are similar in different organisms because they evolved in a similar environment (also known as convergent evolution), rather than inherited from a recent common ancestor. They usually serve the same or similar purposes. An example is the torpedo body shape of dolphins and sharks. This shape evolved in a water environment and thus has hydrodynamic efficiencies, but the animals have different ancestry.

Focusing on mammalian anatomy, we can discuss the commonalities between the limbs as a means of defining architecture. The structure of the limbs is primarily designed for motion. The forelimbs and hindlimbs each consist of a series of bones, meeting the trunk of the body at the pectoral (shoulder, or forelimb) or pelvic (hip, or hindlimb) girdle, respectively.

The pectoral girdle of most mammals consists of a shoulder blade (scapula) and in many, a clavicle. Mammalian pectoral girdles are very much simplified compared to the pectoral regions of their ancestors, which contained a number of additional bones. These bones were either lost or incorporated into the scapula of modern mammals. Monotremes (including the platypus) are an exception—their pectoral girdles include several of these primitive elements. The scapula sits in an envelope of muscles and ligaments which connect it to the rib cage and spine rather than being immovably fused to them. The clavicle, if it is present, runs from the region of the articulation between scapula and forelimb to the anterior part of the sternum. In humans, the clavicle receives forces from the upper extremity and transfers them to the axial skeleton. As the only attachment of the upper extremity to the axial skeleton, excessive forces, such as falling on an outstretched arm, causes all force to be moved into the clavicle. As a result, this is one of the most commonly broken bones in the human body.

The pelvic girdle of mammals is made up of three bones, the ilium, ischium, and pubis. At the junction of these three bones is the socket (acetabulum) for the hind limb. Unlike the pectoral girdle, the pelvic girdle is firmly attached to the spine by a bony fusion between the ilium and sacral vertebrae.

The forelimb itself consists of a humerus (which meets the scapula), a paired radius and ulna (the forearm), a set of carpals and metacarpals (the wrist and the palm), and five digits, each made up of several phalanges (finger bones). The bones of the hindlimb are the femur (which articulates with the acetabulum of the pelvis), the tibia and fibula, the tarsals and metatarsals (the ankle and the foot), and five digits, each made up of two or more phalanges. The first digit of the forelimb (the thumb on humans) is called the pollex; the first digit of the hindlimb is the hallux. A patella lies over the knee joint (junction of the tibia and femur) and functions as a surface for muscle attachments and support. Carpal and tarsal bones are referred to collectively as podials, and metacarpals and metatarsals are metapodials. The calcaneum is a large tarsal bone that extends behind the ankle, forming the heel. It provides an important lever arm for muscles that move the hindfoot.

Limbs are drastically modified to different ends in various groups of mammals. Here, we are concerned primarily with modifications that affect how an animal runs. Several terms describe how and where an animal moves.

Aquatic: Animals that swim (dolphins).
Volant: Animals that fly (bats).
Cursorial: Animals that run rapidly and for long distances (horses).
Scansorial: Animals that are climbers. In the extreme, they are arboreal, spending most of their lives in the trees (sloths).
Saltatorial: Animals that hop. If they use their hindlimbs only and in a fast succession of hops, they are said to be ricochetal (kangaroos).
Fossorial: Animals that dig, usually living in burrows (moles).

A full cycle of motion of a running or walking mammal is called a stride (Figure 10.5). An animal's speed is the product of its stride length times stride rate. There are two ways

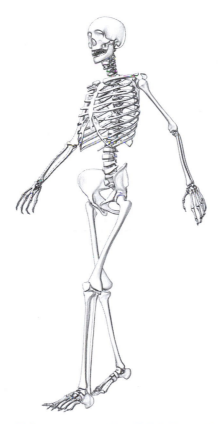

FIGURE 10.5 Human anatomical elements in motion. (Model by cgHuman.)

of increasing the speed of running: increasing stride length and increasing stride rate. Some animals are clearly specialized to increase speed through increasing stride length. The giraffe is an extreme example. Others move rapidly by having a very fast stride rate. These would include, for example, shrews and voles.

10.5.1 Anatomical Case Study: Bird Wings versus Bat Wings

A bird's forelimbs, or wings, are the key to its flight. Each wing has a central vane to hit the wind composed of three limb bones: the humerus, ulna, and radius. The hand, or manus, which ancestrally was composed of five digits, is reduced to three digits. The purpose of the hand is to serve as an anchor for the primaries: one of two groups of feathers responsible for the airfoil shape. The other set of flight feathers, which are behind the carpal joint on the ulna, are called the secondaries. The remaining feathers on the wing are known as coverts, of which there are three sets (Figure 10.6).

The wings of bats give their order Chiroptera its name (literally, "hand-wing"). Functional wings and true flight are characteristics of all bats. The origin of bat wings is most clearly revealed by their skeleton. Every element of its skeleton is clearly homologous with structures in the forelimbs of other mammals as bat wings evolved as a result of modifications to the fore-limbs of their ancestors. The humerus is long and thin compared with the humerus of other mammals, but its articular surfaces and areas for attachment of muscles are fundamentally like those of most mammals. Attached to the humerus are the radius and ulna. The radius is also long and thin, but it is a strong bone that supports the wing. The olecranon process of the ulna (at the articulation with the humerus) is the most substantial part of the ulna, the rest is considerably reduced and fused with the radius. The wrist region is very similar to that of other mammals, although it is less flexible. It is specialized to support the particular motions

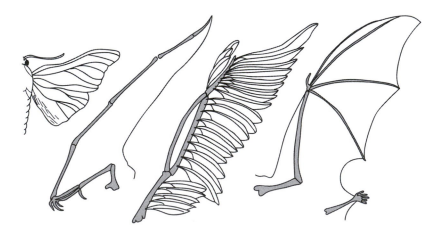

FIGURE 10.6 Comparison of insect, pterosaur, bird, and bat wings.

associated with flying. All bats have a thumb that sits along the leading edge of the wing. It usually has a substantial claw, which is used for climbing, food handling, and fighting. The rest of the digits (digits two through five) support the wing. The wing membrane is an extension of the skin of the body. It is made up of external epidermis and an internal layer of dermis and muscles. These muscles control the curvature of the wing in flight. The membrane is both tough and flexible. Bat wing membranes usually run from the shoulder region to the ankle and over the digits themselves. The wing membrane joins the body along the sides, except in some cases, where it arises near the middle of the back.

10.5.2 Anatomical Case Study: Tentacles

As we will see, the control and coordination of arm movements in 3D space is a complicated task. This is a challenge to both animation systems and biological organisms. Increasing the number of degrees of freedom of the arm makes this task more complicated, and yet most biological movements involve a large number of degrees of freedom. An extreme case, with especially high degrees of freedom, is provided by systems in which muscles are unattached to any internal or external skeleton whatsoever. These structures are much more flexible than jointed limbs and have virtually unlimited degrees of freedom. Examples of such structures are cephalopod (e.g., an octopus) tentacles, or the tongues of some vertebrates, and the trunk of an elephant. These structures are composed solely of muscles used to generate movement and provide the necessary structural support. They have been termed muscular-hydrostats because they are composed of incompressible muscle tissue. The octopus arm is of special interest as a muscular-hydrostat because it combines extreme flexibility with a capability for executing various sophisticated motor tasks. An octopus arm can bend at any point and in any direction, and it can elongate, shorten, and twist.

The biomechanical principles of movement generation differ in animals with and without a rigid skeleton. Those without a rigid skeleton have what is termed a hydrostatic skeleton, consisting mainly of muscles and fluid, which, because they are incompressible, support the flexible body. Hydrostatic skeletons are generally of two types. In muscular hydrostats, muscles and other tissues form a solid structure without a separate enclosed fluid volume such as cephalopod tentacles, elephant trunks, and vertebrate tongues. In a second type of hydrostatic skeletons, muscles compose a body wall that surrounds a fluid-filled cavity, as seen in sea anemones and worms. The biomechanical mechanism that produces reaching movement is a stiffening wave of muscle contraction that pushes a bend forward along the arm.

While an octopus might not have any formal joints, the rigging of such an entity as a digital character would require the placement of many points of articulation to produce the smooth bending motion that is expected. These points of articulation in the animation world are also called joints and are covered in the following section.

FURTHER READING

Some good anatomy references include

Kardong, K. 2005. *Vertebrates: Comparative Anatomy, Function, Evolution*, 4th edition. McGraw-Hill Science, New York, NY, USA.

Standring, S. 2004. *Gray's Anatomy: The Anatomical Basis of Clinical Practice*. Churchill Livingstone, London, United Kingdom.

White, T. D. 2000. *Human Osteology*. Academic Press, New York, NY.

CHAPTER 11

Interview: Lee Wolland, Character Technical Director, Consultant

11.1 BIO

Lee H. Wolland was born in Westchester, New York, and graduated from the School of Visual Arts with a BFA in Computer Art. By the age of 20, he was a lead modeler at a top NYC studio. He also taught advanced modeling and rigging classes at SVA and Prat Institute for 3 years. Lee currently lives in Brooklyn, NY, as a character artist, rigger, and modeler. His company, Asset Factory Inc., has worked on visual effects for films such as *Noah*, numerous high-profile commercials, and widely distributed video games. The Asset Factory rigging

Lee Wolland, Character Technical Director, Consultant

tools are revolutionizing how company's streamline the production process. Lee continues to improve and develop his artistic skills as a respected industry professional.

11.2 Q&A

Q: *The components of character technology are diverse and span the artistic and technical spectrum. How did you get your start in the industry? Based on where you see the field heading what experience/training do you recommend people have?*

A: I got my start in illustration. I was always interested in concept art for films. As more and more characters became CG, I decided to take leap from pen and pad to the fully realized digital characters.

In regards to being prepared for the future, nothing will ever beat a strong fine arts background. Technology evolves everyday, but not being on the cutting edge doesn't stop people from doing great work. It is all about being able to accomplish the most with what you have available.

Q: *Creating compelling digital characters is part art and part science. What is the greatest challenge you encounter on a daily basis? What aspect of character technology keeps you up thinking at night?*

A: Not that this necessarily keeps me up at night, but I see the industry heading towards a broader more casual user group each year. This means that there is a greater challenge for me as a developer to create characters that are user-friendly enough to accommodate a wide variance in technical skills. While feedback is great, I find that it is more effective to dig in and make sure that usability is taken into consideration throughout the development process.

Q: *What are the ingredients for a successful digital character?*

A: Whenever I am developing a character, I always focus on the characters range. Range can lead to surprising the audience and even sometimes the people involved in the genesis of a digital character. You know you are on the right track when you've made something that makes you laugh, or achieve something you did not know was possible.

Q: *While the industry is competitive, it is ultimately respectful of great work. Outside of the work you have been personally involved in the production of, what animated characters have you been impressed or inspired by? What is the historical high-bar?*

A: I can't help but think of this question inside of historical context. *Jurassic Park*, *Terminator 2*, and a few others will always come to mind because they truly represented a quantum leap forward for the industry.

As far as newer work, I was extremely impressed by Davey Jones from *Pirates of the Caribbean*. He was so convincing that I assumed it was footage with 3D elements incorporated for the tentacles. When I realized he was entirely CG, that really blew my mind. An amazing performance topped with incredible CG.

Q: *Where do you see digital characters in 10 years? Where are animated characters for film and games heading?*

A: I think we are at a place now where we have dug ourselves out of the Uncanny Valley, and are faced with an audience that has grown up exposed to successfully designed characters. Great work is the expectation, and I think the industry needs to push towards more interactive experiences to evoke a real sense of wonder in this educated viewer.

CHAPTER 12

Motion Systems

M OTION SYSTEMS ARE THE mechanical architecture—a collection of joints, controls, and procedures—that provide an interface for animation input. Essentially, the motion system involves everything outside the actual deformation of the model. We start with a description of the computer graphics concepts required to implement skeletons followed by some examples of classes, procedures, and constraints to tie the elements together.

12.1 MATRICES AND JOINTS

A joint, in the vernacular of 3D graphics, is essentially a 3D matrix in Cartesian space, often with extra properties that give it special attributes for animation. A matrix is a rectangular array of values subject to mathematical operations (see Figure 12.1). Each individual value in a matrix is called an element. An understanding of joint properties and the mathematics underlying matrix rotations and hierarchical rotations are crucial to the production of character animation.

Joints are the building blocks of animatable skeletons. Some 3D animation programs are "joint-based," whereas others are "bone-based." Autodesk Maya, for example, is "joint-based," which means that the bone, or the link, is visualized between two joint nodes. Bones are defined by two joints and serve a visualization purpose only. Other programs, such as Autodesk 3D Studio Max, are "bone-based," which means that a bone is visualized based on a starting location, direction, and bone length and a child joint node is not necessary for a bone to be visible. The action of a bone attached to a joint is controlled by the joint's rotation and movement. In both cases, various joint attributes determine how joints behave. Rotation can be limited or restricted along certain planes. For the purposes of this book, we will think about joint hierarchies and skeletons as being joint-based. An example class definition for a joint is illustrated in Figure 12.2.

If we think of each joint as a matrix that stores its position and orientation in 3D space, we have the basics of what is required for developing a skeleton. A matrix is described as having

$$A_{m,n} = \begin{pmatrix} a_{1,1} & a_{1,2} & \cdots & a_{1,n} \\ a_{2,1} & a_{2,2} & \cdots & a_{2,n} \\ \vdots & \vdots & \ddots & \vdots \\ a_{m,1} & a_{m,2} & \cdots & a_{m,n} \end{pmatrix}$$

FIGURE 12.1 A matrix can have any number of rows and columns.

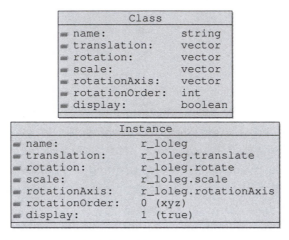

FIGURE 12.2 Class and data diagram for joint object.

m rows by n columns, or being an $m \times n$ matrix. A row is a horizontal grouping of elements read from left-to-right, whereas a column is a vertical, top-to-bottom group.

12.2 JOINT ROTATIONS

Joint rotations are the core method of character transformations in an animation system. Rotations around the x, y, and z axes are called principal rotations (see Figure 12.3). Rotation around any axis can be performed by taking a rotation around the x-axis, followed by a rotation around the y-axis, and followed by a rotation around the z-axis. That is to say, any spatial rotation can be decomposed into a combination of principal rotations. In flight dynamics, the principal rotations are known as roll, pitch, and yaw which are mapped to x, y, and z in a z-up coordinate system. Most animation systems work with a y-up coordination system. As a point of comparison, in aeronautics, positive z is down, toward Earth. Rotation is a rigid transformation—we

$$R = \begin{pmatrix} 0 & 0 & 1.0 \\ 0 & -1.0 & 0 \\ 1.0 & 0 & 0 \end{pmatrix}$$

FIGURE 12.3 A simple rotation matrix.

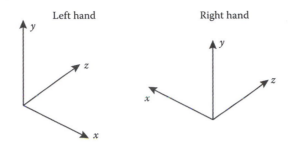

FIGURE 12.4 Left- and right-handed coordinate systems.

are rigidly changing the direction of a joint around an axis without changing its length. The rotation of joints around their local axes, thus transforming their hierarchical children, forms the basis for character motion. It can be helpful to use the "right-hand rule," which is a convention for determining the relative directions of vectors (Figure 12.4). First, the hand is held flat with palm up and positioned so that the index fingers points straight out representing axis y. Then, the middle finger is extended halfway and perpendicular representing axis z. The thumb then indicates axis x.

Rotation matrices around the x-axis, y-axis, and z-axis in a right-handed coordination system are shown in Figure 12.5. The fourth row is usually reserved for "shear" but character setup

$$\begin{bmatrix} x' \\ y' \\ z' \\ 1 \end{bmatrix} = \begin{bmatrix} 1 & 0 & 0 & 0 \\ 0 & \cos\theta & -\sin\theta & 0 \\ 0 & \sin\theta & \cos\theta & 0 \\ 0 & 0 & 0 & 0 \end{bmatrix} \begin{bmatrix} x \\ y \\ z \\ 1 \end{bmatrix} \quad (12.1)$$

$$\begin{bmatrix} x' \\ y' \\ z' \\ 1 \end{bmatrix} = \begin{bmatrix} \cos\theta & 0 & \sin\theta & 0 \\ 0 & 1 & 0 & 0 \\ -\sin\theta & 0 & \cos\theta & 0 \\ 0 & 0 & 0 & 1 \end{bmatrix} \begin{bmatrix} x \\ y \\ z \\ 1 \end{bmatrix} \quad (12.2)$$

$$\begin{bmatrix} x' \\ y' \\ z' \\ 1 \end{bmatrix} = \begin{bmatrix} \cos\theta & -\sin\theta & 0 & 0 \\ \sin\theta & \cos\theta & 0 & 0 \\ 0 & 0 & 1 & 0 \\ 0 & 0 & 0 & 1 \end{bmatrix} \begin{bmatrix} x \\ y \\ z \\ 1 \end{bmatrix} \quad (12.3)$$

FIGURE 12.5 Rotation around the x, y, and z-axes.

FIGURE 12.6   *XYZ* rotation order for $x = 45$, $y = 45$, $z = 45$.

FIGURE 12.7   *YZX* rotation order for $x = 45$, $y = 45$, $z = 45$.

artists work hard to avoid accumulating values for shear as they have unpleasant effects on joint rotations and character deformations.

12.3 ROTATION ORDER

As we mentioned previously, rotations can be broken down into their principle rotations, but the collected rotation is created by an accumulation of rotations in a specified order. This rotation order may be *x*, then *y*, then *z*, or *xyz*, but this can be specified in the animation system. Possible rotation orders include: *xyz*, *yzx*, *zxy*, *xzy*, *yxz*, *zyx*. It is important to recognize that an object with a rotation of $x = 45$, $y = 45$, $z = 45$ will have a different end result depending on the order with which those principle rotations are carried out (Figures 12.6 through 12.11).

12.4 EULER VERSUS QUATERNIONS

There is an important distinction to be made between Euler (pronounced "oiler") and quaternion rotations. Euler rotations are the standard, but quaternions provide a more versatile solution for the complex rotations required for character animation. It is increasingly available in animation systems, but Euler angles are the most common rotation implementation.

Euler's rotation theorem states that any rotation may be described using three angles. The three angles giving the three rotation matrices are called Euler angles. Euler angles have the disadvantage of being susceptible to "gimbal lock," where attempts to rotate an object fail to appear as expected due to the order in which the rotations are performed. Gimbal lock is the phenomenon of two rotational axes of an object pointing in the same direction, thus appearing to "lose" one degree of rotation. This is a common problem with inverse-kinematics (IK) solvers

FIGURE 12.8   *ZXY* rotation order for $x = 45, y = 45, z = 45$.

FIGURE 12.9   *XZY* rotation order for $x = 45, y = 45, z = 45$.

FIGURE 12.10   *YXZ* rotation order for $x = 45, y = 45, z = 45$.

FIGURE 12.11   *ZYX* rotation order for $x = 45, y = 45, z = 45$.

that attempt to find the position of middle joints based on two end joints, or combined rotations over joints. As the solution crosses the 180° mark, the joint position is solved from the reverse angle and flips. This is a major problem for character animators and it is the responsibility of the character setup artist to solve this issue in most situations either by adding controls to counteract this joint flipping or, if possible, to implement quaternions, which are one solution to this problem.

Quaternions allow the rigger to rotate an object through an arbitrary rotation axis and angle, instead of rotating an object through a series of successive rotations. The rotation is still performed using matrix mathematics, however instead of multiplying matrices together, quaternions representing the axes of rotation are multiplied together. The final resulting quaternion is then converted into the desired rotation matrix. Because the rotation axis is specified as a unit direction vector, it may also be calculated through vector mathematics or from spherical coordinates (longitude/latitude). Quaternions offer another advantage in that they may be interpolated. This allows for smooth and predictable rotation effects. This is particularly useful when you need to interpolate between arbitrary orientations without suffering from gimbal lock and the order-dependent problems that are seen with Euler rotations. Quaternions are useful in areas where interpolation between varying orientations are common (like the human shoulder) but may not be as useful and might even look unnatural where a simple rotation interpolation is suitable (like the human knee). There is not one rotation method that works best in all situations, and quaternions are not the magic bullet that solves all problems. This is an admittedly high-level glossing-over of a complex subject, but as quaternions are implemented into animation systems, a basic knowledge of their advantages is crucial to character setup artists.

12.5 JOINT PLACEMENT AND NAMING

Drawing on our discussion of anatomy, we delve into the placement of matrices in space. By doing so, we define the origin of the joint rotation for the purposes of character articulation. Joint placement within a character model may be a tedious process but it is, of course, a necessary one. Our knowledge of anatomy combined with our understanding of matrix rotation informs our decisions as to where to place our joints.

For realistic characters, once the model is created, in an ideal world, the placement of joints starts with the creation of a reference polygonal skeleton that fits the model and represents the underlying anatomy. This also acts as a motion reference for the motion system to drive. Once your control system is in place and driving the motion of the bones correctly, the model can be confidently attached to the joints as outlined in the next chapter. For stylized or more cartoon-derived characters, a polygonal reference skeleton may not be needed and the position of joints is based on the ideal point of rotation. In most cases, the reference skeleton is stripped out of the model either way when it is handed off to the animators or exported to the game engine. The luxury of time to create a modeled skeleton for that character does not usually exist, so the rigger jumps into placing joints based on the design and volumes of the model.

In certain cases, it is conceivable that the polygonal reference skeleton could be used as part of anatomically influenced deformations as a way to drive the muscles (and in turn the skin) by providing multiple points for surface attachment.

Once we have a good sense of where we would like to place the joints by analyzing the model and, if time permits, placing a model skeleton in it, we are ready to start placing the true kinematic joints. As we have noted, the rotation of joints has a direct connection to the motion of the model and therefore the placement of joints is critical. For example, at the area of the human knee, the placement of the joints along the orthogonal plane (as seen from the side of the model) will determine the amount of pinching that occurs when the leg is flexed. Similarly, for the human knee (Figure 12.12) or any area where the resulting surface is a complex of two articulating surfaces with a bone floating within the connecting tendon (usually called a sesamoid bone), finding the middle area can be difficult and a single joint will not suffice. The optimal solution is to place two joints, one at the bottom of the proximal bone and one at the top of the distal bone. This leaves a surface area about which a volume can be preserved when the leg is bent. The volume of the deforming area will be proportional to the amount of space between the joints, so the more distance between them, the more that center region will be preserved. It is important to note that it is crucial to plan motion systems with the downstream deformations of the model in mind.

For regions which require smooth and detailed motion along a fairly straight articulating surface, it is best to place the joints procedurally via a curve. The process for this is straightforward. A two-point curve is drawn from where joint placement is supposed to start to the point where the last joint should be placed. This curve is then reparameterized so that a control point is placed at equally spaced intervals along the curve for the number of joints desired (see Figure 12.13). The joints can then be placed at the locations of these points along a curve with fine resolution. This method is useful for joint hierarchies which are controlled or managed by

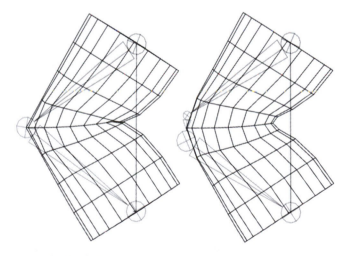

FIGURE 12.12 Example of articulating one versus two joints.

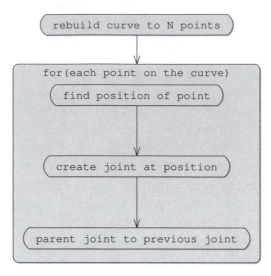

FIGURE 12.13 Method for a curve-based joint placement.

spline interpolation, such as tails, tentacles, even long necks, and spines. Procedural placement of joints can speed up setup and is more accurate in some situations.

From a pipeline point of view, the naming of joints is a paramount part of character standardization and the creation of support tools. Any number of conventions can be developed as a joint naming strategy but the most important decision with regard to naming is to decide on one convention and stick to it. Reliable naming provides information about that joint's position and role in the character rig. Consistency across characters also allows other character setup artists to more easily debug a rig that they did not create. A typical structure uses the side of the body as the first naming element for the sides left ("left," "lt," "L," "l"), right ("right," "rt," "R," "r"), or middle ("middle," "mid," "M," "m"). The descriptive term that follows can be thought of in two different ways: it is either the term for the area of placement of the joint or the name of the structure that is moved by transformation of that joint. The tag "loleg" could mean the lower part of the leg to one person or the knee to another. Production standards and documentation are the only way to enforce consistent naming for a production. The last part of the name is typically an indicator that this is a joint, such as "JNT," "j," or "jnt," so that joints can be queried procedurally and easily. Other suffixes might signify a control ("CNTRL," "cntrl," "CTL," "c"), a group ("grp," "GRP," "g"), or any number of other objects such as locators, curves, and so on. Depending on the system and the production pipeline, the character name may be prepended to each of these joint names as a means of avoiding name clashing within a scene (see Table 12.1). Personally, my preferred naming convention is characterName_side_element_type resulting in hawkshaw_l_hand_cntrl, but every artist, studio, and production has its own preference or standard.

TABLE 12.1   Naming Convention Variations

Name	Position	Element	Type	Combined
Rob	l	uparm	grp	rob_l_uparm_grp
Dave	M	back2	JNT	daveMback2JNT
Todd	r	hand	IK_CNTRL	todd_r_hand_IKCNTRL
Daniel	l	foot	c	daniel_l_foot_c

12.6 JOINT HIERARCHIES

Connecting joints to each other with the intention of creating a cohesive hierarchy is the next step. The most basic functionality of our rig comes from the parent–child relationship of the joints and the way that joints rotate around each other. Early digital characters were animated solely on the basis of simple hierarchies, but modern rigs rely on a complex network of joints, even when not directly connected to each other and are instead connected by constraints.

Hierarchies go hand-in-hand with joint placement, but they also provide the logic to the connections between joints. All characters require a "root" node that controls their basic transformation position in 3D space. The rest of the character is a child of this node, as this node acts both as a hierarchical container and a namespace indicator of that character in the scene. A namespace is an identifier for objects in the scene that might have the same name. For example, all characters will likely have the same joint and control names but the unique namespace for each character distinguishes them all. All of the elements in a character rig should be thought of as their own modular systems that are then connected to each other logically. Where character skeletons have traditionally been composed of a single unified hierarchy of joints, the trend today is to build discrete hierarchies for each element where the joints do not directly connect with each other to associate these modules. These "broken hierarchy" rigs not only provide flexibility by allowing elements to act independent of each other (leaving the animator to have more control), but they also support the idea of the character rig being a set of modular units that can be improved on individually without impacting other regions of the rig. Single-chain joint hierarchies are still used heavily in games and on rigs which depend on motion capture. Often this simple hierarchy is an output of a more complicated nonhierarchical rig.

For rotations between joints to behave as expected, the artist must define the orientation of the axes for their joint chains. Once determined, all of the joints for that element should adhere to the convention for expected results. Defining the axis that should point at the child joint and the axes that should be pointing laterally and perpendicular to that will ensure that all of the joints follow the same directions of rotation. This is particularly important for long chains that define a spine or tail, but no less important for regions with sparse joint layout.

For example, to create a joint chain that moves and rotates like the human neck, you would place the desired number of joints to define the neck's articulation, then set the degrees of freedom for the joints so that they rotate only within the limit of each joint's range of rotation. The cumulative effect of the rotations for each joint should add up to the desired limits of rotation for the whole neck. Limits are something to be used carefully. Often character motion must be extreme for the purposes of exaggeration or to cheat a shot. Therefore, the usual practice is to forgo limits or give the joints a wide range in order to give the animator the freedom to put the character into an extreme or "broken" pose, if even for a few frames. Because joint placement ultimately defines the biomechanics of digital characters, it is helpful to undertake this process with anatomy in mind.

12.7 ANATOMICALLY INFLUENCED HIERARCHIES

With knowledge of joints and constraints coupled with observed biomechanics, one can create a motion system that is informed by and behaves like natural skeletal anatomy. In this section, we describe the articulation of the human shoulder and implement it in 3D. The human shoulder, or the pectoral girdle, serves as the articulation between the free limb and the torso, or axial skeleton. The girdle is made up of two bones: the clavicle and the scapula, connected by a strong ligament and articulating at a single point. This connection allows for slight motion between the bones. The scapula has no articulation with the axial skeleton, and instead floats in a complex of muscles. The humerus, or upper arm, connects to the scapula at a shallow cup-shaped depression called the glenoid fossa. It is the muscular movement of the scapula and clavicle that moves the shoulders. This motion translates the humerus (and the rest of the arm), producing shrug (shoulders up) and slouch (shoulders down) motions, in addition to being able to rotate the shoulders forward and back.

Taking these articulation points into consideration, the 3D joints can be placed (see Figure 12.14). We would place a joint at the most medial point of the clavicle as the point of rotation for the shoulder complex. All rotation of the shoulder should emanate from this point. The child of this joint should be coincident with the lateral end of the clavicle, thus a 3D bone traverses the length of the skeletal bone. The scapula needs to be able to be controlled by the rotation of the clavicle. It also needs its own rotation controls for independent posing beyond the derived automatic motion from the rest of the system, so a joint is placed on the medial edge of the scapula on the character's back. The child of this joint travels up the back to the point where the clavicle articulates with the scapula. A joint is placed at the center of the proximal head of the humerus and its child traverses the humerus down to the most distal end. In a basic way, we now have the joints in place for proper articulation.

12.8 CONSTRAINTS AND HIGH-LEVEL CONTROL

Expressive motion requires complex interaction between joints in the motion system. This is the realm of constraints, where systems are created to solve the motion of joints by relating them to each other or using procedures which manipulate the joint based on factors external to that joint. Joints can be aimed at objects, animation controls, or other joints. Rotations can be limited. The motion of joints can be offset based on interactions in other parts of the rig. The functionality of a complex rig lies in the constraints created by the setup artist and it is this level of sophistication that often separates a basic rig from one suited for production. In

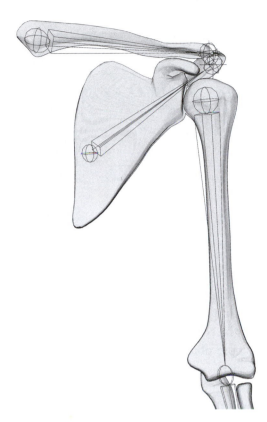

FIGURE 12.14   Human shoulder girdle.

short, constraints are relationships among objects that are maintained automatically by the system [21].

When a character animation pipeline is being developed, a number of constraints need to be implemented to streamline solutions and satisfy animation requirements. Constraints can maintain the position, orientation, or scale of an object with other objects, impose specific limits on objects, and automate animation processes. Other constraints to consider are those that rotate a succession of joints (e.g., curl) and subsets of those constraints that compensate the end node so that end-node orientations (like the head) can be maintained through a rotation. For example, a character can bend over while keeping their head level.

Position constraints are those which maintain the translation offset (or distance) of an object with that of another object. The offset is typically managed so that the constrained object does not move or it can be removed so that the constrained object becomes coincident with the constraining object. When a position constraint is created, this offset can be removed (set to 0, 0, 0) so that the constrained object matches the position of the object it is being constrained to or it can be maintained and the offset value is stored by the constraint. When the position constraint is activated, the constrained object's translation values are updated to maintain the

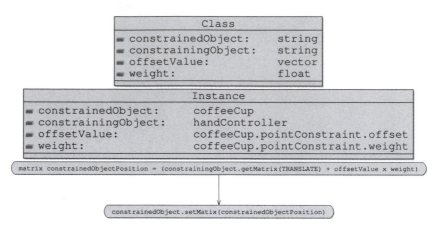

FIGURE 12.15 Class, data, and method diagram for a position constraint.

positional offset from it and the constraining object, thus moving it relative to that object (see Figure 12.15). A similar structure is in place for an orientation constraint where the rotational offset is maintained between the constraining object and the object being constrained, unless it is removed, in which case the object matches the rotation of the constraining object and rotates exactly as it does. As can be inferred, a scale constraint performs the same function by maintaining a connection with regard to scale between objects. All of these transformation constraints add a non-hierarchical connection between objects that may simulate a parenting relationship between objects. Combining position and orientation constraints creates a control that mimics a hierarchical parenting situation, which in an animation system is very powerful. Utilizing a constraint instead of a hierarchy integration means that an object can be temporarily connected, in other words, parented to the rig. This is crucial for props and objects that need to be added and removed from the character without becoming part of its hierarchy. The weight of the constraint can also be blended on and off for a smooth transition because, as with any constraint, making sure that the activation does not "pop" an object into place is an ever-present concern. In animation, nothing breaks the illusion of natural movement more than an object linearly popping into place. Even if it happens at a subframe interval, objects popping into or out of place may be picked up by the motion blur function of the renderer and be evident.

Combinatory rotation constraints provide a means of rotating multiple joints at once, ideally with a weight attached to each one so that the rotation is not uniform. This is ideal for rotating anatomically similar parts of the body, such as torsos, and necks. When chains are cumulatively rotated, it is important to have controls that maintain the orientation of the end node (head and/or shoulders). Once important elements like the head have been positioned and the character's line-of-sight with elements on or off screen have been established, it is important that rigs allow for animation up the hierarchical chain to not affect them. In fact, any region can be set to "compensate" for the motion that has been applied to the joints below (see Figures 12.16 and 12.17).

Class	
objectsToRotate:	string array
rotateWeight:	float array
compensatedObject:	string
compensationWeight:	float
rotationInputValue:	vector

Instance	
objectsToRotate:	neck01
objectsToRotate:	neck02
objectsToRotate:	neck03
objectsToRotate:	neck04
objectsToRotate:	neck05
rotateWeight:	0.20
rotateWeight:	0.30
rotateWeight:	0.40
rotateWeight:	0.50
rotateWeight:	0.60
compensatedObject:	head0
compensationWeight:	head.headNeckComp
inputValue:	head.compNeckRot

FIGURE 12.16 Class and data diagram for a compensating rotation constraint.

Other constraints go beyond the reference of one transformation to another. Often times, an object will need to be constrained to a geometric surface, thus riding along the surface and maintaining its orientation normal to the surface to which it is attached.

The real power of these discrete constraints is the combination of them on a joint or joint hierarchy to form high-level animation controls. The term "high-level control" refers to the

FIGURE 12.17 Method for a compensating rotation constraint.

ability to control complex systems with a minimal amount of attributes. "Low-level control" usually refers to a single control that manipulates a singular discrete element, like bending a single section of a human digit. Complicated anatomical regions such as human hands and feet are areas which typically have a wide range of intricate motion contained in a compact space and as such are typically controlled via both low- and high-level controls. Low-level controls provide the direct access to the individual components, whereas high-level controls allow an animator to pose the entire element quickly and with the manipulation of few attributes (e.g., a fist control). Because of the many working pieces in a human hand and all of the delicate operations it is called on to undertake, it is a complex system that requires layers of control. As we mentioned previously, low-level controls for the hand give the animator fine control for individually posing sections of the fingers into the desired position. This is powerful and specific control, but leads to a tedious workflow if this is the only control for manipulating the fingers. Higher-level controls will give the animator the ability to curl individual fingers from a single attribute which is essentially an interface for simultaneously manipulating multiple low-level controls.

At an even higher level, being able to control all the fingers of the hand through descriptive controls, such as "fist," "spread," "splay," and "bend," provide the animator with the ability to quickly pose the hand and then offset individual fingers with lower-level controls. An even higher level than multi-finger controls are character-specific pose controls which take a character from a default position to an animator-defined pose. In the case of a character's hand, a typical attribute-driven pose is a fist. The construction is based not only on the final positioning of all the fingers curled with the thumb on top, but is also the timing of the curl of those fingers so that, when animated, the thumb does not cross through the other digits. Controls such as this are usually attributes on a continuum from 0-1 or 0-100, the higher number being the hand in its final fist position. As such, these controls are often composed of animation curves mapped through the attribute value continuum so that as the attribute is manipulated, it is mapped to the proper place on the curve for each finger moving it from a default position to the fist position as coordinated by the animator.

In addition, the human foot needs the ability to roll from the heel to the ball of the foot (just before the toes), through the toes, and onto the tip of the foot in succession. This is often programmed as a continuous motion where a single attribute rolls the foot from heel to tiptoe as the character is animated to walk. The three points of articulation of the foot at the heel, ball, and toe are also points where the foot should be able to pivot around all three axes. The ankle and toes also need independent control from this high-level foot rocking system to be able to pose them either on their own or as an offset from the effects of this system. As such, the foot control for a human will be the goal of the IK solver, allowing the motion of the leg to be controlled from the foot and also the interface for all the attributes of the foot pivot system. This high-level system provides a singular interface for the control of the entire foot. Other high-level actions, such as character breathing, are often controlled through a single attribute.

Class		Instance	
▬ rootJoint:	string	▬ rootJoint:	shoulder
▬ middleJoint:	string	▬ middleJoint:	elbow
▬ endJoint:	string	▬ endJoint:	wrist
▬ preferedAxis:	int	▬ preferedAxis:	0
▬ goalPosition:	vector	▬ goalPosition:	handGoal.translation

FIGURE 12.18   Class and data diagram for a simple IK constraint.

12.9 FORWARD AND INVERSE KINEMATICS

Rotations on a hierarchical set of joints result in a forward kinematic (FK) movement where rotations are applied down the joint chain. The position of the final joint in the chain is based on the accumulation of the rotations of all of its parent joints. This is counter to the most common constraint in an animation system, inverse kinematics (IK), in which a joint chain has a root and an end effector and the middle of the chain is solved based on the position of the end effector (see Figures 12.18 and 12.19).

FK motion is reminiscent of stop motion puppet manipulation, where each joint is positioned and the children are moved relative to the motion of their parents. There is little surprise to FK animation. Each of the rotation values (angles) on the joints in the hierarchy result in the pose of the chain. This allows for direct manipulation of the joints, but also makes it difficult to update or change the animation of a chain controlled by FK. Small changes to upstream joints will place the end joint (say a hand) in a very different place. Often FK is reserved for driving animation where the force and energy comes from the top of the chain, like the arms swinging during a walk or run cycle, as opposed to the end of the chain, like the legs making contact with the ground during a walk or run cycle.

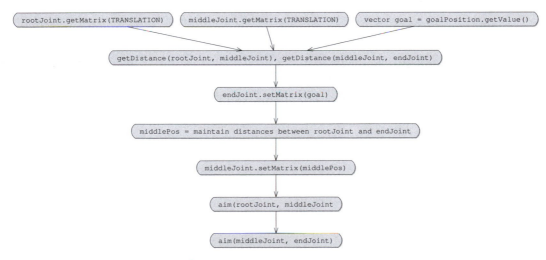

FIGURE 12.19   Method for a simple IK constraint.

With this in mind, we can briefly describe the difference between FK and IK. The term inverse comes from the joint's rotations being solved from the end joint, up the chain and back to the root node. IK constraints are typically the first constraints learned by animators as they are easy to add to a joint chain in animation systems and provide a lot of functionality. Animators typically find it simpler to create a pose as dictated by the position of the end goal, possibly the hand, rather than joint angles that culminate with the position of that end node based on the nodes above it. IK is often overused and reliance on it leads to animation looking weightless and "floaty" which is a common problem for most new animators. The resulting "floating" animation is due to the animation curve attached to the end effector (often called the "IK goal"), which often leads the goal, and thus the appendage, through a spline-based interpolation. Typically, a limb, in space, being affected by gravity, would not follow such paths. There is definitely a place for IK in digital character animation—it is an essential constraint for animation systems. Typically, the IK goal lives in world space (the coordinate system of our 3D scene), which allows it to be parented to objects that exist outside of the character. In more complex situations, the IK goal's parent can be dynamically changed so that it can be in world space or local to the character's shoulders, chest, or other "body parent."

There are a variety of IK solutions and every animation system offers a small variety of solvers for the user to choose from, depending on the setup situation or issues that arise. Some IK solvers are designed to be more efficient for a hierarchy of two joints, others three, whereas others are optimized for many joints. Common differences among implementations is the manner of rotating the system and the level of dependance on a plane for orienting and aligning joints. In its simplest form, two link IK (also known as three joint IK), is merely an application of the Law of Cosines (a generalization of the Pythagorean theorem), whereby you can use the Law of Cosines to find a third side when you know two sides and their included angle. The two link IK is always forming a triangle, so the calculation of the middle joint's position can always be solved using

$$a^2 = b^2 + c^2 - 2bc \cos A$$

A common accompanying constraint is the pole vector, often described as the knee or elbow goal. The pole vector of an IK constraint applied to an arm joint chain is constrained to a control object which is placed behind the character, in line with the elbow. A pole vector constraint for a leg chain IK is placed in front of the "knee" joint. Because joints controlled by IK can reach an unlimited number of solutions in a circle along the axis, the pole vector defines the reference plane for solving the IK. This leaves the IK solver with two solutions, and the preferred angle defines the angle at which the joint chain should bend and effectively limits which of those two to select. The combination of a preferred angle and a pole vector allows the IK solver to produce a singular solution and thus avoids the joint chain from flipping between multiple valid solutions.

As we discussed, the method of rigging a long tentacle-like appendage is via a spline curve-based IK constraint. In this case, the shape of the spline curve dictates the orientation of the

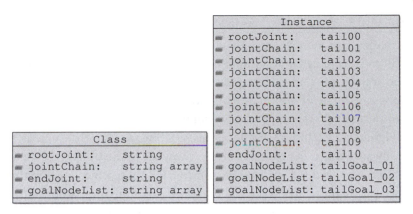

FIGURE 12.20 Class and data diagram for a spline IK constraint.

joints in the hierarchy. Each control vertex of the curve acts like a goal which, when moved, the joint rotations in the hierarchy are solved to match the shape of the spline. Each vertex should ideally be controlled by a transformation control so that the motion of the spline occurs in a space that is local to the character (see Figures 12.20 and 12.21).

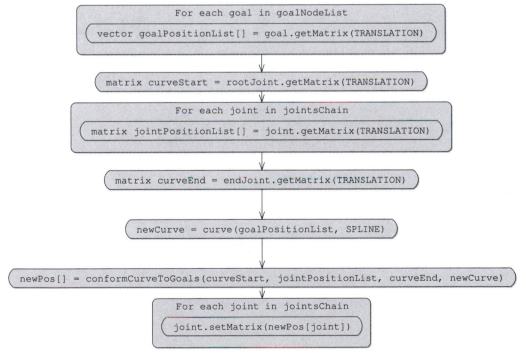

FIGURE 12.21 Method for a spline IK constraint.

12.10 DYNAMICS AND SIMULATION

Secondary animation (reactions to the movement of primary motion) is often produced procedurally by adding a layer of dynamic simulation on top of animatable controls to have the joints react to motion trajectories and forces applied to them. Used sparingly, dynamic joint chain implementations can add a lot of functionality to a rig, but must be a complement to the animation and not necessarily a simulation-only component. The application of dynamics could include tails (Figures 12.22 and 12.23), tentacles, clothing accessories such as a feather on a cap, or practically anything that needs to move in response to the trajectories of the established character motion. The need for animatable controls for these objects is paramount because simulation is very difficult to art direct and therefore the more animator control there is, the faster it will reach the desired result. The dynamics on top of animation should compliment the primary animation that drives it.

Dynamics are usually implemented by maintaining coincident chains of joints; one for the animation, another for the simulation, and often a third which is controlled by the blending of the first two and is the resultant chain that deformations are attached to. Applying rigid-body (nondeforming) dynamics to a joint chain allows for forces to influence the chain's motion. Forces such as gravity, when applied to animated actions, cause the secondary motion created by the simulation to be grounded in the reality of that world. Taking a character tail as an example, we first define the animation control for this structure to ensure that the animator has enough control to pose it within the needs of the production. The most likely control set for tails is a spline-defined, IK goal-based system. Each animatable node on the hierarchy is controlled by an animation controller which the animator interacts with to place keys as needed. Once the animated motion is in place, the dynamics profile (the attributes of the system that define its behavior) can be edited to suit the need of the secondary motion. Dynamic simulations are often a matter of trial and error in the beginning, but as the animator becomes more familiar

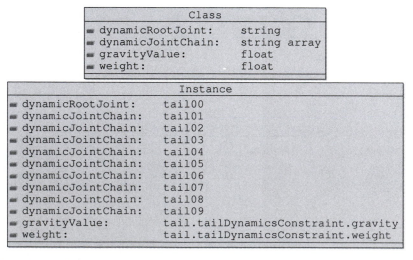

FIGURE 12.22 Class and data diagram for a tail dynamics constraint.

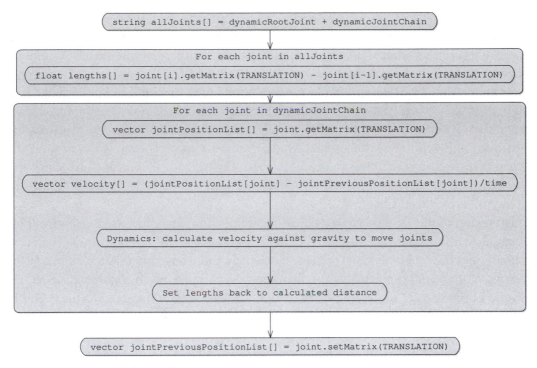

FIGURE 12.23 Method for a tail dynamics constraint.

with how the attributes affect the final motion, predictable and desired results are achieved faster and with less iteration. Tolerances should be implemented to deal with how much the simulation is able to stray from the keyed position of the controllers. It is important to be able to visualize the simulation (even if in a "debug" mode) on its own without the influence of animator motion. In addition, attributes should be in place to blend between full animator motion (no dynamics) through full simulated dynamic motion (no animator influence) on a temporal basis. This allows the normally blended motion of the two to hand off to fully simulated or fully animated throughout the course of the shot. This controls and eases the process of art directing as the motion can be fully controlled by the animator at any time. With simulation also comes the possibility of collisions. Collisions allow the simulated element to have a physical knowledge of the character and the environment of the scene and to avoid intersections with those objects to give the appearance of interacting with them. This is a costly solution but in many complex cases it can be a better solution than an animator maintaining and posing those physical responses.

12.11 USER INTERFACE AND VISUALIZING THE MOTION SYSTEM

All of the constraints imaginable are useless if there is not a means of manipulating the rig. This manipulation is carried out by either an animator, the input of motion capture data, or a procedural system. For an animation system, the goal and challenge is to be truly interactive and allow an animator to produce the performance required by the system, while at the same time it should have fast user feedback and be an accurate representation of the poses animated. A "control" is a means of manipulating the motion system. This can be interfaced via numerical input or via click-and-drag of a manipulating object within the 3D environment. These control objects are created, by default, to not be renderable and are often built to be indicative of the motion possible. Utilizing an array of icons, curves, arrows and symbols, a manipulatable user interface is key to creating a rig which is reliable and intuitive. Character controls are usually planned in conjunction with the animators and that same control set is used across all characters in the production. This even comes down to the individual control icons. Once these have been established, an animator knows what each icon will do by its appearance instead of needing to learn by trial and error.

Each region of the rig needs a special set of controls. In many cases, each region will have a different set of icons depending on what mode the character is in. For example, an arm in FK mode requires a different set of controls, namely those that rotate the shoulder, elbow, and wrist at their point of articulation, than the goal and pole vector (elbow goal) required of the same arm in IK mode. In addition to attaching animation curves to these controls for the animator, these animation interfaces can also be controlled via code in the form of simple expressions or more complicated procedural systems. Actions such as procedurally derived walk cycles and goal-based path-finding of appendages can be easily attached to a set of controllers.

When it comes to motion capture and procedurally controlled rigs, the key is having animatable channels free for animation to be attached to. These channels are often on the joints themselves and not the controlling objects so that the motion capture performance is "baked" onto the joints. Later we will discuss motion capture and the means for offsetting this data by hand-animated controls to add animator nuance to the base-line motion provided by the motion capture performer.

A key component to consider when creating controls is that characters are rigged in their default position and all the controls must be free of transformation values. This is often referred to as being "zeroed-out." This allows the animator to get back to a default pose quickly and to tell, numerically, how much the controls have been transformed. It is also important for procedural systems that, in effect, the starting point of a simulation or solved system is zero.

Joints and character controls do not provide enough accuracy for the animator to pose the character within the limits of the shape and proportions of the character model. Part of the motion system process is defining a means of visualizing the deforming model surface in a fast and light-weight manner. This often requires turning the model into a collection of broken up polygonal elements that are then parented to the joints that best represent how those parts of the model will move.

These surfaces provide a nondeforming guide to the animator (Figure 12.24). These rigid surfaces being transformed by the joints are only an indicator of the final deformation of the character model. A step above this could be a low polygon deforming version of the model

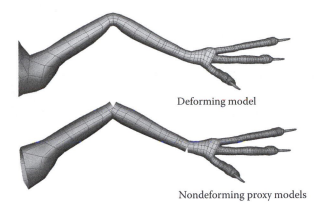

Deforming model

Nondeforming proxy models

FIGURE 12.24 Deforming model versus nondeforming proxy models.

that provides a higher level of feedback for the end result of the character motion. A character's silhouette is a critical aspect of animation and defines the strength and read of the key poses by stripping away all of the details. Being able to read a pose or sequence refers to the clarity of the action despite the amount of complex motion. By providing a fast responding proxy of the character's volume, animators can quickly get a sense of its silhouette. This also requires that the proxy be maintained through model changes to the deforming model so that the two, or more, levels of details match as best as possible. We will discuss this more in the next chapter where we cover character deformations.

12.12 REAL-TIME ENGINE CONCERNS

For real-time characters, it is important to keep the number of objects in a rig to a minimum; this includes using as few joints as possible. The fewer the joints that must be stored in memory and calculated in real-time, the faster the responsiveness of the character interaction. As we have mentioned, motion capture provides much of the animation in real-time game engines, so the hierarchy is often tailored to work with the skeleton defined by the specification of the system, studio, or project that it is being used in. This is often a simple hierarchical structure that has extra joints added and controlled via constraints. In real-time engines, where deformations are controlled by skinning (attaching the model to joints) alone, special joints, termed secondary joints, are often added to control deformation-specific functions. Actions such as flexing muscles are controlled by the motion of these joints which are driven by constraints. As game engines are able to process more and more data, the number of joints allowable increases, but it is still best to keep this number to a minimum. There is always a trade-off in game production with regard to processing power. For example, if you wanted to add a new feature to the calculation of the environment, then character joint count or other features might be affected or vice versa.

12.13 CONCLUSION

Motion systems form the mechanical architecture for digital characters. They rely on knowledge of anatomy paired with an understanding of computer graphics principles to recreate the mechanics of articulation and motion. The combination of joint hierarchies, constraints, and user interface form the motion system. By providing an intuitive interface, complex operations can be hidden from the animator, allowing them to focus on the performance of the character in the scene.

Integrating this motion system with the character model is the role of deformation systems.

12.14 EXERCISE

In this exercise, you will learn about the conceptual and technical process of creating a character motion system. Split into groups of two or more. One of you is the animator and the other team members are the character setup artists. Follow the steps below.

1. Draw a character using nature as a guide (or use one you created in a previous exercise or from your own portfolio). Think about appendages and how they relate to locomotion. The character's mechanics should be physically plausible even if they are outlandishly designed.

2. Based on the design, the project you think this character will be a part of, and the animator's specifications, determine this character's motion and needed actions.

3. Design its skeleton on the model sheet. Design the skeleton by drawing the joints in the place appropriate for the needed points of articulation and rotation.

4. Build the skeleton in either an animation system or procedurally.

5. With the help and feedback of the animator, design an interface for it.

6. The animator should generate 10 poses for the character using the low polygon (nondeforming) proxy models attached to the motion system as a guide.

7. Based on these poses, supply the setup artists with feedback to be addressed.

8. Maintain this test/fix feedback loop until satisfied.

FURTHER READING

There are a few technical resources that every character technical director should have on their bookshelf. The first is a text which provides a solid baseline understanding of the principles of computer graphics.

O'Rourke, M. 2003. *Principles of Three-Dimensional Computer Animation: Modeling, Rendering, and Animating with 3D Computer Graphics*, 3rd edition. W. W. Norton & Co., Inc., New York, NY.

The second is a solid implementation of those principles as applied to animation.

Parent, R. 2012. *Computer Animation, 3rd Edition: Algorithms and Techniques (The Morgan Kaufmann Series in Computer Graphics)*. Morgan Kaufmann Publishers, Inc., San Francisco, CA.

The third reference to own is a math text for when you want to bend the rules or get deeper into constraint development.

Van Verth, J. and Bishop, L. 2008. *Essential Mathematics for Games and Interactive Applications: A Programmer's Guide*, 2nd edition. Morgan Kaufmann Publishers, Inc., San Francisco, CA.

CHAPTER 13

Interview: Cara Malek, Character Technology Supervisor, DreamWorks Animation

13.1 BIO

Cara grew up in Rochester Hills, Michigan, but left the snowy midwest to pursue a Digital Arts and Sciences degree from the University of Florida. She continued her studies at the Ohio State University, acquiring a Master of Fine Arts degree in Design + Digital Animation. An

Cara Malek, Character Technology Supervisor, DreamWorks Animation

internship with DreamWorks Animation turned into a career, and Cara has been a Character Technical Director at DreamWorks for 7 years. Her credits include *Madagascar: Escape 2 Africa*, *How to Train Your Dragon*, *Megamind*, and *How to Train Your Dragon 2*. She is currently supervising the DreamWorks Character Technology team, helping to provide robust solutions to rigging problems across all studio productions and setting the direction of future character technology.

13.2 Q&A

Q: *The components of character technology are diverse and span the artistic and technical spectrum. How did you get your start in the industry? Based on where you see the field heading what experience/training do you recommend people have?*

A: In graduate school, I was fortunate to participate in a master class taught by DreamWorks artists. It was there that I fell in love with rigging, spending long nights in the computer lab perfecting my character rig for the class. The detail-oriented nature of the work appealed to me, as well as the feeling of building something almost mechanical through a digital medium. After the course, I was interviewed and I secured an internship with DreamWorks, where I spent the summer helping to program components for their new rigging software. After the internship, I was offered a full-time position, and I have been at DreamWorks ever since.

If someone wants to work at a big studio like DreamWorks, it is important to have an expert grasp of the basics, like managing complex controls and creating clean deformations. However, like several other big studios, we work with proprietary software, so we especially need people who are flexible and able to learn new techniques quickly. It is not enough to just know how to use a piece of software (like Maya). You also need to have an understanding of the fundamental processes that the tool is doing for you—like what a constraint does, how skinning works, etc. so that you can translate that knowledge to a different toolset. It is also imperative to be able to work on a team and communicate well about technical and artistic topics. Often, students will create a short film as a school project. While this is a good exercise to widen your skill set and experience all parts of the pipeline, I always recommend that instead student riggers try to focus all their energies on rigging and just build rigs for their fellow students. It gives them more rigging experience with a wider set of design requirements, as well as the chance to work on several teams with different dynamics and goals.

Q: *Creating compelling digital characters is part art and part science. What is the greatest challenge you encounter on a daily basis? What aspect of character technology keeps you up thinking at night?*

A: My biggest challenge is managing character complexity. While we have developed many great solutions to the various problems we encounter with our characters, we need the solutions to be easy to install on multiple characters and to be optimized for high performance. With a large crew of riggers and many films in production concurrently, we need to be as efficient as possible in developing and maintaining characters.

It's hard to believe, but even after 20 years of making movies, every new show at DreamWorks has new challenges. The problems I enjoy the most are weird, complicated motion systems, like the pegleg for Hiccup on *How to Train Your Dragon 2*. It had lots of little moving parts, but ironically, the most difficult aspect of that rig was the lack of an ankle joint. It's actually really hard to keep a foot in contact with the ground when all you have is the ability to bend at the knee!

Q: *What are the ingredients for a successful digital character?*

A: As riggers, we're serving two main goals: aesthetics and usability. We need to achieve the look that was specified by the character design, and we need to make it easy for animators to get the poses they are after. Pretty much everything we do (creating controls, tweaking deformations, ensuring good rig speed) serves at least one of these two goals. Success relies on good communication between the rigger, the animator who will use the rig, and the person who is approving the rig artistically (a director, production designer, animator, or rigging supervisor).

Q: *While the industry is competitive, it is ultimately respectful of great work. Outside of the work you have been personally involved in the production of, what animated characters have you been impressed or inspired by? What is the historical high-bar?*

A: I have never worked in VFX, but the work coming out of studios like Weta, Digital Domain, and MPC is consistently amazing. I love watching the FX reels from those studios to see how much of the films I didn't even realize was CG.

I don't think you can talk about historically significant animated characters without talking about *Avatar*. The musculature and skin simulation on those characters was unlike anything we had seen before, and brought new levels of realism to the screen by leaps and bounds. In the realm of non-photoreal characters, I actually really admire the simplicity of design in *Cloudy With A Chance of Meatballs*. Making a complex character rig generate shapes that are so flexible while being graphic and clean is remarkably difficult.

Q: *Where do you see digital characters in 10 years? Where are animated characters for film and games heading?*

A: While photorealism will continue to improve, I feel like we have already made great strides there in the VFX world, with films like the Marvel and *X-Men* movies and *Life of Pi*. What I find even more interesting are the steps being taken to bring 2D characters to 3D while still making them appealing and true to the original design. Films like *Popeye* and *Peanuts* look really fantastic—the characters are adorable, and the rigs are able to really stretch to achieve the wacky, cartoony spirit of the comics. With Disney's *Paperman* and *Feast* we're doing more and more to bridge the gap between 2D and 3D to create really interesting hybrids. I can't wait to see more.

Deformation Systems

D EFORMATION SYSTEMS ARE RESPONSIBLE for how a model is impacted by the actions of the motion system. Deformations can be abstractly thought of as the muscles that stretch and bend skin in response to the motion of the body. In actuality, for animals, the muscles drive the skeleton, but for the purposes of animation, the inverse is true. Deformations can be as simple as a per-vertex connection to the joints that drive them and as complex as an anatomically based layered muscle system that drives successive layers of geometry. This chapter discusses the physiology of muscles in addition to the physical attributes of skin and the relationship between skin, muscle, and bone. An overview of deformation methods, including skinning, spring meshes, and shape interpolation taking into account the theory and code put these anatomical concepts into practice.

14.1 PHYSIOLOGY OF MUSCLES

Muscles can be thought of as motors which actively generate force and produce movement through the process of contraction. Skeletal muscle comprises one of the largest single organs of the human body (with skin being the largest). It is highly compartmentalized and we often think of each compartment as a separate entity, such as the biceps muscle. Each of these individual muscles is composed of single cells or fibers embedded in a matrix of collagen. At either end of the muscle belly in skeletal muscle, this matrix becomes the tendon that connects the muscle to bone.

The basic action of any muscle is contraction. For example, when you think about bending your arm, your brain sends a signal down a nerve cell telling your biceps muscle to contract. The amount of force that the muscle creates varies. In effect, the muscle can contract a little or a lot depending on the signal that the nerve sends. All that any muscle can do is create contraction force. As that contraction force dissipates, the biceps muscle (Figure 14.1) relaxes and in the case of the arm, the triceps muscle at the back of the upper arm contracts and acts to extend the arm. The biceps and triceps are a good example of working pairs of skeletal muscle that work

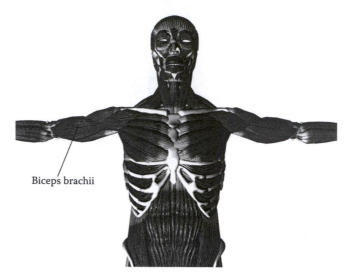

FIGURE 14.1   Bicep muscle. (Model by cgHuman.)

together to perform the actions needed for that range of articulation. These working pairs are also classified as antagonistic pairs.

Digital characters for use in visual effects often include complex muscle systems as a means of creating complex deformations for realistic characters. Studios and projects differ as to how anatomically realistic a muscle system needs to be (Figure 14.2). The common belief is that the visualization of structures moving under the skin is critical to the creation of complex characters. This leads many studios to create abstract surfaces and deformers that look like

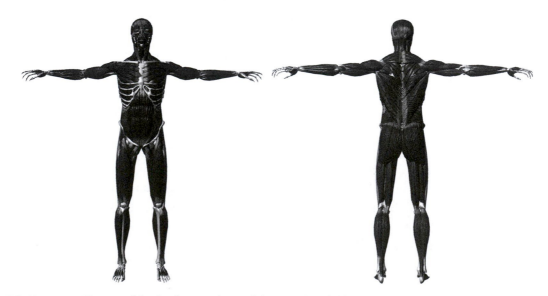

FIGURE 14.2   Front and back of a muscle model setup. (Model by cgHuman.)

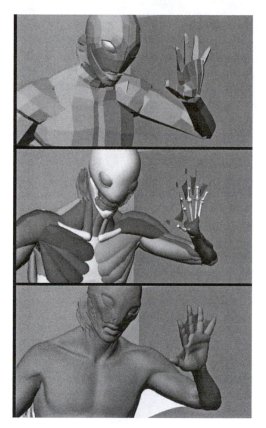

FIGURE 14.3 Abe Sapien muscle setup from *Hellboy*. (Photo credit: Tippett Studios.)

muscles (Figure 14.3), thus creating a more simplified setup that achieves the desired visual results.

Something to keep in mind is that in nature the brain fires a signal which triggers a muscle to act which, in turn, manipulates a bone. For digital characters, the muscles are implemented for a visual result and not a kinematic one whereby the bone is moved and the muscles trigger to produce the desired look. There is biomechanical research that is going into creating a simulated neuron-to-muscle relationship, but at this point that is still not feasible for production.

14.2 THE POLYGONAL MODEL AS SKIN

The manner in which skin slides over skeletal and muscular structures is intrinsic to its mechanical properties. When the deformation of the model surface, in this case, our character skin, reveals an anatomical structure moving under the surface, we are clued into its structure and the complexity of the character. The topology of our model defines the anatomy of our character. The shape of muscles is reflected in the surface of the model (Figure 14.4). The way in which polygonal edges flow and loop over the character define the first level of how the

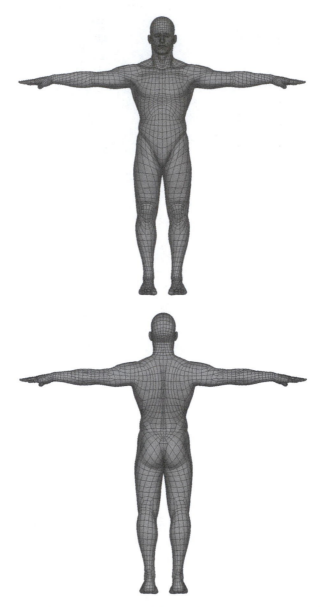

FIGURE 14.4 Front and back of a character model with defined muscles. (Model by Lee Wolland.)

character should deform when in motion. Therefore, character modelers with a strong sense of anatomy and character deformations are key to developing complex characters.

The model is the initial manifestation of all of the design and planning for the character. Proportions, points of articulation, and musculature are all contained in the layout of the vertices (Figure 14.5). This is the starting off point for the character setup artist whose first task for a new character is to provide feedback about the model to the modeler. This feedback usually

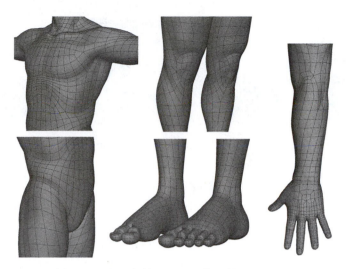

FIGURE 14.5 Close-up model views. (Model by Lee Wolland.)

includes issues with resolution of regions (too much or too little), general flow of the edges with regard to how they will deform, and adherence to surface naming, scale, or position conventions that may be standard for the production. Obviously, catching character model issues early can save a lot of time later. Once the model is approved, motion systems and basic deformations can be applied. Model changes, from a design perspective, happen often, so there are many times that motion systems will need to be updated while the model is in flux. It is best to hold deformation system development until these changes are complete, but it is not unheard of for character design changes to be drastic enough to require reworking portions of a completed deformation system.

14.3 DEFORMATION

For digital characters, deformations are implemented to reach the desired shapes of the regions being moved. Once a motion system is developed for a character, and taking the notion of skin dynamics into consideration, a plan is put into place for how that system will deform the model it was built to fit. Depending on the final output, there are a number of options available for methods of deformation. Game engines rely on joint-based manipulation of the model, often termed "skinning," while animation systems used for film and non real-time production have a few more options at their disposal. These include skinning, layered deformations, relaxation deformers, and shape interpolations. But before a method is chosen for a character, there needs to be an understanding of exactly what mesh deformation is and the type of variation that can be achieved depending on the type of character you are developing. In the interest of clarity, our discussion of geometric deformation will be limited to polygonal surfaces.

FIGURE 14.6   Undeformed, bent, stretched, and sheared polygon plane.

The elements of creatures such as robots and other mechanical characters can usually be implemented with rigid nondeforming parts that are constrained to the most logical joint. For situations such as this, each part is transformed by its joint matrix independently. Thus, parts of the character are parented to exactly one matrix as defined in $v' = v \cdot W$, where v is defined in the joint's local space and W is the transform matrix. These transformations, while sometimes all that is required to attach a model to the motion system, are not technically a deformation.

In the most generic terms, deformation is the modification of a geometric surface shape from any previous state. Deformation is typically a combination of bending, stretching, and shearing a mesh of polygons (Figure 14.6) in relation to the methods enacted on them. Bending the surface of a polygonal mesh involves the rotation of those vertices about the axis of the joint that they are weighted to follow. Stretching the surface is a way to describe the motion of vertices away from other points that are static or moving in an opposing direction. This will cause the polygonal faces to grow in size as they move apart or shrink as the vertices move toward each other. Shearing is the motion of vertices moving in opposite parallel directions from each other, possibly due to twisting rotational forces.

There are numerous methods for deformations and many more being developed. The challenge is the development of methods that are stable, reusable, efficient in terms of user setup, and calculation speed. As computation speeds increase, we are able to calculate methods which would have seemed incomprehensible only a few years ago.

14.4 SKINNING AND ENVELOPING

If we think about deformations from the simplest solution, where the vertices of a polygonal mesh are uniformly constrained (nonweighted) to a joint matrix in motion, we get what is often referred to as rigid-skinning. Similar to the rigid transformation described above, the motion of each individual vertex is constrained to a single joint. Now every vertex of a continuous mesh is individually moved by the transformation of the joints as they are moved by the motion system. This "rigid skinning" approach is used extensively in games.

The maintenance of offsets between the vertices of a surface and the default position of joints is the simplest form of deformation system. Typically called "skinning" or "enveloping," this basic form of deforming the model is effective for film animation and necessary for the

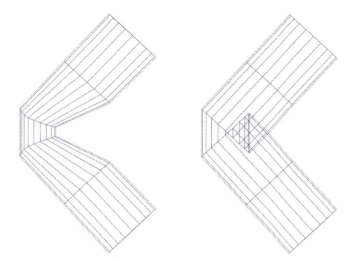

FIGURE 14.7 Smooth (weighted) versus rigid (uniform) skinning.

implementation of deforming characters in games. The term "enveloping" comes from the idea that the model is enveloping the joint set that controls it. The use of the word "skinning" is contrary to the traditional usage, in that it refers to the attachment of the model, or skin, to the joints. In modern animation systems, the influence of joints can be defined as uniform (with each point having one parent), or weighted (where points on the surface share influence from multiple joints). The careful adjustment of skin weights to associated joints creates the appearance of general skin sliding, where the model seems to be be moving as a whole with the motion of the body, as skin would naturally respond. This is contrary to uniform or rigid skin weights where each vertex on the model is associated with one joint which tends to have a more localized deformation appearance. Weighted skinning allows for a falloff from the joint's influence so that joints appear to have a gradation effect on the skin which is a simulation of the falloff from the mechanical elasticity of skin (Figure 14.7).

However, because of the elastic properties of skin, we realize that the motion of a point on the surface should actually be controlled by multiple joint matrices at the same time. This "smooth skinning" is a weighted mapping between a surface vertex and a series of joint matrices where adjustable weights control how much each joint affects it. The speed limitations of these operations are proportional to the number of vertices and the number of influences acting on them, as each vertex is transformed for each influence and the results are averaged to find the ending position for a vertex

$$v' = w_1(v \cdot M_1) + w_2(v \cdot M_2) + \cdots + w_N(v \cdot M_n)$$

or

$$v' = \sum w_i(v \cdot M_i)$$

where the resulting vertex weight is a normalized value with all of the weights of the influences adding to 1:

$$\sum w_i = 1$$

With rigid parts or rigid skinning, v can be defined locally to the joint that it is constrained to. For smooth skin, several joint matrices transform a vertex, but the vertex cannot be defined locally to all the joint matrices, so they must first be transformed to be local to the joint that will then transform it to the world. To do this, we use a binding matrix B for each joint that defines where the joint was when the skin was attached and premultiply its inverse with the world matrix:

$$M_i = B_i^{-1} \cdot W_i$$

After each frame of the animation and after the motion system executes, the deformed vertex position is calculated as a weighted average of all the influences of the joints that the vertex is attached to

$$v' = \sum w_i v \cdot B_i^{-1} \cdot W_i$$

where W is a joint's world matrix and B is a joint's binding matrix that describes where its world matrix was when it was initially attached to the skin model. This is often referred to as the bind pose position. In some animation systems, this position must be returned to in order for the skinning to be edited, but this is becoming less and less common. Skinning is always tested by posing the character in various extreme positions and watching how the model responds. When moved, each joint transforms a vertex as if it were rigidly attached and then those results are blended based on user-specified weights. The normalized weights, as mentioned earlier, must add up to 1:

$$\sum w_i = 1$$

When coupled with creative motion systems, smooth skinning can often be the final solution for character deformation setup. The weighted influence often provides enough smoothness to create appealing results, particularly for less detailed characters. For cartoon-derived characters, the realization of sliding skin is not a crucial issue, but for realistic ones it is a critical component of deformation setup. The alternative is that cartoon-styled characters generally need to be able to squash and stretch, maintaining volume as they extend and compress through extreme motions. This squash and stretch is essentially a scaling of the joints or deformation influences in the regions that are being effected (Figure 14.8).

Realistic characters should avoid stretching joints, but this is often handy to cheat shots. These characters require a more subtle reaction to underlying surfaces, such as wrinkling and

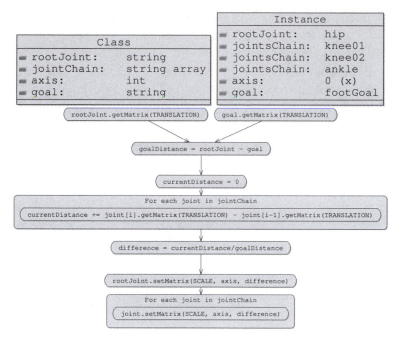

Class	
▬ rootJoint:	string
▬ jointChain:	string array
▬ axis:	int
▬ goal:	string

Instance	
▬ rootJoint:	hip
▬ jointsChain:	knee01
▬ jointsChain:	knee02
▬ jointsChain:	ankle
▬ axis:	0 (x)
▬ goal:	footGoal

```
rootJoint.getMatrix(TRANSLATION)        goal.getMatrix(TRANSLATION)

            goalDistance = rootJoint - goal

                currentDistance = 0

           For each joint in jointChain
currentDistance += joint[i].getMatrix(TRANSLATION) - joint[i-1].getMatrix(TRANSLATION)

           difference = currentDistance/goalDistance

      rootJoint.setMatrix(SCALE, axis, difference)

           For each joint in jointChain
        joint.setMatrix(SCALE, axis, difference)
```

FIGURE 14.8   Class, data diagram, and method for stretching joints in a straight line.

the motion of structures under the skin which we will discuss ahead. Weights associated with character skinning are usually adjusted through a painting interface (Figure 14.9) that creates weighted maps, where values are associated with vertices per joint matrix based on a gray-scale map. This map will display black for the points that are unaffected by the joint selected and white for a point that is fully weighted to that joint. Gray values in between illustrate a

FIGURE 14.9   Painting interface for editing skin weights for the left knee joint.

value between 0 and 1 for that joint. It is best for artists to paint the area based on the most direct influence, then add others as needed to avoid making areas a muddy region of various character weights. Joint falloff is usually smooth and seamlessly overlapping with the next joint influence. Methods and best practices vary based on the artist's preference and style, but it is usually agreed upon that painting weights should happen from the middle of the body outward (e.g., down the arm, or down the leg) and that for most characters, extreme bending should avoid resulting in the surfaces intersecting.

Since skinning is based on weight maps for each joint, these maps can be exported and stored on disk. This can be used to store or version character skin weights, to transfer them to another character with identical or similar topology, or to export them before a major change that may require unbinding the character model from the skin. Once a deformation system change is complete, the weight maps can be reimported and changes can be addressed as needed, but the original state of character skinning is intact. Character skinning can, for feature characters, often take weeks to perfect, so whenever possible that hard and tedious work is preserved as disk-based weight maps. Similarly, the amount of detailed weight painting incorporated into the character should be taken into account when exporting maps. Since these maps are generated procedurally, the user can set the resolution for output. There is no harm in exporting at a higher resolution to retain the small details that a lower resolution map may not retain in an effort to save disk space.

14.5 THE DEFORMATION RIG AND PIPELINE

The character deformation pipeline is responsible for the motion of all the character surface points throughout the entire project, from creation to motion and rendering. This is a huge amount of data to keep track of and therefore a clear plan and architecture is a critical component of production planning and technical pipeline design. As the motion system and the deformation system for a digital character are essentially two interconnected systems, it is often helpful to consider them as two different rigs. At some studios, the two systems are individual tasks carried out by potentially two different artists; this is especially true with regard to complex "hero" characters. In the end, the idea is that the deformation system "hangs" on the motion system. The deformation is the interface between the animation applied to the motion system and the response of the model surface that is rendered in the final image. Often times the deformation system is a complete hierarchical rig that has all the procedural controls designed to manipulate the surfaces associated with the deformations.

The set of joints associated with the deformations should be denoted with a special string in their name, such as "def," as these will be the only ones used for skinning or whatever method is used to attach the model to the rig. These are also often referred to as "secondary joints." Joints can be placed with procedural controls to recreate muscles or just to create smooth transitions for certain regions. For example, in the human forearm, we can bend our hand at the wrist and we can move our hand from side to side at the wrist, but the twisting motion, such as turning your hand over, is produced by the rotation of the radius bone around the ulna. This motion starts just below the elbow and works its way down to the wrist. As such, the deformations for the twisting motion of the human forearm should be weighted from the wrist to the mid-forearm. In the deformation rig, this can be accomplished by a series of joints that start with full rotation weighted at the wrist and then fade down to no rotation as you get closer to the elbow. The joints in between will have a logical falloff depending on the number of joints.

When in place, the deformation rig adds a layer of abstraction between the motion and the model. Deformation rigs can be updated on the fly, without impacting the animation (the overall motion and poses) already produced. This is a critical point because as we previously stated, the deformation system is responsible for the look of the model topology that is handed to the renderer. Therefore, it is very possible, and unfortunately very common, that once animation is finished for a shot, the deformations may need to be tweaked to achieve the desired look for the character. This harkens back to traditional animation where no matter what a character did, it was critical that they always "stay on model" and appear familiar. The distinction between the motion system and the deformation system allows a character technical director to work on character deformations without impacting the functionality of the motion system and risk altering approved animation.

Studios must also take into consideration the fact that deformation systems need to be calculated and that the calculation of the deformation system is dependent on many factors. Even small changes in any of these factors can result in different model result. In the same way that character motion is approved, character deformation can be approved. These approved deformations for a particular shot are often preserved on disk so that changes to the deformation system down the line do not effect them. Deformation system changes are intended to be nondestructive, but when a lighting team is art directing the placement of light and shadow in a shot, a small change to the curvature of a surface can have major effects. To preserve character deformations, the deformations are executed per frame and the models for each frame of the animation are stored to disk. This cache of models is then associated with the shot and loaded into the animation software, instead of the full character rig when the shot goes to the lighting. This is also a valuable time-saving device for the rendering of frames. If the renderer just needs to load the appropriate model and not execute the motion and deformation systems, valuable time can be saved off the computation of that frame. These models take up a lot of disk space, however, as the cost of hard drive space decreases, and this solution is becoming more and more viable for smaller studios as well.

As we will see later, other systems can piggy-back onto the deformation system as well. As the deformation is responsible for the final form of the model, systems responsible for character clothing, for example, could be run on the resultant models. Character clothing can be simply attached to the models via skinning, or be simulated. Simulated clothing requires that the resultant character model surface be used as a collision surface which the clothing surfaces would be collided against over the course of the animation. More commonly, because it is more efficient, a low polygon single surface collision proxy model will be attached to the deformation rig and used as the collision surface. The collision proxy model is often smoothed out to not have any extra creases where clothing simulations may get caught. The artist who sets up the character's main deformation setup is usually also responsible for binding this collision proxy and making sure that it ends up in a very similar position as the character model surface. One can imagine the computational difference between colliding against a production quality character model and a simplified surface that merely represents the volume of the character. Depending on how far that character is from the camera, the simplified solution may be the right choice. If the hero is close to the camera and the clothing response is evident, then the full-resolution character skin may be the only option as a collision surface.

Character texturing and shading is another important aspect playing into the depiction of the model on screen. In many ways, the approval of the model is in the hands of the character shading artists and the character technical directors. Changes to the model once either of these teams have started their work can be time-consuming.

14.6 DEFORMERS

Animation software packages are continually adding new deformation methods and stand-alone deformation tools. These are usually push-button functions that are applied to an object. The user is then given attributes to tune the influence and relationship between objects. Free-form deformations (FFDs), for example, are usually defined as a rectangular three-dimensional lattice of points that surround an object (Figure 14.10). When transformed, the points of the lattice apply a weighted local transformation to the points of the affected surface. FFDs can be applied to regions of the character that need special localized deformation. They are often used for muscle bulges, to twist or untwist regions of a limb, or even to smooth out unwanted creases at points of articulation. The points of the lattice can be animated and controlled based on properties of the rig.

Shrink wrap deformers are another important tool for character setup. This method, often just called a "wrap" deformer, attaches one surface to another regardless of the resolution. In

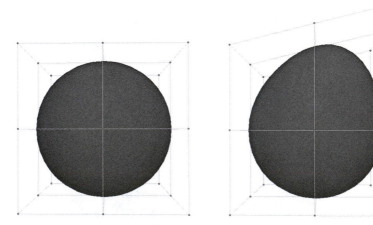

FIGURE 14.10 Sphere modified by a lattice.

many ways, a wrap deformer acts like a lattice, but where a lattice is geometrically cubic, a wrap deformer can be any polygonal surface. Implementations have been developed for NURBS and subdivision surfaces as well, but as stated previously for the purpose of clarity, we are restricting our discussion to polygons. Wrap deformers connect to other surfaces by generating a weighted relationship between all the points of the target mesh and all the points of the wrap surface. This surface connection proves valuable when a high resolution mesh is to be controlled by a lower resolution mesh. This relationship between high and low resolution meshes also opens the door for the low resolution mesh to be the control source for complicated solutions such as dynamics. As we will discuss later, methods such as dynamics and spring meshes can be effective and powerful tools to generate secondary motion on deforming surfaces. The ability to carry out these computationally expensive operations on a low resolution mesh is one of the only ways to make such methods feasible for production.

Algorithms can also be applied to surfaces in the form of deformers. Functions that curve a surface or warp it (in some manner) are often used for the quick deformation of props and objects in a scene without the use of complex joint setups and controllers. Often termed "non-linear deformers," these functions are typically volumes of influence with defined regions, such as top and bottom, that modify the position of the vertices of a model based on the parameters supplied to it. For example, a deformer programmed to bend a surface will define a curve that travels through the deformation volume. When the bend value is modified, the curve is bent, visualizing the amount of bend requested by the user, and the points associated with the curve bending are rotated to match the curve. Compression-based methods such as squash and stretch have also been implemented. These create a curve or a volume of a particular length and the model is constrained to it. As the curve or volume is stretched or squashed, the compression value applied is used to deform the surface in a volume-preserving manner. Squash and stretch, as we have discussed, is the idea that as something elongates, it thins out and as it is compressed, it expands in the direction perpendicular to the compression. An elastic container filled with water, such as a water balloon, is a perfect representation of squash and stretch in the real world.

14.7 LAYERED DEFORMATION METHODS

Our understanding of weighted skinning can be extrapolated, such that a series of underlying skinned models would produce the appearance of surfaces sliding under each other. This not only visually provides the sense of bones and muscles, but also allows for more control over the final model deformations. The style and design of a project dictates the level of abstraction for the anatomical model required (Figure 14.11). Animation systems allow for the layering of surfaces with the resultant deformed surfaces driving the final visible skin of the character. The visible effect of surfaces moving under the surface of the skin adds a layer of visual complexity that is required for creating realistic characters (Figure 14.12).

Layering underlying structures is easier said than done and there are a number of techniques for attaching surfaces to each other. These methods range from UV surface attachment, where

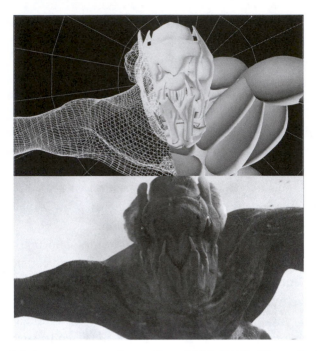

FIGURE 14.11 Layered deformation setup from *Cloverfield* (2008) by Tippet Studios. (Image copyright 2008 Bad Robot. All rights reserved. Photo credit: Tippet Studios.)

the vertices of more complex surfaces are mapped to the UV co-ordinates of simpler deforming surfaces, to collision-driven layers. None of these solutions, at this point, can run in real time and most rely on simulation and solving. Often times, the surface connection is achieved through what is conventionally called a "wrap" deformer (as previously discussed), in which the

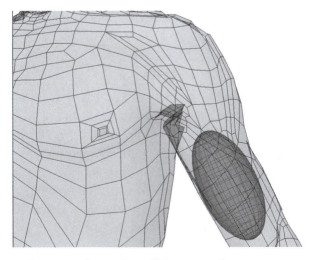

FIGURE 14.12 Surface acting as an abstraction of biceps muscle.

vertices of a driven mesh are controlled by the deformation of a driving mesh based on a falloff value. These types of deformers are difficult to edit and are usually used for push-button solutions where a low resolution mesh controls the deformation of its high resolution counterpart. A more efficient means to work with surface-to-surface attachments is on a regional basis where course deformations on low polygon models propagate up to more and more refined surfaces. The higher surfaces deform by maintaining the established offset, leaving only the lower ones to be manipulated. The point is that the fewer vertices that need to be hand weighted, the faster and more comprehensible the process is. It is inefficient (and painful) to craft deformations on extremely high resolution surfaces.

If an anatomical setup is required for the production, then we take our deformation cues from nature. The layers to be considered for an anatomical model include bone, muscle, fat, and skin. These are made up of geometry and potentially particles. A skeleton model set is created and parented to joints so that all the actions of the motion system translate to realistic articulations. The skeleton model need not be accurate down to each realistic anatomical feature, but the proportions and general shape should be modeled adequately for attaching muscle surfaces where needed.

Muscles have points of origin (where they start) and insertion (where they end). Muscle surfaces are defined as influences on the model surface layer above them. They are attached to the joints and often have procedural controls and callbacks to define the motion expected of them in various situations. For example, as the arm bends, the biceps muscle is supposed to flex and bulge. This can be set up either through a triggered shape deformation (see Figure 14.13), a triggered procedural code to change the surface, or even as simply as procedurally moving a set of joints to deform the muscle surface. The process to set up these muscles is time-consuming and tedious, so the effort must be justified by the end result. Many production studios are

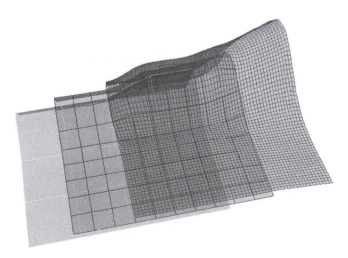

FIGURE 14.13   One low-resolution surface controlling two subsequently higher resolution surfaces.

developing simplified abstract muscle structures for characters that are fewer in number, lower resolution, faster to calculate, and have a very similar visual result to more complex setups.

The fat layer is typically a modeled surface or even dynamic particles that form a regionalized implicit surface. This layer is simulated once animation is carried out to shift the loose connective tissue found just below the skin. As will be seen later, the dynamic jiggle associated with this layer can be represented at the skin layer as a spring-based deformer, but the notion of a layer-based solution is worth noting.

The skin layer is the character model itself. While this rendered surface in layered deformations is, most of the time, just the result of the deformers acting on it, there are opportunities to apply callbacks directly to this surface. These callbacks should be applied to the lowest resolution representation of this model when possible, as the highest resolution model could be prohibitively heavy and slow to evaluate for procedural control.

14.8 SHAPE INTERPOLATION

Shape interpolation is the transformation of a set of vertices from one state to another. Usually termed "morphing," the technique is heavily used in computer graphics and will be covered again with regard to face setup in the next chapter. The common term associated with the creation of a series of models that are stored as a library and called as needed in the animation system is "blend shape" or "morph target." These shapes are sculpted by the artist into the configuration required based on copies of the original model. When called, these shapes are blended via normalized weights from 0 to 1, with zero being the default mode and one being the target blend shape. The transition between states is typically linear, meaning that points move in a straight line from default to target shape. Blend shapes are an effective technique for character face setup, but they are also increasingly helpful for character body deformations. When combined with triggered events, surface interpolations can be combined with particular character motion. Pose-based deformations, or pose–space deformations (PSD), are often used for simulating the effects of body rotations on the skin to create muscle bulges or on cloth to create wrinkles (see Figures 14.14 and 14.15). For example, as the character's body twists, the diagonal wrinkles that would appear naturally on clothing are created as a blend shape and triggered based on the rotation values of the spine joint matrices. Thus, a PSD is a deformation that is created within the context of a character pose. This is a common replacement for dynamic

Class		Instance	
▬ jointTrigger:	string	▬ jointTrigger:	knee.rotateX
▬ defaultShape:	string	▬ defaultShape:	characterMesh
▬ maximumShape:	string	▬ maximumShape:	bodyShapes.kneeBent
▬ minimumValue:	float	▬ minimumValue:	0
▬ maxiumumValue:	float	▬ maxiumumValue:	90

FIGURE 14.14 Class and data diagram for pose–space interpolation.

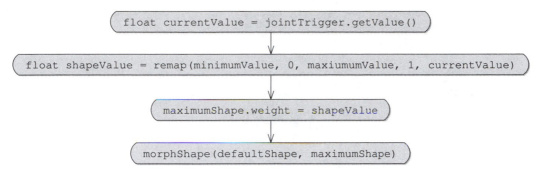

FIGURE 14.15   A method for a pose–space interpolation.

clothing. Wrinkles in clothing provide the visual richness and sense of material weight associated with natural fabrics. Without wrinkles, computer-generated wrinkles will often have the appearance of the stretchy, form fitting neoprene used in wet suits for surfing or diving.

Further, PSDs have a more general application in the deformations of the body. Take, for example, the human knee which rotates along one axis and has a very distinctive appearance when both flexed and when extended due to the motion of the floating knee cap (patella bone). In this case, the rotation of the knee joint can trigger and blend a shape from one state to another depending on the rotation.

This pose-based deformer is essentially a "blend shape" that is activated on the mesh when triggered by the rotation of a specific joint. The benefit of such a solution is that the resulting shape is reliable and art-directed. The shape needed can be achieved at the desired time and is not based on an accumulation of deformation processes. The downside is that creating blend shapes to fix body deformations is a slippery slope. Their use can lead to the need to create and apply corrective shapes depending on the state of the trigger joint and the other influences on the model surface. These can be difficult to keep track of, so it is best if this method is either used as a last step to fix an area not controllable by other means or planned from the start. In areas of complex articulation, such as the human shoulder, the amount of shapes and joints required might make this solution inefficient. On the other hand, it would be difficult to get the shapes desired from the knee or elbow region without a sculpted model solution. Shape interpolation and PSDs are a useful addition to the options in the deformation system toolkit.

14.9 DYNAMICS AND SIMULATION

The elastic properties of skin allow for the stretching and local motion caused by the reaction of the movements of the character. Looking at any high-speed film footage of athletes in action, it is clear that our skin reacts to all the small and large motions produced by the body. Even the leanest runner's skin reacts to the extreme forces applied to the body during vigorous motion. These reactions range from small vibrations to large ripples and are magnified depending on the amount of body fat present. The jiggle of muscle and skin adds a necessary secondary motion to the animation of realistic characters. In particular, large characters benefit from the perceived

Class		Instance	
inputSurface:	string	inputSurface:	face_GEO
magnitude:	float	magnitude:	jiggleMesh.magnitude
damping:	float	damping:	jiggleMesh.damping
gravity:	float	gravity:	jiggleMesh.gravity
weight:	float	weight:	jiggleMesh.weight

FIGURE 14.16   A class and data diagram for a jiggle deformer.

weight that comes along with skin rippling in reaction to heavy motion. In fact, for animals with column-like legs such as elephants and sauropod dinosaurs, the reaction of the skin to the impact results in the skin rotating around the muscles. This rotational inertia is crucial to characters who are bearing a large amount of weight and appear large on screen. This motion is often carried out by callbacks within the deformation setup. Callbacks are pieces of code that are triggered by a system when certain conditions are met. For characters, those conditions might be the rotation value of a joint, or the compression or stretching of the polygons of a model. For example, a point jiggle deformer applied to a mesh can provide a slight secondary motion to a subset of the mesh points based on the motion of the rig kinematics (see Figures 14.16 and 14.17). Dynamic simulation adds the real-world effects that are impossible to hand animate at the surface level. The foremost of these is gravity which acts on the skin in relation to the motion of the body action.

Callbacks such as these work as a post animation dynamic deformation stage. They are run after the animator has completed the shot and are tuned to the appropriate values for the motion of the shot. These values often must be animated, as extreme motion may require that dynamic motion be damped to maintain a stable solution. This method is a surface-based approach where the effect is computed based on per vertex surface motion. A spring-based solution can also be implemented where each vertex is connected to adjacent vertices by springs. These

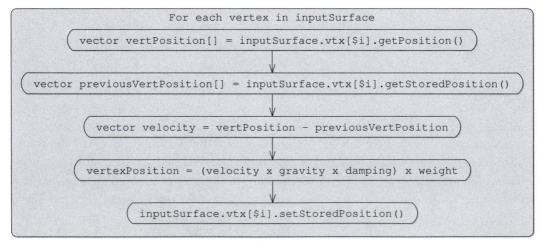

FIGURE 14.17   Method for a jiggle deformer.

springs create a similar result to a jiggle deformer, but per spring attributes, such as stiffness and damping, provides the user with more control. In methods such as these, each vertex can be visualized having a weight attached to them. Each weight has its own mass, and the connections between each of them have an elastic property. As the motion system is executed, the mesh is moved by the skinning deformer to follow the rig. After skinning is executed, the dynamics pass is run to compare the previous position against the current one. Often it is compared to multiple frames in the history to calculate more accurate, albeit slower to compute, simulations. The points are then moved relative to their mass, gravity in the scene, the spring connections to other vertices, and the velocity and direction of the motion applied.

14.10 SPRING MESH AND RELAXATION DEFORMATION METHODS

As joints rotate, they move the deformation surfaces, like muscles, and pull the skin across them. In humans, there exists an elasticity to the skin which stretches and pulls to meet the demands of the underlying movement. In an animation system, the skin layer can be represented by a spring mesh surface composed on a low resolution mesh with its vertices connected by springs. These springs can be uni- or bidirectional. They can also be rigid to represent areas where skin does not slide. The purpose of such a system is to provide smooth regional motion falloff as the rig is articulated.

Skinning alone is a time-consuming and tedious process. The addition of a relaxation step often makes basic skinning all that is necessary. The application of a relaxation step, after a joint-based deformation, smooths out the surface and dissipates the influence of the articulated region. Relaxation methods are iterative, meaning that they are run successively for a defined number of times. The more times a relaxation is run, the smoother the final result will be, but keep in mind that the surface also stabilizes and cannot relax any further after a certain number of steps, depending on the algorithm. Thus, finding the balance between the final visual result and the number of iterative relaxation steps is critical to final deformation efficiency.

When combined with a spring mesh, relaxation methods are powerful. Spring meshes, as we mentioned earlier, are surfaces where each vertex is connected to adjoining vertices by a spring. As an initialization step, the springs determine a tension that will balance them against the others surrounding it to maintain the surface in its initial position. Once surface balance has been reached and mapped to the initial settings, the system is ready to run. The implementation of this system is done based on a copy of the input mesh. The duplicate mesh is created with the balanced springs and the true character mesh is shrink-wrapped to this mesh. The spring mesh has per vertex attributes related to the point's status. Points can be defined as mobile, or floating, or rigidly attached, or fixed, to the joints. The edges between the vertices have attributes related to the springs between the points, namely the elastic value that defines the tension of that spring. A vertex connected to a series of loose springs will be very active during motion, whereas one attached to very rigid springs will have limited secondary motion during motion. A point with three loose spring attachments and one rigid spring will be pulled toward the vertex from which the rigid spring originates. This allows certain points and regions of points to have more influence, and literally "pull" over other regions. Assigning certain regions to contain fixed points means that they will have limited to no stretch. On the human face, the bridge of the nose has limited motion during expressions, so those points would be more likely fixed, whereas areas around the nostrils, forehead, and brows are very active and inherit a lot of motion and therefore have loose attachments. The purpose of all this is to cause small motion in one region and have logical smooth motion in adjacent regions. Think about the human back and how the skin stretches to accommodate the raising and lowering of the arm. The motion is centered around the shoulder, but also shows up down the middle of the back. Results using this method are very similar to what you would expect from skin. The little nuances like this add the visual complexity we are accustomed to seeing in humans and strive to recreate in digital characters.

14.11 DEFORMATION ORDER

The order in which deformation methods are executed has a bearing on the end result. If each is thought of and designed as a discrete function that is called one after the other, then each deformation method begins with the topology of the model resulting from the previous method. If each method is discreet and specific to its task, the user can expect predictable results and its effect can be readily seen when it is deactivated (Figure 14.18). One of the best examples of this is in the interplay between joint-based skin weights and blend-shape deformers on the character's head. In every case, you would need to run the skin weights operation first to put the head geometry into the right place, then run the blend shapes to modify the point's local position from there. Running these in reverse will often result in the head moving back to the origin when the blend shapes are enacted. In animation systems, this ordering can be a simple change to the order of inputs on a surface. On a procedural system, programmed deformation steps are run in the execution loop of the character and can be reordered, but the interplay between methods can take some tuning. Ideally, if each method returns a reference or handle to the deformed surface, then this handle can be passed down the line efficiently.

Switching between functional deformation orders midproduction can often result in slightly different output meshes at the end. Even if the result is generally the same, one can expect subtle variations between results. Changing deformation order should be done carefully and only if absolutely required by the production.

Deformation Order

1. Rigid-Skinning

2. Pose–Space Deformer

3. Spring Mesh Relaxation

FIGURE 14.18 A sample deformation order.

14.12 REAL-TIME ENGINE CONCERNS

In games, and depending on the engine in use, animation is generally baked out to the joints and similarly all deformations ultimately fall under the category of skinning. All deformers created for a particular character are not carried over. This drastically changes how the character setup is conceived and executed. A number of techniques have been developed to overcome this limitation. One solution is to bake complex deformations to joints, so the motion of the surface mesh is baked to a set a joints, one for each vertex. This is a joint-heavy solution, but the baked motion of these joints carries a lot of information. This technique allows the results of methods like pose–space deformers, and muscle and cloth simulations to be maintained in the character deformations in a format that is game engine compliant.

For real-time characters, it is important to restrict the number of objects in a rig to a minimum, as these things must be executed at every frame. One way to do this includes using as few joints as possible. This includes primary joints for the motion system and secondary joints for the deformation system when they are available. A balance between character execution speed and realistic deformation must always be struck. In recent years, character execution speed has always won out over character deformations, but thanks to fast processors we are starting to see a shift toward richer character deformations. Limiting the number of vertices in the skin is a given for real-time engines. While the "polycount" limits are rising with each hardware and engine iteration, there are ways of faking detail on a low resolution model. A highly effective way to do this is the use of normal maps, which are a form of bump mapping that store the normal information of a higher resolution mesh. This allows the detail of a high resolution mesh to be applied to that of a lower resolution at the shader level, taking the responsibility off the deformation system. These normal maps can also be triggered in the same manner as PSDs where instead of a mesh being swapped out, a different normal map is blended into place.

The amount of joint weights used per vertex during skinning is another concern for real-time engines. As described earlier, the position of a vertex needs to be solved for the number of joints associated with it. Thus, four joint weights require that vertex to calculate its weighted position based on the result of the influence of each of those joints. The less joints a vertex must solve its position in relation to, the faster it finds its position per frame. Many practitioners suggest not using more than four joint weights per vertex when skinning but these limitations are increased, with each advance to game engines and graphics processing hardware.

14.13 CONCLUSION

Deformation systems manipulate the character model to result in the final posed mesh. Digital characters for films rarely rely on a single method to achieve the desired deformations. As new techniques emerge, it is likely that they will be integrated into the character deformation pipeline and not revolutionize it immediately. It is the intelligent combination of techniques that has found the greatest success. In many ways, this is akin to the way that living organisms work, with multiple systems working together.

On the horizon, we can expect new techniques for elastic deformations and even deformations produced without the influence of joints. These shape-filling algorithms are an alternative, albeit a costly one, to deforming a model based on the standard character technology conventions. In this method, multiview video streams are used to create a volume. This volume is analyzed and the digital character model is deformed to fill the volume, maintaining the initial proportions of the character. Techniques such as this might have a major impact on our workflow in the future. The immediate challenge ahead is the integration of complex deformations into realtime engines.

Integrating motion and deformation system concepts into expressive faces is the next hurdle in the successful setup of a digital character.

14.14 EXERCISE

In this exercise, we go through the conceptual and technical process of creating a character deformation system. Split into groups of two or more. One of you is the art director, and the other team members are the character setup artists. Follow the steps below.

1. Starting with the character you developed in the last section, design the manner with which the character deformations should behave. Should the character bend with smooth cartoon-inspired motion or be more realistic and detailed?

2. Determine the methods you need to implement the deformation design and list out the order of deformations.

3. Implement the deformations using the motion system and animation poses developed in the previous section.

4. The art director should provide feedback on the look of the character and how "on model" the character remains while in extreme poses.

5. Maintain this review/fix feedback loop until satisfied.

FURTHER READING

Christopher Evans of Crytek has a great collection of resources that relate muscle anatomy to rigging ranging from technical papers to practical implementations:

http://chrisevans3d.com/

A good physics introduction:

Bourg, D. M. 2001. *Physics for Game Developers*. O'Reilly Media, Inc.

Some technical references on deformations:

Lewis, J. P., Cordner, M., and Fong, N. 2000. Pose Space Deformations: A Unified Approach to Shape Interpolation and Skeleton-Driven Deformation. *Siggraph 2000, Computer Graphics Proceedings*. ACM Press/ACM SIGGRAPH/Addison Wesley Longman, Boston, MA.

Nedel, L. P. and D. Thalmann. 1998. Real Time Muscle Deformations using Mass-Spring Systems. *CGI'98: Proceedings of the Computer Graphics International 1998*. IEEE Computer Society, Washington, DC.

Scheepers, F., Parent, R. E., Carlson, W. E., and May, S. F. 1997. Anatomy-based Modeling of the Human Musculature. *SIGGRAPH'97: Proceedings of the 24th Annual Conference on Computer Graphics and Interactive Techniques*. ACM Press/Addison-Wesley Publishing Co., New York, NY.

Sheffer, A. and Kraevoy, V. 2004. Pyramid Coordinates for Morphing and Deformation. *3DPVT'04: Proceedings of the 3D Data Processing, Visualization, and Transmission, 2nd International Symposium*. IEEE Computer Society, Washington, DC.

CHAPTER 15

Interview: Robert Helms, Lead Character Technical Director, DreamWorks Animation

15.1 BIO

Robert Helms graduated from Clemson University in 2003 with an MFA in digital production and a BS in electrical engineering. Since then, he has worked as a character rigger and an occasional R&D team member for Rhythm & Hues, and as a character rigger for Double Negative and Dreamworks Animation. Project highlights include *The Chronicles of Narnia*, *Hellboy 2*, *Madagascar 3*, and *How to Train Your Dragon 2*. He especially enjoys working on projects which bridge the gap between production and development.

15.2 Q&A

Q: *The components of character technology are diverse and span the artistic and technical spectrum. How did you get your start in the industry? Based on where you see the field heading what experience/training do you recommend people have?*

A: I received my BS in electrical engineering from Clemson University in 2000. Just as I was finishing that up, Clemson was starting a Digital Production Arts MFA program. I was quite interested in computer games at the time, and the new program seemed like a good way into that industry. I didn't expect at the time that I would get sidetracked into the film industry instead. In that program, I got involved in character rigging as part of a team project. Mixing my engineering and programming skills with some artistic hobbies, and drawing on the anatomical

Robert Helms
Lead Character Technical Director, DreamWorks Animation

knowledge I absorbed from my biologist parents, rigging was a natural fit. I was also fortunate enough to graduate at a time when Rhythm & Hues was in the market for a character rigger. I of course, took that job and am still doing it 11 years and three companies later.

For new students looking to break into this field, math and programming skills are very important foundationally. You will need those for operator, tool, and plug in development, as well as pipeline integration, and motion system work. Even if somebody else does all that for you, technical skills will still help you understand how to make the best use of the tools and systems provided. For the actual creation of a character, a rigger needs a critical eye for shapes and deformation, not just in pose, but especially in transition between poses. Both technical and artistic knowledge are necessary in some degree, and it's nigh impossible to pick up enough of both through either art or science degree programs. At the moment, I think the balance of value favors artistic skills, but the industry is currently undergoing a shift towards producing real time high-fidelity rigs. Building those requires some significant technical skills and understanding of parallel architectures. If I were planning to break into rigging now, I'd probably go for a CG focused art school undergraduate degree with a minor (or masters) in computer science. Making sure I picked up one class on linear algebra and learned C++ and Python along the way. Remember that you get out of college only what you put into it. It's very possible to graduate having learned virtually nothing of value if all your focus is on just passing the courses.

Regardless of which set of skills you break into the industry with, continual learning in both areas is absolutely essential. This is not a static industry, and those who rest on their laurels will quickly be dismayed to see the amazing skills new students are graduating with in a few years.

Q: *Creating compelling digital characters is part art and part science. What is the greatest challenge you encounter on a daily basis? What aspect of character technology keeps you up thinking at night?*

A: My most tricky daily challenge is probably just explaining to an animator why one request is easy and another is very hard. Helping to steer the requests without upsetting anybody so that my client ends up with the best possible rig for their needs (and budget) is a tricky balancing act. It helps quite a bit to talk face-to-face with a client whenever possible. Starting out with a meeting or phone call is better than an impersonal ticketing system. I prefer to use those systems for recording and tracking what was discussed in person.

As a more technical character rigger, the creation of new operators and motion systems tends to get stuck in my head and often does keep me awake at night. Figuring out a slick, yet robust, solution to one of those sorts of problems is an amazing feeling—even if it comes at 3 AM while tossing about. It does not get much better than sharing new technology with my co-workers to make their workflows easier or help them improve the quality of their rigs. Having worked on the occasional truly awesome character, like Cloudjumper from Dreamworks' *How to Train Your Dragon 2*, and seeing it onscreen for the first time is the only other thing competing for my REM cycles.

Q: *What are the ingredients for a successful digital character?*

A: A successful digital character starts with the design. The design sets the limit on how good a character can get. Doing justice to the design requires a well laid out model, and clear understanding of the intended performance for the character. In order for the animator to do justice to the character you built, he or she needs a rig which doesn't get in the way. To this end, it is critical to prevent counter animation due to overzealous automation. A rig should also inform the user when they're doing something beyond what it was designed for, but generally not prevent them from doing it. It's amazing what an animator can get away with during action sequences or whilst hidden from the camera's view when a rig isn't locked down too tightly. Lastly, it is usually better to provide robust and predictable behavior before adding extra functionality. As long as the design is great and the animator can remain in the flow without being hindered by the rig, any digital character should come out looking amazing.

Q: *While the industry is competitive, it is ultimately respectful of great work. Outside of the work you have been personally involved in the production of, what animated characters have you been impressed or inspired by? What is the historical high-bar?*

A: Animation and VFX are such different beasts. I have great respect for both, though my heart is probably a bit more for the VFX industry. With technology improving constantly, choosing a historical high-bar is somewhat unfair. Each new high point stands firmly on the shoulders of past greats. I would say that, for the moment, the "best of" distinction goes to Rhythm & Hues' *Life of Pi*, especially their gorgeous work on the tiger for that film. It was so believable that it didn't take me out of the story even once. That is not an easy thing to achieve with furry photo-real quadrupeds!

Other animated creatures I've been especially impressed by include Sentinels from *The Matrix*, heavily muscled characters such as the *Hulk*, and early Uncanny Valley evaders like Gollum. Taking a few steps back in time, there's a huge amount of pre-CG work which I still

142 ■ Digital Character Development

admire. Looney Tunes, Harryhausen stop motion, early Disney cartoons, etc. I actually think it's rare for any character to make it all the way to a screen without offering something inspirational. Too much care and work goes into them for it to be otherwise.

Q: *Where do you see digital characters in 10 years? Where are animated characters for film and games heading?*

A: There's so much going on right now in both industries. Obviously things will get faster, better, or cheaper (pick two). That will happen both in terms of asset build times and evaluation times. Beyond that, game technology is quickly catching up to movie quality. Both industries have something to offer to each other, and I expect a blurring of the distinction between the two formats. Games offer amazing immersion and replayability while movies offer a better curated story experience. My guess is that, for both industries, we're headed for a world of photo-real quality rigs being evaluated and rendered in real-time. With technology like that, I could imagine finally opening up the first person perspective in movies properly. It's always been problematic because the camera doesn't move as you turn your head, breaking suspension of disbelief. Perhaps with real time rendering and virtual reality headsets, it could be possible to enable free look first person film experiences.

CHAPTER 16

Face Setup

16.1 INTRODUCTION

Our faces serve to visually communicate emotion and are also a vehicle for spoken language. Digital character development of the face requires a setup which is capable of creating the shapes associated with emotional expressions in tandem with the shapes needed to visualize the sounds required for lip-sync. Lip-sync is the process of animating the character's face to match the voice or sounds present in the character's voice-over audio track. By incorporating the anatomy and psychology of faces into our setups, we gain the ability to create compelling, emotive characters no matter how fantastic they are.

16.2 ANATOMY

As humans arguably have the most complex range of expression known in any organism (that we can comprehend), we will focus our discussion of face anatomy on ourselves, while at the same time maintaining a generality of terms and concepts to be able to port these ideas to characters of any design. The complexity of the human face starts with the skull and the muscles attached to it. The only moving part of the cranium is the jaw which attaches with the two temporal bones on the skull just in front of the ear. The jaw has the ability to rotate from this temporomandibular joint (the point at which the temporal bones on the skull articulate with the mandible) allowing for the opening and closing action. Translation is also possible thanks to the articular disk which allows the jaw to slide forward, back, and side-to-side. The jaw is a critical rigid object that defines much of the look and feel of the face, so it must be incorporated in some manner, whether through a modeled geometry surface or just a carefully weighted joint. The articulation point for where the head attaches to the neck is toward the back of the skull, around the foramen magnum where the spinal cord enters the skull and connects with the brain. This leaves the head weighted toward the face and free to rotate about from this posterior position. The skull also contains the eyes, a critical piece of the human expression puzzle, as we will discuss ahead.

Fifty-three muscles are responsible for the wide range of expressions and face shapes available to humans. These muscles fire in patterns to produce the conceived result. Human expressions cross cultural, regional, and linguistic boundaries. Emotion and the ability to classify emotions is a debated subject. There is a categorical model which defines a number of discrete emotional states and there is a dimensional model which maps a range of emotional phenomena onto an explicitly dimensioned space. References for these approaches are listed at the end of this chapter. Looking at emotion categorically, we express happiness, sadness, anger, fear, surprise, and disgust, the so-called six basic emotions, in addition to all the more complex emotional reactions with the same sets of muscles. Facial muscles function similar to skeletal muscles in the rest of the body. Below is a list of muscles which may be a relevant starting point for a muscle-based facial setup (Figures 16.1 and 16.2).

As we will see later, there are research and tools that attempt to quantify and describe the association between the action of a muscle and the resulting facial motion. While character setup artists should be versed in musculoskeletal anatomy and have a general sense of the muscles responsible for the motion of different regions of the face, what is more important is a working knowledge of the general regions of the face and the motion possible for each. For example, the list below contains the major muscles responsible for facial expressions and the regions they effect.

- *Epicranius, frontalis, and occipitalis*: controls eyebrows and scalp

- *Orbicularis oris*: closes the lips

- *Zygomaticus*: raises the corners of the mouth when a person smiles

- *Levator labii superioris*: elevates the upper lip

- *Depressor labii inferioris*: depresses the lower lip

- *Buccinator*: compresses the cheeks against the teeth

- *Mentalis*: elevates and wrinkles the skin of the chin and protrudes the lower lip

- *Platysma*: draws down the lower lip and the angle of the mouth by lowering the corners

- *Risorius*: draws back the mouth angle

- *Orbicularis oculi*: closes the eyelids

- *Corrugator supercilli*: moves the eyebrows downward and medially, and vertically wrinkles forehead

- *Levator palpebrae superioris*: elevates the eyelids

FIGURE 16.1 Major facial muscles and the motions for which they are responsible.

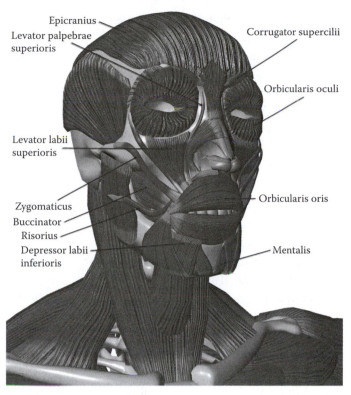

FIGURE 16.2 Major face muscles responsible for motion (platysma not shown). (Model by cgHuman.)

16.3 PSYCHOLOGY BEHIND FACIAL EXPRESSIONS

Facial expressions are a window into the mind of the character. Our discussion of the Uncanny Valley in Section 2.1 illustrated that the subtle motion of the eyes and the face are one of the keys to a convincing performance by a digital character.

Emotion and emotional responses are a highly debated and controversial subject in fields ranging from anthropology, to psychology and philosophy. The fact remains that a big part of our emotional response to the world is communicated by our faces and the subtle interplay of regional muscles. Further, the same is true for successful digital characters where the emotional response is reflected across the face and not limited to one region. Take, for example, this question:

Q. So how do you tell a fake smile from a real one?
A. In a fake smile, only the zygomatic major muscle, which runs from the cheekbone to the corner of the lips, moves. In a real smile, the eyebrows and the skin between the upper eyelid and the eyebrow come down very slightly. The muscle involved is the orbicularis oculi, pars lateralis. [22]

This quote reveals a common problem that is also seen in digital characters where a smile effects only the mouth region. The question is answered by Dr. Paul Ekman, a psychologist and expert on the intricacies of facial expressions and their relationship to our emotions and even our thoughts. Since the 1970s, Ekman has been working to break down and quantify facial expressions into discrete coded entities. This work is invaluable to our discussion of digital character faces, and Ekman's "Facial Action Coding System" (FACS) has been increasingly used in animation productions to lay a foundation for the expressions that will be needed for a particular character. Ekman's system breaks down the facial behaviors based on the muscles that produce them. This reveals directly how muscular action is related to facial appearances. Ekman and colleague W.V. Friesen developed the original FACS in the 1970s by determining how the contraction of each facial muscle both individually, and in combination with other muscles, changed the appearance of the face. Their goal was to create a reliable means for skilled human observers to determine the category or categories in which to fit each facial behavior.

Also from this research, which included the analysis of high-speed video of interviews, the notion of microexpressions emerged. The term microexpression denotes a brief facial expression that lasts less than a quarter of a second. They often occur involuntarily and can reveal emotions not deliberately expressed. These microexpressions generally occur right before the more voluntarily expression that the individual wants to convey. Take, for example, your reaction to someone's cooking. If something is grossly unappealing to you but you do not want to insult the cook, you may convey a split-second expression of disgust followed by something more concealing, but ultimately false. A person trained or inherently able to read microexpressions would be able to tell your true feelings about the experience. Microexpressions are presumably a pathway to an individual's real emotions and are critical knowledge for animators.

16.4 FACE SHAPE LIBRARY

In developing a character's face, it is critical to conceive and design the face shapes expected of that character. Character bibles, the document that describe the overall design of the character, should include sketches of what the character is supposed to look like in different emotional states and may even go so far as to design the shapes related to speaking. Once approved, these sketches become the basis for the library of actions and controls that must be created for the face rig. With an eye on the future, our discussion of these shapes will be done regardless of the techniques used to create them. Suffice it to say, these could be blend shape models, collections of controls for manipulating a joint system, or the animated tensions on a spring mesh. No matter how they are made, the character setup artist will have to implement shapes associated with both emotions and speaking (Figure 16.3). The core functionality of a good facial setup is the ability to lip-sync to dialog effectively and in tandem with existing expressions.

16.5 EMOTIONS THROUGH FACE SHAPES

Psychologists often say that emotions are most clear in human babies. Taking some basic emotions as a starting point, the shape descriptions for happiness, sadness, anger, fear, and disgust

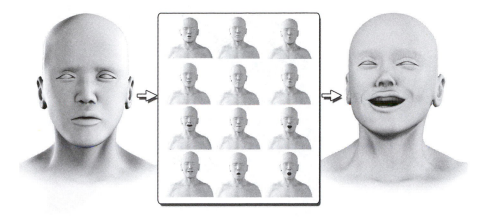

FIGURE 16.3 A neutral face model with blend shape inputs results in an output face with a wide range of emotion. (Original model by Lee Wolland.)

can be described. As with all face shapes, and blend shapes, in general, the idea is to be able to build up complex shapes from smaller, more discreet ones. One must also keep in mind that an animator will rarely use the full shape and in most cases will only use a portion of it. Face shapes will also need to be asymmetrical, meaning that the left and right sides can be controlled independently but be designed to have a smoothly interpolated, seamless middle region. All of these generalizations will of course vary based on the description and design of the character, but there are some core ideas that will transcend design. The Figures 16.4 through 16.9 below were generated using Ken Perlin's "Responsive Face" applet (mrl.nyu.edu/~perlin/facedemo/).

Happiness Happy expressions are universally recognized and are interpreted as conveying feelings related to enjoyment, pleasure, a positive outlook, and friendliness. It is said that one can train themselves to depict happy expressions, so these are often used to mask true emotions. Real or faked, the hallmark facial attributes of happiness include the following features:

- Corners of the mouth up
- Mouth slightly opened, teeth possibly showing
- Eyes partially closed
- Eyebrows up

Sadness Sad expressions convey messages related to loss, bereavement, discomfort, pain, helplessness, and the like. Many psychologists contend that sad emotion faces are lower intensity forms of crying faces which can be observed early in newborns, as both are related to distress.

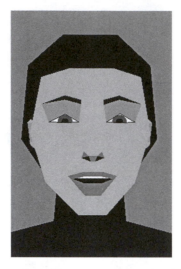

FIGURE 16.4 A basic happy expression. (Image created using Dr. Ken Perlin's "Responsive Face" applet.)

- Corners of the mouth down
- Eyebrows down

Anger Anger expressions convey messages about hostility, opposition, and potential attack

- Eyes very nearly closed
- Eyebrows pointed down and inward
- Mouth corners in, teeth possibly showing
- Nostrils raised

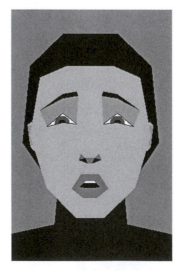

FIGURE 16.5 A basic sad expression. (Image created using Dr. Ken Perlin's "Responsive Face" applet.)

FIGURE 16.6 A basic angry expression. (Image created using Dr. Ken Perlin's "Responsive Face" applet.)

Disgust Disgust expressions are often part of the body's response to objects that are revolting and nauseating. Obnoxious smells are effective in eliciting disgust reactions.

- Mouth asymmetrical and sneering (one corner up, the other slightly down)
- Eyebrows pointed down and inward
- Nostrils up

Fear Fearful expressions can be described as a feeling of agitation and anxiety caused by the presence or imminence of danger, a feeling of disquiet or apprehension such as a fear of looking foolish or extreme reverence or awe.

FIGURE 16.7 A basic disgust expression. (Image created using Dr. Ken Perlin's "Responsive Face" applet.)

FIGURE 16.8 A basic fear expression. (Image created using Dr. Ken Perlin's "Responsive Face" applet.)

- Eyes wide

- Pupils dilated

- The upper lip raised

- Brows drawn together

- Lips stretched horizontally

Surprise Surprise expressions are fleeting and difficult to detect or record without high-speed recording. They almost always occur in response to events that are unanticipated

FIGURE 16.9 A basic surprise expression. (Image created using Dr. Ken Perlin's "Responsive Face" applet.)

FIGURE 16.10 Sarah and Joel from *The Last of Us*. (The Last of Us © 2013/™ SCEA. Created and developed by Naughty Dog.)

and they convey messages about something being unexpected, sudden, novel, or amazing. A surprise seems to act like a reset switch that shifts our attention. Surprise can be neutral, pleasant, or unpleasant.

- Eyebrows raised, becoming curved and high.

- Stretched skin below the eyebrows.

- Horizontal wrinkles across the forehead.

- Open eyelids, the upper lid is raised, and the lower lid is drawn down, often exposing the white sclera above and below the iris.

- Dropped jaw, lips and teeth are parted, with no tension around the mouth.

There are many more subtle and complex emotions that we experience in life including contempt, shame, and startle. The basic ones described above should form a baseline that your character can achieve. Emotion, as portrayed by the human face, is a subtle and nuanced collection of elements that are impossible to boil down but when care and attention are invested in the performance, at this level, you can get your audience invested deeply in your character because we start to feel for them (Figure 16.10). These emotion shapes, as well as the visemes for speaking described below, should start to produce a character that is capable of a basic facial performance.

16.6 VISEMES AND LIP-SYNCING

In human language, a phoneme is the smallest unit of speech that distinguishes meaning. Phonemes are not the physical segments themselves, but abstractions of them in the acoustic domain. An example of a phoneme would be the "t" found in words like tip, stand, writer, and cat (Figure 16.11). In animation, sounds are associated with the arrangement of the mouth,

- M, B, P

- EEE (long "E" sound as in "sheep")

- Err (as in "earth," "fur," and "long-er"—also covers phonemes like "H" in "hello")

- Eye, Ay (As in "fly" and "stay")

- i (short "I" as in "it" and "fit")

- Oh (as in "slow")

- OOO, W (as in "moo" and "went")

- Y, Ch, J ("you," "chew," and "jalopy")

- F, V

FIGURE 16.11 The basic sounds that need visemes to do lip-sync.

tongue, and teeth to produce visemes. A viseme is a basic unit of speech in the visual domain that corresponds to the phoneme, the basic unit of speech in the acoustic domain. It describes the particular facial and oral movements that occur alongside the voicing of phonemes (Table 16.1). Phonemes and visemes do not share a one-to-one correspondence; several phonemes will often share the same viseme. In other words, several phonemes look the same on the face when produced. For digital characters, it is essential to be able to create all the visemes (Figure 16.12).

16.7 EYES

The eyes are a portal to the mind. They reveal so much about what we are feeling when our spoken language may reveal otherwise. For digital characters, the eyes have the same benefit and responsibility, whereas at the same time unfortunately pose one of the greatest challenges. We often encounter digital characters with "dead eyes." As we discussed previously in Section 2.1, when this occurs for realistic characters, the illusion is broken entirely. When it comes to stylized characters, it is often just the animation that is responsible for characters' eyes looking alive. For realistic characters, we need to explore the small nuances that make eyes believable from the point of view of both setup and motion. From the perspective of setup, the construction of the eye surface should represent the iris, pupil, and eyeball (Figure 16.13). The iris needs to be able to adjust and impact the radius of the pupil to dilate the eye. Keep in mind that the iris and pupil make up a lens that is slightly more convex than the general sphericity of the eye.

The shading and texture of the iris must communicate the color, micro-structure such as veins and capillaries, and the wetness of the eye (Figure 16.14). Often artists will surround the eye, iris, and pupil surfaces with a larger semitransparent surface that gives the impression of wetness and acts as a surface to render specular highlights and reflections. The area around the eye is also highly detailed and provides a lot of visual information to the viewer that is often overlooked. These details come from the micromotions that occur around the lids when the

TABLE 16.1   Phoneme to Viseme Mapping

P		K	
B	/p/	G	
M		N	
EM		L	
F	/f/	NX	/k/
V		HH	
T		Y	
D		EL	
S		EN	
Z	/t/	IY	/iy/
TH		IH	
DH		AA	/aa/
DX		AH	
W		AX	/ah/
WH	/w/	AY	
R		ER	/er/
CH		AO	
JH	/ch/	OY	
SH		IX	
ZH		OW	
EH		UH	/uh/
EY	/ey/	UW	
AE		SIL	/sp/
AW		SP	

eye moves. Looking at someone closely or at yourself in the character setup artist's ever-present computer-side mirror will reveal that as the eye looks left the skin around the eye shifts slightly to the left. The same is true for the right and, of course, the lids react to the motion of the eyes looking up and down. These motions are critical to realistic characters, as they provide a physical relationship between the eyes and the face which for a long time were treated as separate unconnected entities. The motion of the lids and area around the eye should be mostly automated so that the animator's control of the eye logically triggers the motion of the skin around the eye.

The motion of the eyes is complex. Rotational motion based on the direction of gaze causes the eyes to look at the object of interest. This is usually controlled via a constraint that causes the eyes to aim at an external object. This object, usually an animation controller, is normally parented to the head, but can also be constrained to objects in the world. This is important so that character's eyes can be fixed as needed on animated objects. The setup usually involves each eye being controlled individually, each with their own goal, and those two goals are parented to a single controller. Independent eye movement is important for cheating the look of a character in a shot. A believable gaze is difficult to recreate for digital characters and must often be modified to look correct in the render and not necessarily what looks correct in the shot. This

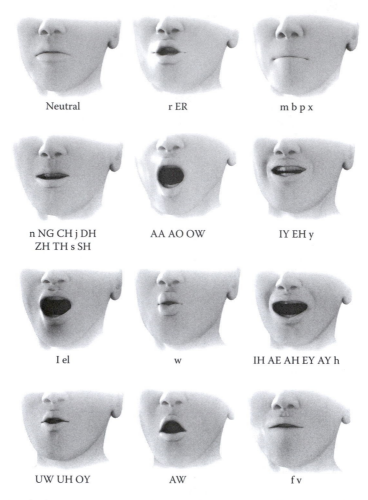

FIGURE 16.12 Mouth shapes representing the basic face visemes. (Original model by Lee Wolland.)

is sometimes due to the reflectivity of the eye surface and how the iris and pupil look at the time of rendering. Other times, it is just the camera angle and how the pupils read in the shot.

Eye blinks happen normally at regular intervals and are usually animated over a couple of frames. They also occur, as needed, as a reaction to a surprising moment and are used in animation often as a means of transitioning a character from one emotional state to another. In general, the weight of the eyelids is a prime vehicle for expressing a character's emotional state and are, of course, expressed in a heavy manner for a tired character. Blinks also occur during the start of a head turn motion. Lid motion is not linear, so setting up a proper eyelid requires that the geometry of the lid surface rotate around the eye geometry. Often a spherical deformer of the same dimensions of the eye is constrained to the eye geometry and programmed to deflect lid geometry points so that the lid surface never penetrates it.

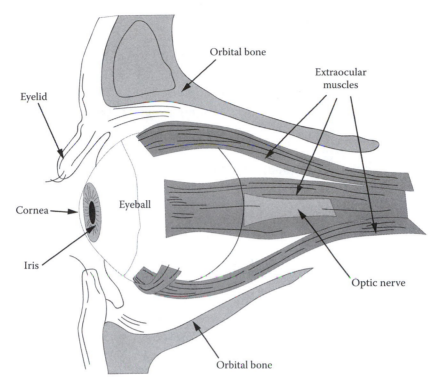

FIGURE 16.13   Eye anatomy.

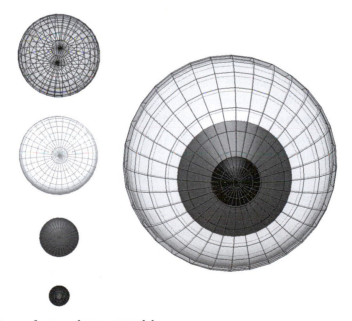

FIGURE 16.14   Eye surfaces and an eye model.

When humans are talking or thinking, our eyes look around the environment in quick bursts of motion. This motion is typically referred to as "eye darts," or saccades. Saccadic motion is involuntary eye movement that occurs when your brain is trying to draw in more information. The information can be visually evident or not. Many people will produce eye darts when visualizing something imaginary from memory. "Look-at" constraints are a relationship between the character's eyes and the object that they are looking at. This is usually in the form of a controller sitting out in space in front of the eyes. It is usually composed of three objects: a master controller, and a controller for each individual eye which is a child of the master eye controller. The individual eye controls give the animator the ability to cheat the gaze direction to the camera. Sometimes, to keep both eyes on camera and look correct, they must be oriented in an unnatural direction (if viewed from another camera angle). Eye look-at controls are often implemented in a character's local space relative to the head controller so that the eyes move with the head as expected and do not need to be counter-animated with the motion of the head. There should also always be the option to globally constrain the position of the eye look-at controller to something else in the scene.

The motion of the eyes is quick and loaded with meaning. The subtle motion of the pupils as they dilate can tell a whole story in an instant. Luckily, eyes and eye controls are typically very portable systems and can be moved from character to character. This means that lengthy research and development for one character will have benefits for all the characters in a production.

16.8 INTERFACES FOR FACIAL ANIMATION

Because the face is often a small area to work in, mapping out the regions and the systems implemented is critical. In many cases, one of the most effective techniques is a mix of blend shapes and joint-based transformations. Blend shapes provide direct access to the desired poses via a sculptural workflow, whereas a point-based offset allows for those shapes to be additionally modified. This ability to hit an art-directed expression through blend shapes and then to be able to offset the shape with a point-based method allows the animator to generate asymmetry quickly and to create interesting in-between shapes that the linear interpolation of geometry morphing will not account for. With this in mind, the notion of high- and low-level controls comes into play. High-level controls allow you to manipulate multiple attributes for a system at one time to reach a descriptive goal. This might include a control that ranges from "happy" to "sad" which triggers all the needed underlying controls to reach the predefined mark. These high-level controls are often the starting point for an animator to block out expressions. As high-level controls are merely manipulating or nondestructively modifying attributes, an animator can drill down to lower-level controls to tune individual attributes as desired.

In the same manner that the motion system for the body has an interface for animation, facial controls need a combination of ease-of-use and direct control of the high- and low-level controls. Typically, a separate camera is fixed to the face or parented to the head joint so that animators always have easy access to a front view of the characters face no matter what configuration or position the body is in. User access to the controls is the next step. Much of this is preference or historical depending on who you talk to, but there are many schools of thought when it comes to facial controls. Some artists prefer controllers which reside directly on the face surface so that selecting them and manipulating them will affect the face. Imagine the corner of the mouth having a controller associated with it; its motion in an upward direction triggers blend shapes for the position of the mouth corner to move up accordingly. Better yet, the motion of that controller moves a joint that the face surface is weighted to. No matter how the face is deformed, face controllers need to be accessible and move with the deformations of the face so that they remain unobstructed by surface geometry and always reside in a logical place (Figure 16.15).

Another form of interface is the control panel which is a nonrenderable set of handles or curves representing the elements of the face being controlled and that contain all available options for the user. This control set is often parented to the head, but exists just beside it so that it can be easily seen in connection with the face geometry. The simplest form of interface is merely the attribute spreadsheet that lists all the controls associated with the face rig. While this

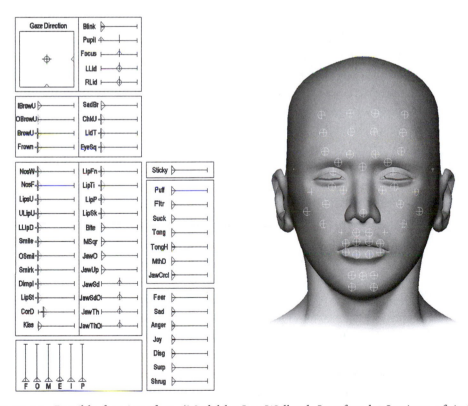

FIGURE 16.15 Possible face interface. (Model by Lee Wolland. Interface by Institute of Animation, Filmakademie Baden-Wuerttemberg.)

is not the most intuitive control strategy, an experienced user can navigate an interface such as this quickly and efficiently. As the spreadsheet is the raw visualization of control attributes, it is usually accessible in tandem with other control systems.

16.9 DYNAMICS AND SIMULATION

The face goes through its contortions at a rapid rate and the anatomy of the face contains many regions that remain flexible. These two conditions result in a structure that jiggles, even slightly, as it goes through its motion. This secondary motion adds a subtle cue that the structure is alive and affected by forces in the world it inhabits. With this in mind, like deformations on the body, it is worthwhile to consider a dynamic simulation pass once animation is complete. Because the resulting face is geometry, all of the same jiggle and postanimation spring dynamics developed for the body are possible and similar systems can be implemented. What is important to consider for the face is the ability to tone down simulated motion that interferes with the visemes for lip-sync or the general read of the emotions of the face. This involves mostly damping vibrations during moving holds where the characters motion is minimal. On the contrary, for a cartoon-styled character, the stretching and pulling of the face while in motion will need to be exaggerated for full effect.

16.10 REAL-TIME ENGINE CONCERNS

Facial animation shares the same limitations within a game engine as the body motion. Historically, facial animation has been the area most affected by the lack of support for deformers and, because of the fine detail required for effective facial motion, has been the area least developed for digital characters in games. Similarly, and possibly a consequence of this, games spend less time looking at faces with the player looking at the backs of their player's head as they run around. As we discussed with regard to deformations in real-time engines, there are a number of ways to work around this. It is entirely possible to have each vertex of the face mesh be attached to a joint. These joints could contain the motion required for each of the face shapes as triggered curves, thus baking the motion of the deformers to the motion of the joints. This essentially gives the game developers access to techniques such as blend shapes. When used in tandem with normal maps for wrinkles and other details, the quality of facial shapes can be very high as seen in the example from *Ryse: Son of Rome* (Figure 16.16).

16.11 CONCLUSION

For a character's face to fill a movie screen and convincingly convey emotion, it requires a sensitivity and understanding of all the factors going into that moment. For stylized characters, we have a chance to see into the mind of a designed character that is intended to make us laugh or cry. For realistic characters, we have the opportunity to put something or someone recognizable into an unbelievable situation and feel through the expressed emotions of a digital double. As artists strive for realism, human faces are one of the hardest aspects of digital character technology to be convincing to audiences. It is inevitable that digital characters will eventually be

FIGURE 16.16 Characters from *Ryse: Son of Rome*. (Courtesy of Crytek GmbH © 2014. All rights reserved.)

visually indistinguishable from reality, but getting them to act right (and in real time) will be the hurdles beyond that.

The combination of motion systems, deformation systems, and the interplay of those components into facial setup all amount to a rigged character that is ready for animation. As we will see in the following chapter, there are many ways to create and attach motion to a rig depending on the type of project, production resources, and creator preference. What does not differ is that the time and effort that goes into the development of a digital character is nothing without the motion and acting that creates the performance.

16.12 EXERCISE

In this exercise, we go through the conceptual and technical process of creating a character facial setup. Split into groups of two or more. One of you is the animator, and the other team members are the character setup artists. Follow the steps below.

1. Starting with the character you developed in the last section, sketch out a plan for the face shapes that the character needs to produce and your method for creating them.

2. List out the steps that need to be carried out to create the controls and deformations for the character's face.

3. The animator should find a piece of audio, break it down, and list out the shapes required for the performance.

4. Implement the deformations and test the results against your initial sketches from the first step.

5. The animator should begin lip-syncing the character's face to try to hit the performance. They should also provide feedback on the interface for animating and the shapes they

are able to achieve, or not. Can lip-sync and expression poses be layered together in a complementary way?

6. Maintain this review/fix feedback loop until satisfied.

FURTHER READING

The controversial aspects of classifying emotion run the spectrum from Ekman's categorical model to Russell and Mehrabian's dimensional model:

Ekman, P. 1992. An argument for basic emotions, in *Basic Emotions*, N. L. a. O. Stein, K. (Ed.), Lawrence Erlbaum, Hove, UK, pp. 169–200.

Mehrabian, A. and Russell, J. A. 1974. *An Approach to Environmental Psychology*. MIT Press, Cambridge, MA.

Russell, J. A. 1997. Reading emotions from and into faces: Resurrecting a dimensional-contextual perspective, in *The Psychology of Facial Expression*, Russell, J. and Fernandez-Dols, J. (Eds.), Cambridge University Press, Cambridge, United Kingdom, pp. 295–320.

A great practical overview into the theory and practice of face setup is Jason Osipa's *Stop Staring*:

Osipa, J. 2010. *Stop Staring: Facial Modeling and Animation Done Right*, 3rd Edition. SYBEX Inc., Alameda, CA, USA.

CHAPTER 17

Interview: Nico Scapel, Creative Director, Faceshift

17.1 BIO

Nico is a creative director at Faceshift, heading their new London office. Faceshift software enables detailed and real-time facial tracking using off-the-shelf and integrated 3D cameras. During his career, Nico has pioneered techniques for procedural rigging, anatomy simulation, and performance capture on high-end CG creatures and digital actors. Nico's previous role was Head of Rigging at Framestore, where he lead the rigging team on over 20 VFX films including the Oscar-winning film *Gravity*. Prior to Framestore, Nico was a lead rigger at DreamWorks Animation in Los Angeles and San Francisco. Born in Marseille, Nico holds master's degrees from École Centrale, École Normale, and Stanford University with a specialization in artificial

Nico Scapel

intelligence, graphics, and computer vision. Nico is also a keen drummer and painter, and lives in vibrant Camden with his wife and two children.

17.2 Q&A

Q: *The components of character technology are diverse and span the artistic and technical spectrum. How did you get your start in the industry? Based on where you see the field heading what experience/training do you recommend people have?*

A: Character technology is a new field, but in many ways an echo of the Renaissance period: both creative and deeply rooted in arts and science. On the artistic end of the spectrum, key skills are observation, abstraction, craft, and communication, and on the science end is understanding, analysis, engineering, and implementation. The limits of our craft and knowledge are always shifting, as we are dealing with the recreation of incredibly complex life forms such as animals and humanoid beings. As much as Renaissance artists had to explore anatomy as well as drawing techniques, today any breakthrough comes from linking artistry to mathematics, physics, biology, etc.

Throughout my education, I strived to pursue both, even though that can be a challenge within the education system. I did feel though, as I think is still the case today, that mathematics and analytical skills are fundamental and extremely hard to learn without structure so it made sense to focus on that first. After graduating from École Centrale Paris and École Normale Superieure with two Masters Degrees, one in Engineering and Applied Mathematics, and one in Artificial Intelligence and Pattern Recognition (quite a mouthful), I applied to Stanford University for a Computer Science Degree. In the US many universities offer programs which include arts and sciences in one place; the flexible curriculum allows students to freely attend any course and customize their learning path. At Stanford, besides learning Computer Graphics, I also took sculpture, life-drawing, and animation classes with some fantastic teachers. I had been drawing and painting for many years but I essentially learned fundamentals and the need for daily practice. The best advice I received there was from my drawing instructor Pat Hannaway: "You will make a thousand bad drawings, so make them fast." I also enjoyed the emphasis on hands-on projects, presentations and team work, something some european universities seem to miss, even though they have their unique strengths.

The university was just a mile from the PDI/Dreamworks studio in Palo Alto. I met a few people from that studio at Siggraph, and really loved the culture of the company, so I spent a few months preparing my reel and portfolio to apply for a Character TD role. It was rare at the time to join right after university, but I think my unusual profile helped and they offered me a position. I still remember that call, it is so hard to enter the field and getting that first job.

It is not easy for me to give advice these days, with such a large selection of specialized schools and media programs. In the end, choose whichever way gives you that balance of technical and artistic skills—making sure you learn them in depth, not superficially. Make sure you take risks and make your own choices, character technology is first and foremost about creativity. I find Film Akademie to be a great example of a very successful integration of technical and artistic curriculum, with great resources and emphasis on ambitious and collaborative long-term projects.

Q: *Creating compelling digital characters is part art and part science. What is the greatest challenge you encounter on a daily basis? What aspect of character technology keeps you up thinking at night?*

A: A large part of our daily communications are non-verbal. I strongly believe that the greatest challenge at the moment is to create digital characters that are fully expressive, meaning they can communicate our messages and emotional intent, just as we do in daily human interactions. Photorealism is also a formidable challenge, but also requires mastering expressivity to avoid the Uncanny Valley. What does that mean in practice?

Essentially, a digital character is a vessel for communication, which is conveyed via audio (verbal) and visual (facial, gestural) cues. The appeal of digital characters comes from the fact that they use universal cues from the human and animal world, which means that our brain can decode their meaning and emotional intent. We could make an analogy to music, a form of audio communication. The universal patterns in music can be abstracted using musical notation systems. Many instruments can play the same score, each one will sound different but still conveying the intent of a score. However a single note doesn't suffice to communicate, and to explain musical styles we refer to higher level concepts such as scales and chords.

Now looking at the human face, the equivalent to notes being played would be muscles being activated. We all have the same 43 facial muscles, which would be like notes on a piano. A facial expression is essentially a chord being played, for example a fake smile is read from the 'zygomatic major' muscle only being activated, whereas a 'true smile' also includes 'orbicularis oculi'. Designing a digital face which can be expressive is akin to designing an instrument, which can possess a unique appearance (or timbre for an instrument), but must be able to express a performance via muscle activations. However we do not observe muscle activations directly, and rather our brain process the visual information in a different way to recognize patterns of muscle activations. Visual cues probably include the movement of the skin, the appearance of disappearance of wrinkles, the relative placement of features (brows/eyes/mouth) and even blood flow.

With the technology we are now developing at Faceshift, we are getting close to have a universal notation system for facial communication, and we have for the first time the ability to track this data accurately in real-time and play it back on a digital avatar. With such tools the design process is dramatically altered, you can essentially iterate on a digital character by "wearing it," looking at yourself in a virtual mirror or getting direct feedback by interacting with a sample audience using this "work in progress" character.

Q: *What are the ingredients for a successful digital character?*

A: There has to be strong integrity in the design of a character, and a sense of a physical or metaphorical world it could belong to. It also has to be tailored to the performance it has to give. A digital T-Rex will be convincing by having very believable physicality: a sense of weight, balance, muscles, sliding, and folding skin. Creatures which are more physical than expressive can have very extreme and diverse designs, the sky is the limit really. If they do look like a known species, then they will have to be more accurate or stylized in a very careful manner as viewers will have expectations on their appearance and behavior.

As soon as characters need to talk or convey human-related emotions, the design has to follow more and more human cues to remain expressive—the ultimate challenge being to create fully believable digital doubles. I find it fascinating to study the infinite variety of human and animal faces, and think about the most important cues for communication. To produce a rich and easily identifiable range of facial expressions, Paul Ekman's FACS (Facial Action Coding System) has become the basis or inspiration of most facial control systems. Putting aside technical considerations, my key advice would be to focus on the end goal: can you recognize the six universal emotions on your digital character? Can you create a convincing mapping from your separate facial actions to your character facial controls?

Q: *While the industry is competitive, it is ultimately respectful of great work. Outside of the work you have been personally involved in the production of, what animated characters have you been impressed or inspired by? What is the historical high-bar?*

A: In the nineties *Jurassic Park* was a key milestone, enabling us to experience the sight of creatures long disappeared through detailed CGI, based on a careful study of their probable appearance and motion. Sixteen years later, *Avatar* opened a new chapter in digital characters: almost-human avatars able to convey the full range of human expressiveness, mimicking through capture technology and artistic animation the performance of actors on a stage. That film also explores themes which humanity will soon be facing.

Q: *Where do you see digital characters in 10 years? Where are animated characters for film and games heading?*

A: We are rapidly entering the age of virtual reality and avatars. Rather than being a revolution, this is the natural evolution of our communication tools, where we can enjoy full immersion and communication without physical presence.

It has been shown through decades of research that avatars can actually be more effective communication tools than we are. They have already become an essential tool in research, enabling us to better understand human interactions and conditions such as autism which might be related to difficulty in "decoding" human expressions. They will liberate us from many physical constraints in remote working, shopping, learning, and playing environments. In their book *Infinite Reality*, Jim Blascovich and Jeremy Bailenson gave the example of a VR classroom where the teacher can look every student in the eye through an avatar to get their full attention. For better or worse, they explain how avatars might even end up changing the way we perceive ourselves.

Avatar's fiction is supported by science: dozens of psychological experiments have shown that people change after spending even small amounts of time wearing an avatar. A taller avatar increases people's confidence, and this boost persists later in the physical world. Similarly, a more attractive avatar makes people act warm and social, an older avatar raises people's concern about saving money, and a physically fit avatar makes people exercise more.

In conclusion, I expect digital characters to become ubiquitous, as intellectual and artistic creations that people view, wear, and interact with daily. We are witnessing an exponential trend in hardware and software innovation. I expect character technology to be at the heart of this, and fundamentally alter the way we communicate.

Game and film characters will surely retain a lead role, in terms of visual appeal and technical complexity, but many of them will also be accessible through a variety of platforms as live, interactive, or wearable (e.g., avatar) assets.

CHAPTER 18

Rig Synthesis

18.1 INTRODUCTION

Once the motion system, deformation system, and face have been designed and architected, there is the necessary step of combining all these interrelated aspects into a unified digital character rig. These systems should already be working well together, but this last stage is really about polishing and double-checking all the details. The synthesis of the rig also allows for the testing of all aspects of the character by the character setup artist and animators before it is released into production. This process of quality assurance (QA) allows minor and major bugs to be identified and fixed before any animation is tied to the state of the rig.

18.2 THE RIG IN A SCENE

If we forget all of the functionality we have discussed thus far, the most basic function of the rig is to successfully load a character into a scene. The character must exist properly in the scene as dictated by the production guidelines or the established character pipeline. Whether by referencing or importing, the character must be able to be loaded into a scene and have keys set upon its controls and stored. At the rig import stage, it is critical to think about optimization in terms of rig interaction speed, as we have mentioned previously, and general file size. Deleting stray nodes in the rig that have no functionality or purpose will decrease file size and speed up load time. For one character, this may not seem like a big deal, but one can imagine the benefits for a scene with many characters. Each node in the rig should be accounted for and uniquely named.

A character should exist in a scene inventory as a single node, and all of the rig and model components should be children of this node. This "master," "all," or "god" node lives at the origin $(x = 0, y = 0, z = 0)$ and is not only the hierarchical parent for the character, but also acts as the inventory node which can be used to query which characters are in a scene. Attributes about the character and the character's name are often stored on this node. Within any animation system, the character's name must be unique. Therefore, it is a good idea to have the top-level node of the character be something along the lines of `name_char` so that the character is identified and noted as a character. Just the character's name will suffice. Often times, characters will have special attributes on their top-level node that defines them as type "character." To create an inventory of characters that populate a scene, all top-level nodes with this character attribute can also be queried. Not only should the character's name be unique, but also must all of the nodes that make it up, so as to avoid any potential conflict with other characters or objects in the scene. Making sure that all the nodes have meaningful names will make maintenance that much easier down the line. As such, prepending the character's name to all of the nodes that make it up is an easy way to achieve uniqueness. Scripts are often written which analyze a rig to look for node names that repeat and potentially clash with nodes in other characters or itself. Utilities such as this are good to run at fixed intervals in character rig development and ideally at each point that the rig is published.

Since this master node contains all the nodes of the character, and some of the nodes may have multiple influences on them, moving it may have unwanted effects on the rig and therefore it is typically not moved. If the model is moved by the same node that the rig is moved by, then there is a double transform in cases where skinning is used as a method to attach a model to a rig. The skin is moved once by the transformation of its parent space node and again by moving the joints that it is bound to. Other deformation models, including layered surface deformations, can have the same issue. Usually there is a world-space node that is coincident to this node that is used to position the character in world-space. This is often called "body," "world," or "root" and is the most top-level animation control (Figure 18.1). As such, models that are deformed by the rig are stored under the "all" node, but in a sibling group its transformations are unaffected. Once a character rig is under a world-space node, it is critical that the rig be tested away from the origin and rotated about all three axes. Doing this will quickly reveal any hierarchy issues and often even deformation issues that were not obvious when the character was at the origin. With regard to the motion system, if a node is not under the world-space node, it will obviously be left behind, but sometimes less obviously, constraints that are not calculating the position of nodes properly will be revealed when the space that they exist in has

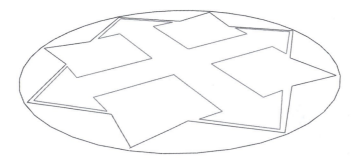

FIGURE 18.1 Top-level nodes are often visualized as a series of curves to give the user a sense of character placement and orientation.

changed. Similarly, for deformations, points not weighted to a joint or other objects in the rig will remain about the origin as the character is moved away from it. It is a common practice for a rigger to include off-origin testing in the evaluation of the rig.

Another factor that a world-space node figures into is the ability for the rig and character to scale uniformly in the scene. In many situations, a character will need to change size to play to the camera for shot composition and as a result, the rig should be able to scale. There are many reasons why a rig may not be able to scale properly: from the misplacement of nodes in the hierarchy and either inheriting the scale twice or not at all, to the composition of the rig may have elements which cannot scale. Some dynamic systems do not have the ability to scale uniformly or accurately because of the functions associated with them. In other cases, geometry which is used to attach joints might need to be specially placed in the hierarchy to scale appropriately. All efforts should be made to allow a rig to scale and this functionality should be tested with the introduction of each system. This is one of those scenarios which can be very hard to fix without major changes to the rig architecture after the rig is finished. In a worst-case scenario, the geometry cache for the rig is output and the resultant models are scaled as needed while the rig itself is not scaled. This is far from an ideal solution, but if the character does not need to make a physical contact with other elements in the scene it can be used to fix the lack of scale.

The control which moves the rig in world-space is also the one that is used to attach the character to other objects in the scene. This is generically called "character parenting." For example, a moving prop, vehicle, or even another character can become a temporary parent of this node so that the character inherits its motion. Vehicles are an obvious example where the world-space transformation of the character is carried out by another entity as the vehicle moves with the character in it. This basic principle of computer graphics can often times lead to issues for complicated character rigs, so it is necessary to test the functionality of a rig when parented to another object in the scene.

All aspects of the rig feed into these top-level nodes. As such, they can also contain controls for rig visibility, character resolution display, or read/write status. Once the protocol for this node is established, all characters can share its functionality with each having their own set. As we will see in the following section, the functionality of all the systems that make up the rig should be tested as they become ready for animation.

18.3 MOTION SYSTEM INVENTORY

As we discussed previously, a motion system is a collection of interconnected elements that define the kinematics of the character rig. Each element is a system in its own right which must connect and interact with its adjoining systems. A humanoid motion system requires systems to control the arms, hands, legs, feet, spine (including the hips), neck, and head. A quadruped would include four-leg systems structured to represent the type of leg required. Other anatomical elements such as wings and specialized feet or hands may be augmented on either standard humanoid bipeds or as building blocks for other animals. A tail and a neck system might also need to be implemented. Returning to the subject of comparative anatomy, all mammals have legs with five major segments articulating at five major joints. Legs typically have a mirror image from front to back, with corresponding joints bending opposite to each other. Certain animals, like horses, have an extended foot that gives them a lower leg segment similar in length to the other segments that, when looked at comparatively, gives them the appearance of walking on their tiptoes with their heels held high. These ideas are revisited to drive home the idea that no matter the character, the same rules apply and much of what we understand about our own kinematics can be ported to nonhuman or partial-human characters. Whether they are biped, quadruped, or something different altogether, the functionality of the rig should be consistent with more traditional characters, isolating idiosyncrasy to where it is needed and relying on the familiar where possible.

These systems can be simple FK hierarchies with controls all the way up to complex multi-chain hierarchies controlled by custom constraints and multiple states of interaction. No matter how they are constructed, they need to be attached to other systems and function normally. As the pieces of the rig are combined into an integrated whole, switches that modify the space that elements exist in can be implemented. For example, an animator might want the shoulder of a character to be in the space of the hips for certain parts of the shot, and the torso (as it would be normally) in other parts of the shot. This influences the space that the object operates in. Hand controls that are controlling IK are also good examples of this. Often these will be most beneficial in the space of the shoulders and at other times world-space.

Control objects and the attributes that they contain (Table 18.1), related to position-, rotation-, and rig-specific attributes, need to be keyed individually and often times together. An animator may want to key all the attributes of a control or even an entire system. This allows them to key the system they are positioning without needing to key all the specific attributes they may have to move unconsciously to achieve the pose. When multiple characters must be animated to interact with each other, it is often useful to be able to key the controls for all characters at the same time. Thus, as the character contact is animated, such as in a fight scene, characters can be posed simultaneously. Attributes are often collected into sets or bundles that

TABLE 18.1 Sample Attributes on an Animation Control

r_hand_control	
Attribute	**Value**
TranslateX	5.6
TranslateY	3.2
TranslateZ	0.4
RotateX	6.5
RotateY	20
RotateZ	2.3
FK_IK	1 (IK on)

can be keyed together. These collections of keyable controls are created by the character setup artist and travel with the character rig into scenes. In an ideal scenario, giving the animator the ability to create their own collection of controls also provides a lot of flexibility.

When the motion system is considered complete, it should be sent to an animator to test. The animator should produce a short animation sequence that puts the rig through its paces. This not only gives the animator the opportunity to provide feedback, but it also creates a piece of animation that can be used to test rig modifications that are made to see whether the animation changes in unwanted or unexpected ways. The animator should keep in mind the rig's consistency with other characters on the project. Is it intuitive and familiar? Are there any controls which do not work as expected? Do any of the controls not hold keys when the file is reopened? Another factor to test is the ability to export and import animation. This is something that should be attempted using generic animation curves of a walk or run to see whether generic cycle animation can be applied to the character. This is especially important for "variant" characters that will be used in a crowd system. Having a number of animated test shots is also necessary for testing and reviewing deformations.

18.4 DEFORMATION SYSTEM INVENTORY

Once the motion system is created and while deformations are being architected, it is a good idea to build a test shot that includes your character going through a series of "exercises" that demonstrate the character transforming through a series of extreme poses. These poses should push the deformations to their limits and beyond and be used to iteratively develop the deformation system (Figure 18.2). With a consistent set of poses, progress can be reviewed and compared at intervals until completion. This test shot, in conjunction with any animation produced by an animator to test the motion system, can provide a good baseline for deformation review. The key features to look for when addressing deformations are volume preservation and the character staying "on-model."

Volume loss is common in areas of great deformation like shoulders and hips that need to exhibit a large range of motion. As points are rotated about a surface, they can be pulled inward and give the appearance that the area is deflating, especially when skinning is implemented as the deformation technique. In reality, the bone and muscle underlying the surface would prevent such things from happening, so collision objects are often placed to stop these regions from collapsing and to preserve volume. With regard to staying "on-model," this is something that must be analyzed at every frame of the test animations when evaluating deformations. There can be no point, even in extreme motion, when the deformations do not represent the designed character. If the character does not appear as itself, then a solution must be found to bring the character back "on-model."

Debugging deformations means looking for not only the loss of volume, but also the smoothness of the deformations in motion. When collisions are used to preserve regions, there is the possibility of vertices popping from frame to frame as the collisions are calculated. This is visible in the animation of the character and may also impact other systems or elements informed by

FIGURE 18.2 Silly as they may look, putting the rig through a series of extreme-pose exercises is an ideal way to test deformations while in development. (Model by Lee Wolland.)

that surface. When collision-related popping occurs, the first thing to check is that the collision is actually giving you desirable results in general situations. This is always valuable to check as removing a collision calculation is a major optimization to the speed of a rig. If this is an isolated incident, then the calculating "pad" that surrounds the surface can be increased to provide a more gentle fall off for this specific shot. The pad is essentially an offset from the actual collision surface that can have an adjustable fall-off distance. If the pad value is animatable, then it can be eased on around the time of popping and then eased off as needed. These per-shot fixes are unavoidable when collisions are part of the deformation system.

As deformations are the end result of a series of systems and influences which start with the model and run through the motion system and whatever tools are used to create the deformations, it is essential to be able to look at a region or single vertex of the deforming mesh and be able to follow its influences back to a nondeformed state. Being able to quickly isolate the influence or collection of influences that are impacting the region in question allows the solution to be reached more quickly. Being able to turn on and off special controls which might affect the deformations via the motion system, such as stretch, is also helpful. As stretch is usually implemented as functions or connections on transform nodes or surfaces at the motion system level, these features can often be overlooked in the deformation debugging process.

Part of the development of the motion system is the creation of stand-in or proxy geometry, so it is important when implementing the deformations that this stand-in geometry reasonably matches the deformations. Any model changes that were undertaken in response to the deformations and change the shape of the model should be reflected in an update to the stand-in geometry that the animator sees.

As with body deformations and motion systems, the character's face system must also be reviewed and tested before it can go into production.

18.5 FACE SYSTEM INVENTORY

Depending on the way the character model was built, the synthesis step at the end may require some special work to attach the face system to the rest of the body. In the past, the head was treated as a separate model and the vertices at the border of the body and head needed to match up and seam perfectly. These vertices needed to be exactly coincident (existing at the same exact point in space), have the same normal direction, and be deformed by exactly the same influences. If any one of these factors was off, a seam would be evident in the deformation and surfacing of the character model. This is still a valid way to work, but the trend leads toward a fully integrated single mesh, or separate meshes that locally affect certain parts of a single-mesh model. With the final model being a single mesh, the risk of a seam between the head and the body is eliminated. No matter the solution, care must still be taken in the neck region which acts as an interface between the body deformation system and the face deformation system (Figure 18.3). Sometimes a layered surface at that region can act to smooth the effects between the systems. Other times, some careful weighting or a small deformation joint set that is driven by the respective systems can act as a blended result to make sure that the neck benefits from both influences.

Once the face, neck, and body have been integrated, it is important to test that the effects of deformers that might carry over from the body onto the face and vice versa to make sure

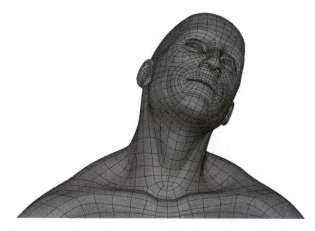

FIGURE 18.3   The neck is a complicated region at the boundary of the body deformation and face systems. (Model by Lee Wolland.)

everything is in order. Due to the discrete nature of these systems, this is rarely an issue. For example, a relaxation algorithm that is applied to the body to smooth out deformations could be through the integration of systems propagated to the face. Relaxation algorithms iteratively smooth out regions by averaging the motion of vertices across their surrounding vertices. Because this changes the resultant shape, something of this nature could lessen the expected effect of blend shapes as it ends up being the target shape plus the effect of the relaxation.

If blend shapes have been implemented as part of a face system, it is paramount to have a plan to manage them through the pipeline. Because blend shapes are offsets from default vertex positions, they can be stored as these offset values as opposed to the models that were used to create them. In many animation systems, once the blend shapes have been added to the rig, the models that they were derived from can be deleted. The blend shapes still work, the file is now smaller and more lightweight as it moves through the pipeline, and the shapes are now protected from accidental modification. The original shapes can be stored in a "workshop" version of the file that the modelers and riggers have access to, but not the published file that is shipped into production.

Testing the face rig is similar to testing body deformations. Test shots should be created that exercise the range of the face shapes going through all the visemes, key emotional states, and put the character through a short performance shot where they must lip-sync and emote at the same time. Eyes should be tested for tracking and expressiveness all the way through the surfacing and rendering stage as much of the communication of the eyes is affected by the materials applied to them. The interpolation of the face through extreme shapes will also test the interoperability of the controls, making sure that they work together as expected. Again, as with the body, making sure that low-resolution animation control meshes reasonably match the high-resolution output is a noteworthy step. But thanks to the advances in processing speed, it is increasingly common for animators to pose with the high-resolution mesh, making an animation control mesh (or stand-in) less important when compared with an intuitive control for the final mesh.

18.6 DOCUMENTATION

At larger facilities where many people will be using a rig and the work has the possibility of existing through multiple projects, documentation of the rig is critical. This can be as simple as a few notes about what makes this rig different from standard rigs at that facility, to a detailed manual that can be modified by the community using the asset. Often times, documentation is a spin-off of the initial specification that was developed for the creation of the rig. This document would have outlined the features and functionality that was desired for the motion system plus descriptions, ideally with images, of the key poses that the designers had envisioned for the character. As the specification evolves into documentation, it takes on the role of animator reference. Often incorporating short demonstration videos, images, and text descriptions to describe the functionality of the rig, the documentation should provide a clear and organized overview of the rig.

When implemented like a wiki or other community-driven document, animators and character setup artists alike can modify it as needed. This then becomes a live and evolving document that is more up-to-date than static pages that might fall behind in the heat of production. These documents inevitably go out of date but, if maintained, can be useful to new employees or team members and are often good augmentation for classes.

Whether it was built procedurally or through an existing animation system, a character rig is ultimately a piece of software. As such, like any piece of software, it will go through QA and through all the stages of development and at times rigs will be described as being in "alpha," "beta," or "release" stages with accompanying version numbers to keep track of revisions. As we described before, QA essentially is just the testing and revision cycle of the rig to make sure that it is working as expected and functions within the established or proposed animation pipeline and able to be exported if needed.

18.7 REAL-TIME ENGINE CONCERNS

Once the rig is synthesized into a complete package, it is time to test the elements needed to export it into the engine being used on the production. This usually involves developing a set of joints that the engine expects, which are constrained to the proper joints in the animation rig (Figure 18.4). The motion of these game export joints are then baked for the number of frames in the shot and exported to the appropriate format. Most game engines have detailed specs for

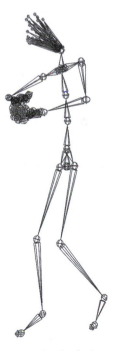

FIGURE 18.4 The rig exported to the game engine includes a stripped-down set of joints representing the body and face.

what is expected or, more increasingly, provide export tools to go from established animation systems directly to the proper format. Because there are limits to the number of weights that can be applied to the skinning of any vertex of a polygonal model, it is mandatory to review that the animation and deformations are best represented at the moment of export. In addition, from a pipeline point of view, issues to keep an eye out for include naming conflicts in the engine for multiple characters. This should be addressed in the setup and export stage.

18.8 CONCLUSION

The synthesis of the rig into a unified whole brings us to the end of our discussion of pure character technology. As a high-level overview of all the concepts related to character setup, we have touched on the anatomical underpinnings of the character motion system, the various techniques possible in building the character deformation system, and the requirements behind a character facial setup. The challenges of first learning this material is understanding the relationship between all the systems and the cause and effect of all of the component pieces. It is very easy to create your first rig with a few joint chains, some simple constraints to handle IK, bind the whole thing to the model, paint a few weights, and call it done. This is the way most people start and usually things go horribly wrong the first time. Those that want to understand how to make it better often get hooked on the subject of rigging, and those who find it overly frustrating often look back on their initial rigging experience with the desire to never do it again. The advice one can offer is to start over and try it again. Your second rig will be better than your first and they will keep getting better. As you work with animators to get feedback, or work with more experienced riggers, your rigs will develop more functionality, ease of use, and complexity. Also, demand more from your own rigs especially with regard to deformations. One can never spend enough time on deformations. As you gain more experience, you will also gain more confidence in fixing issues that come up. As said previously, a large percentage of the character setup artist's job is maintenance of the rig as it moves through production.

18.9 EXERCISE

In this exercise, we get a character ready for the production pipeline and go through the process of QA to make sure it is production ready. Split into groups of two or more. One of you is the lead character setup artist, the other team members are the character setup artists who must work as a team to move this rig into production. It is optimal if someone on the team can be designated as an animator. Follow the steps below.

1. Collect all the nodes in your scene under a single group that defines its position in world-space. Create groups for geometry, the rig, and possibility for other nodes that may or may not fall under the world transformation node of the rig. Move the rig off the origin and keep an eye out for objects that move away from the character. Those are double transforms and need to be fixed.

2. Have one of the character setup artists (or the animator) run the rig through a series of exercises to test out the controls and to evaluate the deformations.

3. If time allows, the animator should also try to produce a short animation of the character in action doing something which might be typical of it.

4. Schedule two review meetings where the animator evaluates the performance of the rig in conjunction with the team. The riggers should prioritize what needs to be fixed and what might not be clear about the rig interface and results. A list of fixes should be produced.

5. With each iteration, emphasis should go on fixes that preserve the animation and test scenes produced. Notes about deformations and user interface should be implemented.

6. Maintain this review/fix feedback loop until satisfied.

FURTHER READING

The references described in the previous chapters should still be a guide through this synthesis stage, but it might also be helpful to wrap your head around some of the concepts behind software project management:

Stellman, A. and Greene, J. 2005. *Applied Software Project Management*. O'Reilly Media, Inc., Cambridge, MA.

CHAPTER 19

Interview: Stephen Mann, CG Supervisor, Shade VFX

19.1 BIO

Stephen started his career working for a small Burlington, Vermont, studio as an editor and VFX creator while getting a Bachelors of Studio Art at the University of Vermont. He then attended USC Film School to get a degree in Digital Art and Animation. While in Los Angeles, he worked for several small studios and for Sony Imageworks on the production of *Stuart Little*. Upon returning to the east coast, Stephen worked for Kleiser–Walczak serving as a 3D artist on commercials, ride films, and on the feature films *X-Men* and *The One*, along with teaching at New York's School of Visual Arts. He then served as CG supervisor for Hornet Inc. for a year, before working as a character rigger for BlueSky Studios on *Robots*. Before joining Shade VFX he was the lead Character TD and Pipeline TD for the postproduction studio Charlex in New York City.

19.2 Q&A

Q: *The components of character technology are diverse and span the artistic and technical spectrum. How did you get your start in the industry? Based on where you see the field heading what experience/training do you recommend people have?*

A: I got my real start as an intern at Sony Pictures Imageworks while at USC film School. Sony was really pushing technical and traditional classes for their artists and I learned a ton. They focused more on traditional skills and good story telling and I really related to that.

The traditional skills are still the most important if not even more so. Computers and software are getting cheaper and faster every day and a lot of major technical hurdles can now be overcome much easier, or don't even exist anymore.

Stephen Mann
CG Supervisor, Shade VFX

Programs like Mudbox and ZBrush are making it much easier to use those traditional skills and be able to explore and experiment more. It's always been said that the technical skills can be easily learned over the traditional skills. I think that's becoming more and more true every day. Form, balance, framing, anatomy, good silhouette, timing, and appeal in modeling, and animation are still the most important skills to focus on. In drawing, the more you draw the better you can become. With the advent of these tools, artists can do more faster and experiment and learn more in the process.

Q: *Creating compelling digital characters is part art and part science. What is the greatest challenge you encounter on a daily basis? What aspect of character technology keeps you up thinking at night?*

A: Some of the biggest challenges right now are keeping things fast and easy to use while being more complex. Models and rigs are becoming more and more data intensive and complex. Keeping all that fast and manageable is the biggest bottleneck. That along getting it all done faster, cheaper, and better for the client. Rather than thinking about technical aspects though, I think more about how wrinkles work, how volumes maintain, and how to get movements driven in pleasing ways.

Q: *What are the ingredients for a successful digital character?*

A: Appeal, appeal, appeal! Form and appeal in the model, and deformation of the movement are key to character. Good anatomy, attention to good shapes and design and not letting all that collapse in the animation are paramount. Maintaining weight and volume help keep the character from falling flat. In traditional animation each frame needs to hold up, it's no different for digital characters.

Q: *While the industry is competitive, it is ultimately respectful of great work. Outside of the work you have been personally involved in the production of, what animated characters have you been impressed or inspired by? What is the historical high-bar?*

A: I tend to lean more toward stylized characters. Weta's work on *Planet of the Apes* is truly amazing and by far the most advanced to date, but I am still enamored with Davey Jones from the second *Pirates of the Caribbean*. It has excellent appeal in design, movement, and acting set in a live action environment.

Disney is killing it lately. For me, *Tangled* is some of the best digital character ever done. The movement and pushing of form is top notch. *Frozen* has a lot of similarity, but I think they put more love and set the bar higher with *Tangled*. I think *Big Hero 6* looks amazing, from what I've seen.

And of course games like *Assassin's Creed* and *Ryse* are really pushing boundaries as to what can be expected in games. It still has some mocap feel to it, but it cannot be denied, it is amazing work.

Q: *Where do you see digital characters in 10 years? Where are animated characters for film and games heading?*

A: Digital humans are super close to having a leading role in films, but I think they will stay relegated to VFX work. I'm curious to see the different takes on *The Jungle Book* and how the audience reacts to those films. I think a realistic human character can be done, but I still believe if you are going to animate something, do it for a reason. So I expect to see animated films with more Studio Ghibli, Disney, Warner Brothers stylization in animation over replicating human actors for leading roles.

With hardware and software becoming more accessible I think we'll see more small studios and low budget films making their way onto the big screen and having larger presences on the internet. These films will be a little looser and have more experimentation in them, which I think is a good thing. There is a movie coming out soon called *The Henchmen* that falls into that category as well as a film *Metegol* from Argentinian director Juan Jose Campanella. I want to see some long format animated films coming out from smaller groups of artists.

I also expect that we'll be seeing more digital characters go mainstream in infotainment and everyday correspondence. I wouldn't be surprised if we get a face to SIRI soon, or we use avatars to talk to each other that are animated from real time motion capture. We'll probably be ordering McDonalds from digital characters pretty soon as well.

CHAPTER 20

Rig Construction

20.1 INTRODUCTION

Once all the requirements of a rig are designed and the animator's expectations are understood, the rigger then needs to construct the character rigs. The process of building a character rig can be a tedious one. Particularly for motion systems, the volume of joints, constraints, and controls can be overwhelming. Coupled with the amount of nodes that need to be managed is the fact that, most of the time, there is a desire to have absolute consistency across characters. Animators typically have little lead time to get to know a character rig, so making rigs as similar as possible to each other minimizes the ramp-up time. With this in mind, many artists and studios develop rigging systems where predefined rig modules or building blocks are created, maintained, collected, and fit to the character (Figure 20.1). Further, many characters can be generalized to a type such as "humanoid biped," or "feline quadruped" and, as such, the motion system and control set for those rigs should be identical. For the rigger, it is also a question of not wanting to "reinvent the wheel" with every rig and risk forgetting something, introducing an error, or just spending too much of their time on manually redoing work. A large benefit to storing motion system components in either file or code form is that it becomes the recorded memory of how characters are created so that time can be spent developing solutions to the unique problems that might not be so easily handled by these preestablished building blocks.

The construction process that takes these building blocks and puts them together can take a few different forms depending on the needs and preferences of the studio or rigger. The two most notable ones are *referencing* and *build* systems. Referencing is the practice of connecting and fitting prebuilt systems while build systems use code to procedurally create and connect rig elements. While both have their pros and cons, build systems are

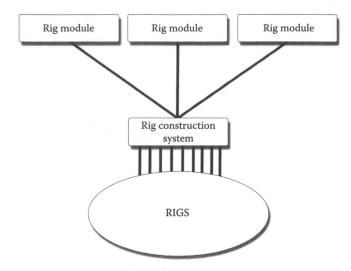

FIGURE 20.1 Scripted rigging systems use predefined modules to generate character rigs.

increasingly found at production studios. The main differences between referencing and build systems are

- How are the rig modules stored: as data or as code? For build systems, the modules can be stored as either data or code, whereas for referencing the modules usually exist as prebuilt data files.

- What is the connection to the original modules: live or baked? Build systems typically bake the data of the modules into the rig that they produce, whereas with referencing you have the option of maintaining a live connection to the modules.

Many third-party animation packages have strong scripting functionality and have had, at times, a cumbersome implementation of referencing. This trajectory has lead to the growing prevalence of build systems. While referencing data across live scenes is a complex problem, as more sophisticated solutions are developed, it is possible that this could become easier and build systems will become less prevalent. There is certainly a large amount of overhead in developing and maintaining build systems but, thus far, for many studios, the benefits have outweighed the cost.

20.2 RIG BUILDING BLOCKS

Regardless of the method of construction, modularity is the key to designing a reusable motion system library and the place to start is with modular building blocks. These building blocks are the core functional components of a rig. They are containers for the anatomical elements that make up the character and associate functionality with the regions of the rig. They should create the joints needed to support the kinematic system, the constraints needed to define the relationships between the joints, and the controls that provide the interface for animation. Having the controls be standardized is one of the strengths of a reusable, modular system in that no matter how many times a system is installed the control names and functionality are always identical. The building blocks should also include any hooks needed for the deformations. There are many factors to determining how granular to divide up the systems. For example, should an arm module include fingers? Usually not, but if your company is in the business of always creating humanoid bipeds, then maybe this is a valid route to take as it saves time and integration steps. Generally, you want to make your modules as discrete as possible.

20.2.1 Modules

- *Arm:* The arm module should support FK and IK posing along with the ability to blend and match between states and a way to pin the elbow to something in world space. It should include an attachment point at the root to connect to the torso and a node at the opposite end to have a hand (or other kinematic collection) attached to it.

- *Leg:* Like the arm, the leg module should support FK and IK posing along with the ability to blend and match between states and a way to pin the knee to something in world space. It should include an attachment point at the root to connect to the torso and a node at the opposite end to have a foot (or other kinematic collection) attached to it. One can imagine that legs and arms could be derived from the same code in a scripted build system.

- *Digit:* The digit module is a useful building block as it can be instanced to create the fingers of a hand or the toes of a foot, but can also be used as a building block for a claw or other simple segmented kinematic structures. The digit module should support FK rotations at each segment and have high-level controls for curling all the segments at once. Constructing a hand is tedious, so a well-formed digit package instanced across the number of digits required along with some glue to connect the functionality across them is a great start and simplifies the process.

- *Spine:* The spine at the most basic level is a series of cumulative FK controls that allow you to smoothly bend the joints. The next level up is a spline IK, and even further is a ribbon spine based on a NURBS surface that has deformation joints associated with it. Usually, an animator needs to be able to move the upper body and the lower body independent of each other and also be able to shape the curvature of the spine.

- *Neck and head:* The head can typically be a single joint, but its connection with the neck makes it a little tricky. You usually need FK and head-driven IK in which the neck follows along. This is also an area where space-switching for the head is important as sometimes an animator will want the head in the space of the shoulders and other times in world space so that body motion does not have an impact on it.

- *Tail:* A tail is composed of a varying number of joints with a mix of high- and low-level controls that give the animator a lot of options for posing and shaping the curvature. Standard, per-joint FK is usually too fine of a control for an animator to keep track of each individual segment. It is best to have higher-level bending controls that work alongside a spline-based IK setup that allows the tail to be posed from a few key points with additional overall curling. The tail is a prime example of a module that is best created through a build system as the number of joints at the base level can vary widely depending on the length of the tail model and the smoothness desired by the production design.

- *Tentacle:* Like the tail, tentacles are composed of a varying number of joints and require a combination of high- and low-level systems to provide effective control to the animator. The difference between the tentacle and the tail is that the tentacle needs support for being a kinematic structure to accommodate locomotion. For example, a character may need to walk on a tentacle. It may also need a finer control at the tip to manipulate the end of the tentacle to be able to pick things up.

- *Wing:* Wings are complex systems that can vary widely between different types of flying animals. Mostly they can be viewed as a collection of digits that provide controls for folding, bending, and flapping.

20.3 REFERENCING

Referencing usually implies that the rig is created via the inclusion of prebuilt modules that are stored on disk. There is usually a chain of files that are collected and brought together into a single file where they are connected and the deformations are hung on them. The building blocks of a referenced rig are often other scene files with rig elements in them. These are referenced into the main rig and adjusted into place to fit the character being set up (Figure 20.2).

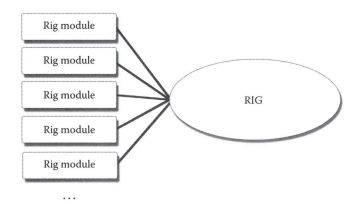

FIGURE 20.2 In referencing, individual rigging modules are collected into the rig to be fit and published.

FIGURE 20.3 An example directory structure (based on OpenPipeline for Maya).

Sometimes, it is a complete rig that can be referenced in and has the configurability to be refit. This data lives on disk and can be opened, inspected, and edited interactively.

The referencing system is usually based on the file import functionally of the software package in which the rig is being built. Referencing is the creation of the live connection to one or more files that lives on disk from a base scene file. When the base scene file is loaded, each of the referenced files are loaded and the data from each is loaded into the scene and local overrides or saved customization data for fitting the rig are applied. When the referenced files are edited, the changes appear in the base file when it is reloaded or when the references are refreshed.

When building rigs with referencing there is at first a desire to maintain live connections between the building block elements and the final rig. The lure is that many rigs can be updated in real time with the modification of those building blocks but this actually adds a lot of room for error. Not all updates will suit all characters and maintaining live connections forces the rigger to work in the dark and leave animators with the possibility of getting broken rigs. The same can be said for many forms of rig development but the solution here is to insulate the changes to the building blocks from the live rigs by maintaining a rig publishing workflow and pipeline. This can be as simple as storing the changes in a workshop version of the rig that is accessible only to the riggers and publishing a more self-contained version (Figure 20.3). This self-contained version would have all the same functionality of the workshop version but the live references to the building blocks would be imported and static so that updates to them do not affect the rig. This notion of importing references is often referred to as "flattening" or "baking" as it flattens all the references and bakes the live dynamic ingredients into a standalone publishable asset.

20.4 BUILD SYSTEMS

Build systems are usually composed entirely of code-based rig building blocks. Creating these blocks through code is an effective method of storing and managing them because they exist as lightweight and well-documented data objects. Rigging is an inherently object-oriented problem, so developing a rig as code and utilizing notions such as inheritance (basing an object on another object) allows the developer to harness OOP principles to develop concise and efficient building blocks (Figure 20.4).

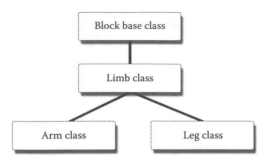

FIGURE 20.4 Simple inheritance structure for building block classes.

Because build systems are created entirely of code, the process of creating the rig is sometimes called "scripted rigging" and the system itself can sometimes be called an "auto rig." A good way to think about scripted rigging is to implement rig building blocks as discreet coded pieces called modules. When scripting them, modules can share a lot of functionality, so the base class can handle much of the rig's input and output. From this class, all the others can be derived. Each module can represent a different element of the character rig such as an arm, leg, hand, head, wing, and so on. This breaks the process of writing the auto rig into logical pieces, but it also creates a modular rig that can be optimized, updated, or modified for the needs of the production. This allows for rigging with options. There may be multiple arm rigs that can be selected and installed for different types of characters. If a module needs an update in the midst of a show, it can be identified and modified across the show quickly through code updates instead of manually editing a potentially large number of character rigs.

Build systems provide the framework which collects these individual building blocks and attaches them to each other based on a user-defined recipe. The recipe is usually comprised of an inventory of the building blocks that are requested, the attributes that specify the parameters of those modules, and a definition of how they connect to each other. The system reads this recipe and calls out to the build modules as directed to execute each one in a sequence (Figure 20.5).

```
<character_build_recipe>
        <module  flip=False>spine</module>
        <module  flip=False>head</module>
        <module  flip=True>arm</module>
        <module  flip=True>human_hand</module>
        <module  flip=True>leg</module>
        <module  flip=True>biped_foot</module>
</character_build_recipe>
```

FIGURE 20.5 A simple character recipe.

There are a number of strong options for storing rig build data in software-agnostic, human-readable formats including XML (Extensible Markup Language), JSON (JavaScript Object Notation), and YAML (Yet Another Multicolumn Layout). While all of these are well-supported, lightweight data-interchange formats, we will use XML as an example here. XML is a structured markup language that sets up a series of fields and stores data in them. Python has a lot of functionality specifically suited to dealing with XML data thanks to the xml module that comes with most built-in Python installations. XML is also an agreed-upon standard that is easily read and managed. It would be relatively easy to write your own file format but, with the multitude of libraries that exist to read and write XML, there should be a very good reason to try to write a new standard even for internal studio use. There is often the desire to write binary data, as it is faster to load and smaller to store on disk. However, since our character data is relatively small already and the ability to have it readable far outweighs the small speed or storage gain that would come from writing it in a binary file. Binary files are also easily corrupted which would leave this valuable data in an unreadable state. With this in mind, our simple recipe might look like a simple XML file (Figure 20.5).

The steps required for creating a procedural rig module:

1. Read recipe

2. Load modules

3. Fit modules

4. Read/set attributes

5. Build joints

6. Build constraints

7. Build controllers

8. Set animation control attributes

The interface for the build system can range from a fully fleshed-out graphical user interface that exposes all the attributes to the user, to a command line or series of scripts that the user calls. The system itself can be fairly simple in that the modules themselves could be coded with the knowledge of what they require as inputs. The system then just installs them and applies whatever customization code is needed to fit and attach them together. Of course, over time, one can imagine the build system itself taking on more functionality to handle lots of special cases and specific expectations but in the beginning the process of building can be quite simple. Taking advantage of the object-oriented nature of motion system development and modern rig scripting, a build developer can create an architecture for a system that is hierarchical and based on increasingly more specific modules. One can imagine all building blocks deriving from a base block class and then like modules being related to each via a hierarchical structure.

Once all the modules are installed in the character, there is typically a process of attaching all of them together to create the completed rig. These "glue methods" at the end typically attach limbs to torso elements, scale controllers based on the size of the character, and clean-up and delete any extraneous data that were created during the build. This area in the system is also a catch-all for the elements that could not be fit cleanly into the build system.

20.5 EXAMPLE BUILD SYSTEM: THE ARM MODULE

In writing a production auto-rigging solution, it is best to start with one element, such as an arm, as it defines all the types of nodes, connections, and logic that will be needed to build the rest of the character. It also asks us to answer the basic questions regarding standards such as naming conventions, mirroring functionality, rig module inventory, and animation data management. This is just to get you thinking about the steps required to build rigs modularly and all the architecture that needs to be built to make the process as efficient as possible.

Procedural rig elements are simply code-generated versions of previously designed rig constructions. Often production-tested rig elements are converted into reusable functions. This not only saves production knowledge into a repeatable function and makes that functionality common to the production and the artists on it, but it also standardizes rig functionality across productions.

Our node naming class is a critical component to our scripted rig pipeline. Since a rig inherently has hundreds of nodes that make it up, it goes without saying that proper naming is essential. A good way to handle this in scripted rigging is to create a node naming class that all node creation passes through. This class takes the incoming data (such as object type, side of the character, region of the body, etc.) and formats it into a node name based on the style that is specified. Along these lines, you can create any number of styles and include varying spacers such as underscores (r_arm_ik_cntrl) or capitalization schemes such as camel case (rArmIkCntrl). This method of naming allows you to define patterns based on the needs of the show, your changing preference, or the direction of the overall character pipeline.

In an ideal situation, the elements should be defined by manipulatable objects that define the locations of points of articulation and the proportions of the pieces of that element. In a simple case, these objects could take the form of a locator or, in a more advanced case, as a more recognizable node-based geometric representation of the element that is being created. Below we walk through the thinking behind scripting a very basic arm rig.

The basic steps to build the arm (which are indicative of building all rig modules) are as follows:

1. Get marker positions

2. Set attributes to define the type of build

3. Build joints

4. Build constraints

5. Build controllers

6. Set animation control attributes

In order to define the proportions of our character's arm, we create a series of markers for the shoulder, elbow, and wrist. The markers are assumed to be symmetrical but the user can change their positions after they are created. Your rig should never be coded in a way that assumes that it will always be symmetrical. This rigid thinking can lead to problems quickly down the line as unique characters are called for. The arm module would get those markers and their positions first and define the space in which the arm will be created.

Next, attributes for the build would be read in. These might define the node naming schema, whether the arm needs IK, FK, or both, and any other attributes that you might want to specify. These attributes often end up being arguments passed to the method that builds the module. Once the build system knows where the arm will be located in space (from the markers) and the parameters that are requested, it can start building the architecture of the arm rig.

The base of the rig would be the joints. The shoulder, elbow, and wrist will likely be created exactly in the place of the markers that we positioned previously but the module might also need to create helper joints at the forearm or between the shoulder and the elbow to assist with deformations later on. These procedurally placed joints are informed by the position of the markers. Once joints are in place, constraints are created to manage the FK and IK behavior and any of the mode switching that might be involved in such systems. In the case of the arm, a pole vector goal might also be created and hooked up. These constraints are often intrinsically connected with the controllers so that step is often interwoven with the creation of the constraints. Controls utilize the position of the markers and the created joints. Through this process, objects are put into their proper place in the scene hierarchy so that all joints and controls are grouped with like objects and constraints are put into the proper location. All of the node hierarchy work is a critical part of rigging to avoid unwanted transformations but one of the real powers of scripted rigging is that the tedious aspects of node management can be automated. As the controls are created, the module should add and connect the attributes on them to the functionality of the newly created rig. Attributes for IK/FK mode need to be added but just as important the module should also lock and hide attributes that an animator should not need access to. Often "default" attributes such as scale and visibility are managed through larger systems, so hiding them from the main interface is a way to make sure that they are not mistakenly animated.

In general, modules should have a consistent hierarchical structure that allows them to be moved and parented without affecting local functionality. This allows them to act like building blocks that can be snapped together to form the rig. When building a module, one must take into account "side," as in: which side does this exist on the character's body? One must also consider that a character may have more than two arms and so the module should be flexible enough to work in large multiples on one rig. When writing a module, it is a small amount of work to make something work in multiples instead of hard-coding functionality for a single right or left arm. This usually comes down to unique naming, making sure that utility nodes work well together and that all the functionality of these nodes is optimized.

Rig version attributes are a handy way to limit the propagation of rig changes and to make sure they do not negatively impact animation. For example, a rig is created with the version attribute set to "1." Animation on a dozen shots is carried out, some shots are finalized, some are in-progress, and some have revealed a bug in the rig that requires a fix. The rigger changes the code for the rig and includes a version switch to "2" at that point. The animator can then set the rig version attribute as they see fit. Anything set to 1 is untouched by the change and anything created afterwards would get the latest rig. For the shots that need the fix, they are asked to change their rig version attribute to 2 and test the shot. Ideally the fix works. Now the default version of the rig is set to 2 for new rig builds, so old shots at version 1 are locked and new shots get the latest version of the rig. This can also allow an animator to roll back a rig's functionality after a fix or test two versions of a rig against each other for how they handle the motion of a shot. Most times, switchable attributes like solver types for IK or dynamics are exposed to an animator but if they are built into a show-wide update, then rig version changes may be the only way to access older solutions. Ideally, all shots should be running the latest rig and much of the time the rig version attribute is locked and set in the character build step so that it can be carefully controlled while maintaining the option to change it. This is an incredibly powerful practice to implement in your scripted rig and is essential for large productions.

20.5.1 Problems with Build Systems

The problems with build systems are mostly centered around the idea that editing and working within a code-based rigging paradigm requires users that are comfortable with reading and editing code. Creating modules for a build system is also often seen as double the work where a module needs to be created interactively, tested, and then recreated in code. Within large teams, there is often an expertise gap between the developers who are creating the build system and its components, and the artists who are building the rigs. Build systems are often seen as "black boxes" by the artists that use them and require a fair amount of technical support to fix bugs and add in new features or building blocks.

20.6 CONSTRUCTING DEFORMATIONS

Once you have a framework in place for constructing motion system components, you may find ways of procedurally setting up the deformations for your character. If you are consistently building similar characters, such as humans, the problem set is reduced and becomes more plausible. For example, you could manage a model that has weighting set up for it and warp it as part of your build process, and then transfer the weighting to your new character model. There is also the possibility of deforming simple surfaces with your build system and then attaching your character model to them to get an initial binding. These methods are available regardless of whether your construction method relies on building or referencing, as deformations are hung on the motion system after it is created.

To create an abstraction between the motion system and deformation system, there are typically a set of joints that are attached to the motion system and are in the domain of the deformation system. These are procedurally implemented and are merely the first stage hooks on which the deformation system hangs. This parallel joint set can be defined as a set of mirror joints that follow what exists in the motion system. In addition, you can introduce joints that sit between existing joints or that are colocated with existing joints but perform a partial rotation. Partial rotation joints are less affected by the absolute articulations of the character and open the door for more options when it comes to attaching layered deformation surfaces or weight painting a skinned mesh.

As we discussed in the chapter of deformations, layered deformations can be as simple as layers of higher-resolution surfaces that build into the final mesh or can be more informed by anatomy and seek to recreate muscles and tendons. The layered surface approach starts with a low-polygon mesh attached to the deformation joints (and as such the skinning data associated with it). That mesh then drives subsequently higher-resolution levels with fixative aspects as needed. This is usually done through a surface-to-surface connection that leaves you relying on a "wrap" deformer that performs a closest-point binding between two models. The build step for this involves reading each of the layers subsequently and applying their wraps and weighting as needed to build the character deformations onto the motion systems.

20.7 ANIMATION DATA TRANSFER

As your rig is scripted, every similar character type should be able to share animation. This means that the animation for a marauding knight should be able to be applied to the friendly ogre with little or no modifications outside of possibly scaling the data to deal with size differences between the characters.

By storing animation as a separate file, it then becomes a modular piece of data that can be stored in a library or database and applied to whatever character is chosen. Whether the animation is created by hand or derived from motion capture, this data can be mixed, matched, and blended to create the performance desired for the character in the shot. For situations where crowds are built, the animation can be art-directed to meet the needs of the shot and rearranged by associating different animation clips with different characters. By building a scripted rig, you have a reusable framework that makes the animation produced even more valuable by turning it into a reusable asset.

20.8 VARIATION SYSTEMS

The idea of building can be extended beyond just creating the rig to creating the variations of a character as well. As such, we can define a character as a collection of build elements that are

```
<character>
        <name>ghoul</name>
        <type>biped</type>
        <proportion>ghoul_proportion.xml</proportion>
        <variation>ghoul_var.xml</variation>
</character>
```

FIGURE 20.6 A simple character data structure.

run to create a variety of characters. This character data (Figure 20.6) is all the information that is needed to build a character in a shot. This includes a pointer to the character template type, its proportion specification file or the data itself, and the variation information. Ideally, this data is stored in external files and in a generic format that multiple applications can read and write. Storing data externally allows you to write tools that exist outside of your production software that can be run independently. These tools can be anything from small shot update scripts to larger production pipeline tools that manage the data in your project from start to finish.

To create visual diversity and populate the project with a crowd of characters, rigs need to be created in large volumes and with variations. Many times these diverse characters are created from one base rig that has switchable attributes that can be mixed and matched to create the variability needed. Variation elements can be clothing pieces like hats, shirts, pants, shoes, accessories like weapons, or even rigging attributes like height or build. Rigging attributes that affect the proportions of the character must be added to the build step at the stage of motion system generation and potentially fitting the model. Clothing must also be warped to fit the reproportioned character but can often be added as a secondary step. These attributes should, where possible, be switchable in the shot so that they can be art directed on-the-fly. If all of the changes need to happen at the character build step, then the iteration loop for shot population is longer.

The variation system relies on a wardrobe or library system where variation selections are stored on disk and accessed to create options for the system. Often, logic can be added to the selection criteria so that there are dependencies between objects. Just like in real life, some shoes only work with some clothes. These dependencies can be added to your build based on the rules defined by your art director, so if certain options are selected, noncomplimentary options are not possible or visible.

20.9 RIG PUBLISHING

Regardless of the method of construction, the rig must be delivered to "downstream" departments including, most importantly, animation, and this process of rig publication is one of the most critical in the character technology pipeline. The newly published rig needs to replace the rig that is currently being referenced into shots. The update to the rig should not change existing animation. If it does, then measures need to be taken so that shots can be fixed as well to deal with the changes. The process of publishing is usually an automated, push-button operation and can be incorporated into a build system so that multiple characters can be built (and rebuilt) and published either in a sequence or in parallel by distributing this work to a group of computers sometimes called a "build farm," a variation on a render farm.

20.10 CONCLUSION

Rig construction is the process of combining all the elements of a rig into a cohesive deliverable with which an animator can create a performance. While it may not be the most artistic part of the process, it is one of the most essential and requires planning and precise execution as the reliability of the rig building and publishing process is a core component of the character pipeline for a production.

With the rig in place and tested within a scene and with the production pipeline, it is time to apply animation to bring it to life. All this work leads up to animation in its many modern forms.

20.11 EXERCISE

Build a simple limb creation script. Using Python, write a simple script that takes three locators as input and creates

- Joints

- An IK solver

- Animation controls

You should be able to pass in the names to be used for the controls or have the script read in a configuration file that describes that data.

Questions to ask:

- Can the limb be installed multiple times?

- Can it be mirrored from side to side easily?

After you complete the tool, think about what you would need to do in order to extend it to a system for building a complete character.

FURTHER READING

Reading about rig construction systems from different studios such as Disney's dRig or ILM's Block Party can be pretty inspiring:

Rose, R., Jutan, M., Doublestein, J. 2013. *BlockParty 2: Visual Procedural Rigging for Film, TV, and Games.* ACM SIGGRAPH 2013 Talks.

Smith, G., McLaughlin, M., Lin, A., Goldberg, E., and Hanner, F. 2012. *dRig: An Artist-friendly, Object-oriented Approach to Rig Building*. ACM SIGGRAPH 2012 Talks.

This is also a good point to pause and take stock of the work that has been done on character technology. "Making of" featurettes on DVDs, books that document the creation or art of a film or game, and articles that might provide more in-depth coverage on the creation of digital characters in production are all good sources. In particular:

CG Channel is a great on-line resource for production articles geared more towards animation: http://www.cgchannel.com

Gamasutra is another great on-line resource but is specific to video game production: http://www.gamasutra.com

Cinefex Magazine is also an industry standard for deep coverage of the making of films and visual effects.

III

Animation Technology

CHAPTER 21

Introduction to Animation Technology

C OMPLEX DIGITAL CHARACTERS and the architecture built to drive them would be meaningless without the ability to make them move. Animation breathes life into these systems and whether it is driven by a talented animator, a motion captured performer, or a procedural system, the skill required is formidable and the technology underlying these techniques is advancing rapidly. In this section, we explore the curves created by animators, the capture of human performance, and the code used to express complex motion for layering these techniques into the character performance required. This is a high-level overview to give the character rigger an introduction to the various ways in which motion is generated and some of the rig concerns related to each method.

21.1 DEFINITIONS OF ANIMATION

As we stated earlier, the word "animation" at its most basic means "physically or graphically moving," and an animated character could be said to have had the divine or magic wind (animus) breathed into it. In this section, we cover the many aspects of introducing motion onto a character rig. All of the techniques covered in this section are forms of animation (Figure 21.1).

Purists will argue that only traditional, hand-generated (even by computer) animation, is real animation. Procedural animation, which is generated through the execution of code, is seen as a different entity altogether. Procedural motion should never be seen as a replacement for animation but as a complement or solution to issues of character volume in a scene. Motion capture, on the other hand, where a live performer's performance is captured and applied to a character, is often thought of as something more imposing. Animators often fear that motion capture will put their jobs at risk. There is the belief that directors see the motion produced by a motion capture performer as providing them with instant results; thus, they direct their

> *Keyframe animation:* The creation of character motion by
> means of hand-creating character poses from action to
> action and controlling the interpolation between those
> actions.
>
> *Motion capture:* Also termed "performance capture," this is the
> recording of motion data from live performance which is
> then used to drive the character rig.
>
> *Procedural animation:* The creation of character motion by
> means of code or simulation so that the animation system
> drives the frame-to-frame motion based on user-defined
> parameters.

FIGURE 21.1 Types of digital animation.

animated characters exactly like the way they direct live actors. Because motion capture records and injects reality into the character instantly, a digital character takes on hyper-real motion and behavior. Often times, the result is off-putting to people, likely inducing Mori's "Uncanny Valley" phenomenon. The truth is that motion capture is a tool that is critical to the recording of realistic motion for characters intended to be integrated with live action actors. It provides a baseline of motion that animators may build upon for realistic digital characters, as in the case of Gollum from *The Lord of the Rings*. As motion capture technology becomes more advanced, it will be possible to record more refined performances. Fine detail regions such as the face and hands will be captured with all the subtlety that we see in humans and make its way into our digital characters.

However, none of this will replace keyframe animation. While movies like *Beowulf* (2007) will push the art of performance-based animation, they are a very different animal from a movie like *Ratatouille* (2007). Motion capture, as it stands now, does not have the nuance of real motion nor does it have the caricature of keyframe animation. The embodiment of an animator in a digital character creates a very different, and some would argue more subtle performance than the application of motion capture. Where a motion capture performance manipulates parts of the rig, everything else must be controlled through triggered proceduralism or through the hand of the animator. This disconnect does not exist in fully key framed animation which relies on the animator as an actor from beginning to end of the character's performance. Many characters will require hand animation entirely, some could be a mix of motion capture and keys, whereas others entirely procedural motion. The decision is based on project types, budget, timeline, and aesthetics. One solution is to develop characters that take multiple streams of motion data and mixing and matching animation techniques to find ways of building up the desired performance from multiple sources.

21.2 INTEGRATION OF ANIMATION TECHNIQUES

Motion is created in a multitude of ways. Motion capture is often used as a reference for hand-keyed animation in the same way that animators would rotoscope film footage to capture the subtlety of human motion. This, however, is rare. What is more common, as we have discussed, is the layering of hand animation on top of motion capture data or procedural animation to create a blended performance. This notion of motion-mixing and input-blending is very similar to film editing where a scene is built up from the montage of shots to create a unified whole. The difference is that all of this editing is manifested as output on the character rig. This can be accomplished in the nonlinear animation editing or on the rig itself.

In the nonlinear animation editing stage, each control gets the result of the current edit of motion through the blending on animation curves for each region of the body. This is accomplished through a process of joint definition and characterization where rig controls are associated with like animation curves on all the incoming animation tracks. Once characterized and associated with each other, for example, the motion of the arm, as controlled by animation, can be blended and edited with the action as derived from motion capture. This mixing and matching of tracks and clips of motion treats the character rig as the playback device performing the results of the editing operations. Similarly, the rig itself can be created with overrides and regions of blended output. Through the construction of an intelligent hierarchy of nodes, portions of the rig can be controlled by different streams of data or the weighted average of multiple streams at once. In this way, the animation all exists on the rig itself and streams are utilized, muted, or blended with other streams as needed. Both of these methods produce the same results and are really just workflow differences for getting multiple streams of animation data working synchronously on a character rig. They give the director and the animator choices when it comes time to finalize a shot. Often motion capture data is too high frequency and needs to be dampened by more smoothly interpolated animation. The inverse is also possible. It is very rare that a shot will have a full motion capture performance and an animation performance so, more often, if motion capture or procedurally generated motion does not hit the mark expected or desired, then it is animated on top to finalize the shot.

21.3 INTERFACES FOR ANIMATION

Animation is a time-intensive process and a grueling amount of work for the artist. The interface that an animator uses can be the bane of their existence. The animator's desk is very different today than in the past when it contained an animator's light table with its pegs to register animation frames. These days, animators might still have those off to the side for use in preliminary pencil work for a shot, but the tools used in general production are similar to those used in any setting where a computer is in use. Digital animation, like so many activities undertaken by humans using computers, is usually created via a mouse and keyboard interface. Tablets and tablet personal computers, with their gestural stylus interface and software to recreate natural media, are also making strides as an interface for 3D animation and as a replacement for the traditional light table for hand-drawn animation. Animators manipulate components of the rig and set keyframes on their transformations and attributes over time using these tried and true user interface devices. Keyframes are the starting or ending positions of an animated transition and adjusting the distance between them changes the timing in which they occur.

As we will see later, there is the possibility of live and recorded performance of a live performer through motion capture.

These tools will likely remain the standard for the immediate future. Looking forward, research is focusing on methods for providing animators with alternative interfaces to produce animation. Apparati, such as mixing board systems for facial animation and performance rigs, like the ones used by the Jim Henson Company, provide a more tactile and real-time performance interface. While these are not ideal for all productions, like motion capture, they are a way to bring real-time gesture to the animation production. Animators often miss the tactile feeling of drawing while working in 3D animation. Animators, and artists, in general, traditionally create quick gesture drawings to capture the essence of a pose. A few prototype systems have been developed that allow an animator to sketch out the pose of a character and let the system adjust the character articulations to propose a fit to match it. This is a difficult problem to solve because a 2D drawing can be ambiguous as to how it should result in a 3D articulation, but when implemented could be a boon to animators. A few examples have surfaced in which the artist draws a stick figure depiction and the 3D character fits itself to a pose. Much of the work in this area deals with the sketch-based posing of a human body. This is a good place to start as the rigid limbs of the human body, once defined, can be fit to the like-length portions of the figure in the sketch. "3D character animation synthesis from 2D sketches" (2006) by Yi Lin of University of Waterloo [23] is a good example of work in this area. There is also research going into the animation of faces such as the case of "Sketching articulation and pose for facial animation" (2006) where Edwin Chang and Odest Chadwicke Jenkins of Brown University implemented a system that converts sketched lines into poses for a rigged facial setup. While no commercial equivalent has emerged and no animation studio has formerly presented such interfaces in production, this is no doubt on the horizon. This is paradigm-shifting technology and a bridge between traditional techniques and modern interface.

FURTHER READING

Chang, E. and Jenkins, O. C. 2006. Sketching articulation and pose for facial animation. *SCA'06: Proceedings of the 2006 ACM SIGGRAPH/Eurographics Symposium on Computer Animation*, Vienna, Austria. Eurographics Association, Aire-la-Ville, Switzerland, Switzerland, pp. 271–280.

Lin, Y. 2006. 3D character animation synthesis from 2D sketches. *GRAPHITE'06: Proceedings of the 4th International Conference on Computer Graphics and Interactive Techniques in Australasia and Southeast Asia*, Kuala Lumpur, Malaysia. ACM, New York, NY, pp. 93–96.

CHAPTER 22

Interview: Javier Solsona, Senior Character Technical Director, Sony Imageworks

22.1 BIO

Javier Solsona is a wanderer, a traveler, a "citizen of the world." He was born in Argentina and grew up in Patagonia. From an early age, he started doing graphics on his Commodore 64 at home, painstakingly painting pixel by pixel. Many years later, still in front of a computer, he got a BSc in Computer Sciences from the University of Cape Town (UCT), South Africa. During his last year at university in 1995, he was introduced to Multimedia and 3D and there was no looking back ever since.

After finishing his degree, he moved to Brazil where he carried on studying 3D animation on his spare time while taking part on various 3D courses. Later, he moved to London, UK, where he worked for three years as a freelance graphic artist for various hi-tech companies including Cisco Systems.

He eventually moved to Vancouver, British Columbia, where after working for a year as a creative director in a small company, decided to leave his secure position and go back to school to complete his education. He studied for six intense months at the Vancouver Film School in their Character Animation program. After his completion, he was awarded a scholarship for his efforts in his final film.

Once out of school, he got a position at Lost Boys Studios in Vancouver working on their 3D department as a visual effects artist doing commercials, Game Cinematics and music videos.

He worked for 3 years at Electronic Arts Canada as a cinematic animators on *Def Jam Vendetta*, *Def Jam: Fight For NY* and a game play animator on *SSX4*. He then moved to

Javier Solsona
Senior Character Technical Director, Sony Imageworks

Propaganda Games (a Disney Interactive Studios) as their Senior Creature Technical Director working on the new installment of *Turok*. He jumped at the opportunity to work at DreamWorks Animation in movies like *Shrek Forever After*, *Puss in Boots*, *Rise of the Guardians*, and was a lead Character TD on *Turbo*. Finally, returning to Vancouver with his family to work at Sony Imageworks for the Rovio movie, *Angry Birds*.

When he is not working on computers, he can be found playing with his kids, exploring the back country is his skis or kite-boarding in exotic locations around the world.

22.2 Q&A

Q: *The components of character technology are diverse and span the artistic and technical spectrum. How did you get your start in the industry? Based on where you see the field heading what experience/training do you recommend people have?*

A: I grew up in Patagonia in a very small town. We were the second family to own a computer and I started playing around at an early age. I would "draw," painting each pixel on the screen. Back then it was very painful—you needed a lot of patience and dedication. All the drawing was done by typing in numbers, running some code and, eventually, you would see the result on the screen. Change, run, repeat, change, run, repeat.

I moved from Argentina to South Africa when I was 15. Even then I knew I wanted to study computers and I was always drawn to graphics. At the time, at least in South Africa, there was nothing computer and graphic related, so I graduated with a Bachelor of Science in Computer Sciences. During my last year at the university I did a course in 3D graphics at a local college and I loved it so much that I knew that was what I wanted to do. I had discovered the blend between art and technology. I spent many years afterwards playing at home, doing small animations. I lived in London, England for 3 years during the dot com boom where I worked mainly as a graphic designer but also incorporated a lot of my technology background. Later in life I moved to Vancouver where I decided to get a proper education in 3D and animation. At the time I thought I wanted to be an animator. I went to VFS for 6 months where I learned to use Maya. This is when I discovered that scripting and rigging just felt natural to me. It was the perfect blend of art and coding.

I got a job at Electronic Arts working as an animator but immediately started scripting things to help us with our pipeline. Back then there were no Character TDs in gaming. I left EA 3 years later to concentrate fully on being a character TD at Propaganda Games, a Disney Interactive Studio.

During a Siggraph conference I was chatting with Jason Schleifer, then Head of Character Animation, at DreamWorks Animation. I had known him from his Character TD days at Weta and he said that I should join DreamWorks. I thought, "Why not?" and a few months later I moved to California.

After spending 6 amazing years at DreamWorks, my family wanted to return to Canada so we made the move back and I'm currently at Sony Imageworks. I am still working on movies and enjoying every day.

Things have obviously changed a lot since I started in the industry. There was almost no formal training—most people were self taught and there were very few resources online. I always felt that it was important to understand the other disciplines (animation, modeling, etc.) before going into rigging since that gives you an idea of what you need the models to look like and what works and doesn't and be able to modify them to get the best results. It also allows you to understand your "client"—the animator. In my opinion, having worked in any of those disciplines before becoming a character TD is very advantageous.

Q: *Creating compelling digital characters is part art and part science. What is the greatest challenge you encounter on a daily basis? What aspect of character technology keeps you up thinking at night?*

A: My kids keep me up at night these days, not CG.

One of the biggest obstacles I encounter today is the software. I often want to do things the software won't allow me to do, or it would take too long to figure out a work around or I would have to spend a long time coding a solution.

In some studios you have privilege of having a big R&D team that can help you out with that or you can be a very good coder and can write plugins, scripts, etc. However, the reality is you are more often than not only be able to use the tools that are in front of you, so you need to be inventive. It helps to always be thinking outside the box, always exploring and always trying to figure new ways of doing things.

Aside from that, it's the constant struggle of getting things done in a timely manner. We are always against the clock. Depending on the production you might not have a lot of time to experiment or figure things out, before you have to move on to the next character. It's a fine balance of quality vs. the amount of time allotted for a certain task. No matter how much time you spend on a character, you always wish you had just a few more days to fix this or that and you are always super critical of every little detail when you see it on the big screen.

Q: *What are the ingredients for a successful digital character?*

A: Attention to detail is the key to a great character.

I believe that a character's hands and eyes are some of the most important parts on a character. Hands are often overlooked.

We empathize a lot too through a character's facial expressions, especially the eyes. We, as humans, have adapted to reading faces very well so our eyes are always directed to the face. A good facial setup is key to portraying life in a character.

Of course we are all part of a team. If you have an amazing character setup but the animation is bad you will not have a successful character. Likewise you could have the best character animator in the world, but if the setup just doesn't allow him to do what he needs/wants to do then you'll fail too. I often like to see a character as part of a tight group belonging to the modeler, character TD and animator. If one of them fails, the character fails. There are other departments too such as surfacing, lighting and rendering, but I think of them as the outer layer, the icing.

Q: *While the industry is competitive, it is ultimately respectful of great work. Outside of the work you have been personally involved in the production of, what animated characters have you been impressed or inspired by? What is the historical high-bar?*

A: I grew up with *Star Wars*, and even though that wasn't CG I loved the creature work on it. Mos Eisley's Cantina was probably one of my favourite places because you could see so many different creatures—that was probably what attracted me to be a character TD, even though they were practical effects.

In CG, one character that still stands out for me is Davey Jones, ILM did an amazing job with him. The eyes were one of the best I have ever seen. Weta has done some amazing work lately too. Smaug was particularly impressive in the latest Hobbit movies and so are all the Navi in *Avatar*. I really enjoyed the effects of the aliens in *The Edge of Tomorrow*—they were something new and refreshing.

When it comes to feature animation, Madagascar was the first show that I thought CG had finally figured out the cartoon look and I saw a whole new world opening up. The work done in Madagascar is what inspired me to join DreamWorks. Of course, my industry colleagues keep on pushing the limit in every single movie and I expect to be continually impressed by all the amazingly talented people that are out there.

Q: *Where do you see digital characters in 10 years? Where are animated characters for film and games heading?*

A: We keep on improving the way characters look. Every movie and game that comes out is better and better than the last. I think we'll see even more details. We are at the point where we are adding a lot of subtle details. You might not be able to see them all but you'll feel them and even though you might not realize it does make a big difference.

The characters in games are finally starting to get over the Uncanny Valley. Gaming is challenging because there are certain limitations, but the engines keep on getting better and better and games are coming out with more and more detail. The biggest challenges in the future, like always, will be time and money: it is a matter of how much can we get done in the time we have to do it in and with smaller budgets.

CHAPTER 23

Traditional Animation Techniques

T RADITIONAL ANIMATION REFERS to the means of creating moving images frame-by-frame without the assistance of a computer. This encompasses hand-drawn animation, stop motion puppetry, and any imaginable technique that uses traditional media over time. In many ways, modern digital 3D animation has a lot in common with stop motion animation. The process of modeling, surfacing, rigging, cinematography, animation, and lighting are very analogous. In stop motion animation, modeling may involve making a sculptural character out of clay. The model may actually be built around a metal armature that serves as the character rig. The model is painted and adorned with clothing and other accessories. The camera is placed along with the lights, and characters are animated. This all sounds remarkably like modern 3D animation.

The fundamentals of character animation, however, were devised on paper for the purposes of hand-drawn animated characters. While animation is filled by strong historical figures and its origins are diverse and worldwide, it is worth delving into the pioneering and defining work Walt Disney Studios undertook to set the stage for how motion is applied to digital characters.

23.1 CLASSIC PRINCIPLES OF ANIMATION

Animation was not a particularly new medium when Walt Disney emerged onto the scene in 1928 with *Steamboat Willy* (1928), but his research and development on how to make characters emote was innovative. Disney and his early animators studied animals and people, copied live action footage (also known as "rotoscoping") both in production and as a study tools, and developed technology to take the art of animation to another level and made it possible for them to produce animation on a large scale. As Disney collected motion and expression into a set of personality types, he and his animators defined these characters, no matter what form they took, for a generation. Along with these personality types, and even more important to modern animators, they outlined the definitive set of animation principles in the classic book *The Illusion of Life* [24]. As we look at the traditional principles of animation as an example, we can discuss ways in which these principles are implemented for modern digital characters. In a 3D animation system, the gestures and arcs that Disney's founding animators (the *Nine Old Men*) defined take a more controlled and calculated posing of character elements than the gestures inherent with pencil on paper, but the principles apply equally. In fact, because of the inherent rigid nature of 3D animation, these rules play an even larger role. The application of traditional principles to modern 3D digital animation is a challenge for every 3D animator. John Lasseter [25] spent some of his early days at Pixar helping to develop tools that would allow himself and the other animators there to have the ability to apply these principles to their work. Since then, animators have added other steps to this process and as character setups have become capable of performing difficult deformation procedures, such as squash and stretch, there is a decreasing discrepancy between what has been typically created in 2D and 3D with regard to formal character animation. The following are known as the *Principles of Animation.*

Squash and stretch is the notion that as an object moves, its shape changes, reacting to the force of the movement. In doing so, it compresses and stretches, preserving the volume of the character shape. Both the axial body and the appendages react to the notion of squash and stretch and can be thought of as a scale along the axis that is aligned with the motion. For elements of a digital character, one can imagine that when something is scaled up in the Y-axis, that it must be scaled down in the X- and Z-axes to stretch. Conversely, scaling something down in Y would require that the object be scaled up in X and Z, giving the impression that the object is squashing. The setup for squashing and stretching characters varies and ranges from scaling joints, translating joints, or even a postprocess on the model itself at the deformation level.

Anticipation is the announcement of an action before it happens—it is the wind-up before the pitch. It allows the viewer to get a sense of the flow of motions, with each motion anticipating the next and presenting a clear performance. A character rig should have the ability to bend and move in all directions equally. The arch of the spine should be flexible enough for the typical bend to be anticipated with a curve at the reverse angle even for a few frames. This often requires that the animator be able to do things that the character setup artist might not have anticipated. Of course, the anticipation of an action happens at the pose level, but every control should be available to move a part of that character in the "broken" direction to some degree.

Staging is the most general principle that deals with the cinematography and framing of the action. The emphasis here is in making sure that the intended idea is clear to the viewer watching the scene. A critical component of staging is creating a clear and strong silhouette for the character. For digital characters, the position of the render camera has the same effect on the audience as it does for live action actors in films. The position of the camera creates a relationship between the actors on screen and their relationship to each other, the set, and our view of them.

Straight ahead action and pose to pose are the two main approaches to animation from the point of view of production. Straight ahead action is produced frame by frame from the start by the animator deciding the motion as they go, always keeping the end goal in mind. Pose to pose is the laying out of key poses and then working out the in-between poses that fall between them. This is more typical among modern digital animators because of the nondestructive nonlinear nature of animation systems which lends itself to this workflow. Modern animation systems also inherently interpolate the transitions from pose to pose based on the curve associated with the keys. The spacing of those poses on the animation timeline informs the timing of the action. As we will discuss later, the type of interpolation chosen for the keys will dictate the transition from key to key.

Follow through and overlapping action are complementary concepts. Follow through is the termination part of an action. When throwing a ball, the hand continues to move after the ball is released. In the movement of a complex object, different parts of the object move at different times and at different rates. For example, in walking, the hip leads followed by the leg and then the foot. As the lead part stops, the lagging parts continue in motion. Heavier parts lag farther and stop slower. Antennae of an insect will lag behind the body and then move quickly to indicate the lighter mass. Overlapping means to start a second action before the first action has completely finished. This is meant to keep the interest of the viewer, as there is no dead time between actions. The ability to manipulate parts of the rig independent of others makes the addition of overlapping action easier to add to a shot. Typically an animator will, for example, want to be able to control the character's hips and not have them affect the upper body. This independent region control allows an animator to modify the motion of one region without impacting another so that motion can be overlapped.

Slow in and slow out refers to the spacing of the in-between frames at maximum positions. Rather than having a uniform velocity for an object, it is more appealing, and sometimes more realistic, to have the velocity vary at the extremes. This is due to our expectations regarding physics and how an object moves, or appears to move, in the real world. For example, a bouncing ball moves faster as it approaches or leaves the ground and slower as it approaches or leaves its maximum height position. The name comes from having the object or character "slow out" of one pose and "slow in" to the next pose. In traditional animation, the speed of actions was based on the number of drawings. In modern digital animation systems, the timing of poses can be shifted around easily and shots can be retimed in a nondestructive manner.

Arcs are the visual path of action for natural movement. Even the fastest motion should happen in curves. There is almost no place in character motion for a linear curve (or interpolation) to look correct. The motion of a hand IK goal is a classic example where linear interpolation reveals its flaw. As the hand moves, no matter how hard one tries to move in a straight line, the force of muscle fatigue and gravity always introduce some form of an arc. In a digital system, as keys are laid out, the curves that represent the path of the action should be separate from the curve that defines the timing of the in-betweens. Spline-based interpolation naturally creates curves between a small number of keys. For noncharacter objects, curves can be drawn in the scene and objects can be attached to them so that the arcing path can be refined and tuned based on the timing desired.

Secondary action is an action that directly results from another action and can be used to increase the complexity and interest in a scene. It should always be subordinate to, and not compete with, the primary action in the scene. Secondary action is where modern animation systems make up for some of the challenges that they create as this motion can be computed automatically. Secondary motion usually includes all the accessory pieces to the main performance and often is contained in props and clothing. Elements such as hair, clothes, tails, hats, swords, and the like can be setup or programmed to move dynamically based on the actions of the main character. If simulation is too costly in terms of time and computation investment, then simple expressions can be created to move these objects based on the motion of other parts of the body or to lag behind these main motions.

Timing for an animator, as in comedy, is something that is part honing a skill and part innate talent. For animation, timing is the spacing between keyframes which sets the tempo of the action and speed of the movements. The more in-betweens that exist within key poses, the slower the action will appear. One or two in-betweens result in almost immediate transitions between key poses. As stated earlier, the spacing of keys in an animation system is easily edited both at the pose as well as the individual element level. This does not make the animators natural sense of timing any less valuable, but it does make their jobs a little easier.

Exaggeration accentuates the essence of an idea via design and action. This is often what is meant when an action is "made bigger" or the moment is said to be "over-the-top." It applies to everything from a single movement, to the arc of a motion, to a sequence of events. Often exaggeration is used to communicate a motion more clearly by amplifying it. As exaggeration lies in the performance and the natural extension of the rig's potential, the setup artist should need to do very little to accommodate this principle. One aspect to keep in mind is the character's face. Most of the time, facial controls are created with the possibility of achieving more range than is exposed to the animator or set in the default range. Ensuring that values outside of the typical range for a character are reasonable and exposing them for use during moments of exaggeration or anticipation gives animators a lot more freedom.

Appeal is about creating a design or an action that the audience enjoys watching, in the same vein of an actor bringing charisma to their performance. While not strictly an animation principle, it is always important to question the appeal of a character's design and performance. Even villains need appeal and this comes down to original character design and the execution of the model. The implementation of an appealing set of shapes for the face to achieve is in the domain of the character rig, but much of this still relies on the design of the character and the appeal of the character's performance as determined by the animation.

23.2 CURVES AND INTERPOLATION

Animation is based on curves. A node's position or rotation in space over time creates a series of points in a Cartesian space as it moves, forming a curve for each channel, usually defined

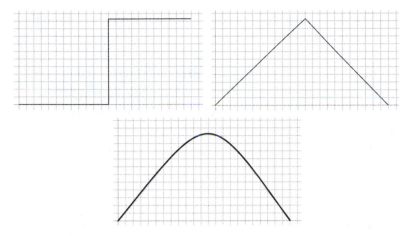

FIGURE 23.1   A curve with stepped, linear, and spline interpolation.

by transformation axis such as translation z or rotation y. During playback, that node travels from point to point based on the interpolation of that curve. The nature of the animation varies widely depending on this interpolation type and therefore the curve type selection is an imperative decision. Since curves are defined by points and interpolation, they are easily described, edited, and communicated through an animation system. Interpolation is the method of constructing new data points within the range of a discrete set of known data points (Figure 23.1). Thus, depending on the interpolation, the curve will construct a different path to follow from one point to the next.

Each point on a curve has an in-tangent and an out-tangent. The in- and out-tangents define how the curve enters and leaves the point and are usually depicted graphically as two vectors originating at the point. The angle of these tangents will modify the direction of the curve based on interpolation. Often times animators, when animating in the preferred pose-to-pose style, will plot out keyframes with a stepped, noninterpolated curve so that they never rely on interpolation from one pose to the next. Poses are the foundation of animation and define the key moments in the course of the action of the shot. They are critical not only for composition, but are also used to block out a shot and to work out the timing based on the time between poses. The out-tangent of points on a stepped curve are flat, thus the curve segment is horizontal so that the values change at keyframes without gradation or interpolation from one to the next. This lets them focus on the silhouette of the poses and to "spline out" the motion later. Splining is akin to what traditional animators refer to as in-betweening or "tweening." Splining out an animation curve involves changing the interpolation type to a spline-based interpolation and plotting out the in-betweens that occur. Specifying a spline tangent creates an animation curve that is smooth between the key before and the key after the selected key. The tangents of the curve are colinear as both are at the same angle. This ensures that the animation curve smoothly enters and exits the key. If tangents are not colinear, a discontinuity will occur not in position, but in velocity (the derivative of position) producing artificial looking motion. A side effect of this interpolation is that the position of the object may overshoot the position of the key in order to smooth in and out of its position. This is detrimental for characters where an interpolation such as this could cause the feet to pass through the ground plane or miss hand contact with an object. Many studios will implement their own brand of curve interpolation to satisfy the demands of animation. For example, the Catmull–Rom Spline is defined as a spline curve where the specified curve will pass through all the control points. Similarly, a clamped Bezier–Spline curve passes through the first and the last control points but the others are not actually passed through unless the previous or successive control point is tangent to it.

23.3 DRIVING VERSUS DRIVEN MOTION

The determination of a character in a scene can be defined by how the motion is carried through the action. One way to break this down is to make a distinction between driving and driven motion. Driving motion is where the character is the one applying weight to the objects or other characters in the scene, while driven animation is defined by the character being influenced by the other elements in the scene. This is not a scene description, but is worth considering when thinking about animation and the selection of controls used in a scene. Driving motion typically comes from the root joints, thus driving the child joints as it moves, as in FK. Driven motion, on the other hand, comes from the manipulation of end effectors and can often have a spline interpolated look about it. A character walking, particularly the motion of the arms, is usually animated with FK as this motion is driving motion originating from the shoulders. IK, in this regard, has the appearance of looking "floaty" or without weight, often requiring careful selection of the interpolation type, but more importantly, the timing of keys set on these goals.

23.4 CLIP-BASED ANIMATION

As is common for video games and for multicharacter animation systems used for crowds, animations are collected into clips which are stored in a library for reuse. A clip is a collection of curves describing a discrete character action stored on disk and triggered by the animation system as needed. It is the building block for a reusable library of motions. For example, generic motions such as clapping, waving, and cheering would be collected and maintained by a company making sports games. Small clips are often looped, such as walks and run cycles, whereas more specific motions must be blended into these loops. Loops are often used as a base to layer performance on top of. An animator might start with a loop, then spin off a variation of it either to create a new loop or a discrete nonlooping motion. A loop is simply a collection of discrete motions which start and end in the same pose. As mentioned previously, a walk cycle is one of the most common loops and is also an exercise that every animator does time and time again. Typically, these are done using local motions so that the character does not travel through space and thus remains in one spot. Translation is then applied to the character and the cycle is sped up or slowed down to match the rate of translation. This higher-level translation is important for characters walking along unlevel or uneven ground so that they can be constrained to the ground and walk as needed. In scenarios such as this, constraints can be built which orient the

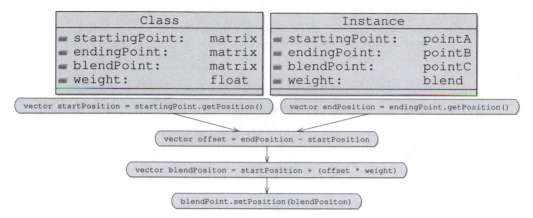

FIGURE 23.2   A class, data instance, and method for a position blending operator.

body and feet to a natural position relative to the angle of the ground. Constraints can also be developed for attaching a particular motion to an object such as a character climbing a ladder.

On top of cycles and constrained actions, the motion clip library can also have specific nonlooping actions that can be applied. These actions would be blended into the existing motion. Blending involves creating an overlapping transition from one action to another. It is carried out on a joint-by-joint or control-by-control basis but is usually cataloged and managed on a character element or whole character level. Creating a normalized blend creates a bridge between motions so that each component of the motion is interpolated smoothly from one state to another (Figure 23.2). Smooth curves are created between the blend points, and the blend value travels along those points to generate the transition. Interpolation is a simple process that cannot easily predict the interpenetration of character elements from pose to pose, like a character's arm passing through its body. Having body regions be "mutable," meaning that you can turn off clips on a per-region basis, allows for edits to be made to the animation of a subset of the character. For the most part, states to be blended must either be fixed regionally or clips must be carefully chosen so as to work smoothly together. At a lower level, poses can be stored as well. Poses are single-frame snapshots of a character. In some cases, an animator may need to go in and manually adjust the transition to be more natural or add an in-between pose or clip if the motions are different enough that they cannot be naturally interpolated between each other.

23.5 SOUND

One component of production that has been tied to animation since the early days is sound. Although tied to all facets of modern animation and game production, since the production of Disney's *Steamboat Willie* (1928), animators have made particularly good use of sound. No matter how motion is produced, sound is a critical compliment and some would argue an essential component to animation. Lip-sync, of course, cannot be undertaken until the voice actor's work is complete. Taken a step further, sound effects help to accentuate and punctuate

FIGURE 23.3 Audio waveform.

motion. Simple events such as a character walking benefit greatly from the synchronized sound of footsteps. In addition, sound helps to enhance the mood of the moment and the character-ization of the actor. By creating theme music for a character or a moment in that character's story, we immediately communicate a richer emotional experience than can be achieved solely by performance.

The waveform (Figure 23.3) of digital audio can also be used as a base-line animating factor for basic characters. For example, the amplitude of the track can be used to control the amount that the mouth is opened. Thus, the opening and closing of the mouth is controlled by the amplitude of the audio track. When the track is silent, the mouth is closed. This can almost be thought of as automatic viseme triggering, but on a more binary scale. An animator might cringe at such a technique, but in a pinch, for low-resolution characters, this can be a production life-saver and can often serve as the staring point for more elaborate lip-sync.

Sound has been used as a time-saver ever since it was available to animators. Even the masters at Warner-Brothers knew when to use the off-screen sound. The sound of a ruckus off-screen could stand-in for the complicated animated brawl that Bugs Bunny might have gotten himself into. Productions geared for the stage also use this convention frequently. How we might imagine that fight could be funnier than actually seeing it but the time-saving aspect of having sound in its place is still a means of streamlining production. When it comes to games, the sound design must be intricately planned, as sound must be programmed to coordinate with character event triggers in the game, like individual footsteps or various styles of jumps. These coordinated sounds, when coupled with a strong music track, greatly enhance the immersive experience and sell the believability of the character interacting with the environment around it.

23.6 REAL-TIME ENGINE CONCERNS

As mentioned earlier, animation for games consists of animation that is stored in a library which is called up by user action and looped, blended, and constrained as needed. Only in cut scenes are characters given specific animation performances to play out that exist outside of the motion library. As we will see in the following chapters, the creation of motion is most varied when it comes to game development as characters need to react to innumerable situations and almost infinite camera angles. This makes animation substantially more difficult for games than for films where motion only needs to work for one particular shot from one particular camera angle. Blending animation in real-time is also far more difficult as the system has little warning about user-triggered events. We will discuss the challenges for real-time animation in more depth in Chapter 29.

23.7 EXERCISE

This exercise is all about timing and gesture. With the character that you have been designing, plan out a single action for it to carry out. The action should be simple and accomplished in about 3 seconds of animation (72 frames at 24 frames-per-second [fps], and 90 frames at 30 fps). You will need drawing material to draw with.

1. With the action in mind, plot out the poses for that action on paper. First, create quick thumbnail drawings that capture the flow of action in a single line. Build up your drawings iteratively until the character is more clearly represented and you can visualize all articulations you will need to manipulate on the rig.

2. Scan your sequential drawings and bring them into a video editing program (something like iMovie is fine) and start timing out the spacing between images.

3. Did you draw enough frames to represent the motion over time? Do you need more? Add in-between images as needed until the rough sequence adequately represents the motion of the character.

4. Get feedback and critique on the posing and timing. Does it work? Does it read in the time allowed? These frames will help you start to layout the keys in your animation software.

5. From largest motion to smallest start blocking out the action.

6. Refer to your image sequence as often as needed. Have you captured the nuance of the drawings? Do you wish you drew more often? We all do.

7. Render out the sequence with rough settings to play it back at the frame rate you chose (24 and 30 fps). Compare it to the drawing sequence and be critical of the animation.

8. Maintain this review/fix feedback loop until satisfied.

FURTHER READING

Three critical resources for the animator or the technician who wants to know about animation (and they all should):

Hooks (Ed.) 2001. *Acting for Animators*. Heinemann Publishing. Portsmouth, NH, USA.

Thomas, F. and Johnston, O. 1981. *The Illusion of Life: Disney Animation*. First Hyperion.

Williams, R. 2001. *The Animator's Survival Kit*. Faber & Faber, London, United Kingdom.

Lasseter's paper that distills down the principles into modern terms for the animator working digitally:

Lasseter, J. 1987. Principles of traditional animation applied to 3D computer animation. *SIGGRAPH'87: Proceedings of the 14th Annual Conference on Computer Graphics and Interactive Techniques.* ACM Press, New York, NY.

And a great modern text from Angie Jones and Jamie Oliff:

Jones, A. and Oliff, J. 2006. *Thinking Animation: Bridging the Gap Between 2D and CG.* Course Technology PTR, Boston, MA.

CHAPTER 24

Interview: Stephen Candell, Lead Character Technical Director, DreamWorks Animation

24.1 BIO

In 2003, Stephen Candell started his career at Sony Pictures Imageworks through the Television Academy of Arts and Sciences' internship program. He was the Lead Facial Rigger on *Surf's Up*, *Cloudy with A Chance of Meatballs*, and Tim Burton's *Alice in Wonderland*. He joined Dreamworks in 2009 as a Character TD and recently completed his work on *How to Train Your Dragon 2* as the Lead Facial Rigger of Hiccup, Valka, Stoik, and Drago Bloodfist. His continuing focus has been on the redesign of the studio's facial animation control set and its underlying core technology for PREMO. He enjoys both the technical and artistic aspects of his career. In his spare time, Stephen enjoys robotics, puppet-making, and woodworking.

24.2 Q&A

Q: *The components of character technology are diverse and span the artistic and technical spectrum. How did you get your start in the industry? Based on where you see the field heading what experience/training do you recommend people have?*

A: I was one of a hundred applicants that applied for an animation internship at Sony Pictures Imageworks through the Academy of Television Arts and Sciences internship program. I wish I could say my raw talent was greater than that of the other applicants, but that definitely was not the case. I was the only applicant that was not an animator. I applied as a Character TD,

Stephen Candell

and my balance of technical and creative skills was what was in high demand at Sony Pictures Imageworks at the time. I felt very fortunate.

I used to, and still may, be of the opinion that students/individuals should focus their skills on a single aspect of the pipeline to appear more marketable. The theory being that the hiring practices of the studios is skewed towards specialist positions and not towards 3D generalists that possess an overall knowledge of the front and back end of the character pipeline. However, in recent years, for personal and professional reasons, I have felt the need to expand my skill set and and knowledge of the entire character pipeline. Like any artist, I hope to increase my creative control over the projects I work on.

Q: *Creating compelling digital characters is part art and part science. What is the greatest challenge you encounter on a daily basis? What aspect of character technology keeps you up thinking at night?*

A: As a creator of three-dimensional facial expressions, I am often faced with the indisputable fact that my work is restricted to live by the physical rules that are established in the initial design of the character. Cheekbones must remain somewhat firm like actual cheekbones. Most of the beautification of the character must require for-thought and planning and it can be difficult for my impatient mind to wait and see the final results until weeks or months down the road. For example: Forehead wrinkles must be planned and discussed months in advance by teams of people. "How many wrinkles does this characters forehead have?" "Are they tight?" "Are they symmetrical?" I am envious of the days where animators could add such details and also take liberties on the design by the sheer power of a pencil.

Q: *What are the ingredients for a successful digital character?*

A: The single ingredient for successful digital characters is: iterations—working and reworking the same character over and over, and refraining from "finaling" your work too early.

Early CG animated characters performance lacked in originality and depth because the computational speed limited the iterations artists could viably take in a production timeline.

Q: *While the industry is competitive, it is ultimately respectful of great work. Outside of the work you have been personally involved in the production of, what animated characters have you been impressed or inspired by? What is the historical high-bar?*

A: Rapunzel and Flynn Rider from *Tangled* are the current high-bar for CG animated characters. They deliver a broad, clean and well designed performance and capture a previously uncapturable level of appeal in CG animation. I left the theater very inspired and angry the day I first saw it.

Q: *Where do you see digital characters in 10 years? Where are animated characters for film and games heading?*

A: In regards to animator's workflow, I predict animators drawing their poses with digital pens that makes for a very organic classic-2D-animation experience. I predict quality levels to continually rise, due to the fact that computers will no longer require a reduction of iterations taken by artists. I imagine gaming and film technologies will collide and become much more similar over time.

CHAPTER 25

Motion Capture

MOTION CAPTURE, OFTEN CALLED "performance capture," is the recording of motion in the real world through various sampling means to drive the action of a digital character or representation of a performer. Historically, motion capture is descended from rotoscoping where the motion of an animated character is derived from the frame-by-frame tracing of pre-recorded video or film footage. Motion capture, often simply called mocap, and often jokingly referred to as "The Devil's Rotoscope," is the sensor-based capture of performance motion in 3D. Sensors range from magnetic markers to video and essentially try to keep track of the motion of the performer over time. Motion capture is used for animation production, video games, and real-time interactive installations. For a variety of reasons ranging from time constraints to budget to aesthetics, motion capture is a powerful and complex means of adding motion to digital characters.

25.1 MARKER-BASED MOTION CAPTURE

Motion capture is typically accomplished through the placement and tracking of physical markers attached to the performer's body (Figure 25.1). Many technologies have been developed to capture marker motion ranging from magnetic, optical, and electro-mechanical. Different markers are used for each of these methods. This is a thoroughly explored technique that is used to capture body and face motion with consistent results on human and nonhuman subjects. Marker-based motion capture takes place in a calibrated space embedded with sensors. Sensor technology has evolved over time, ranging from magnetic to infrared, but the concept remains the same. Markers are applied to the performer based on a specification for the system. Depending on the amount of resolution required, more or fewer markers are included in the set. Motion capture artists seek to resolve markers as consistently animated points over time. Marker positions are triangulated by the sensors in the space at a high frame rate. Occlusion of the sensors and environmental factors such as the composition of the floor or wall are all sources of noise that can affect the quality of the motion captured. For example, a magnetic

FIGURE 25.1 A motion capture performer. (Courtesy of Worleyworks, Brooklyn, NY.)

system in a room with metal beams under the floor may make it difficult to resolve critical foot-to-floor contact. Many systems are optical and therefore the visibility of the markers by the sensors is essential. The motion of the performer and their position and orientation in the space can occlude a marker and thus its motion needs to be reconstructed for those frames. The more cameras in the system, the more field of view is available to create the 3D volume and to minimize occlusions. Complex parts of the body often utilize special setups and equipment to capture the motion. For example, hands are often captured via gloves with sensors for measuring the bending of fingers in this area of complex motion. Regardless of the method, motion capture almost always requires processing and the issue of motion capture cleanup is covered in the following section.

There is a large amount of research going into capturing motion information from actors using markers through video in a noncalibrated space. For two of the *Pirates of the Caribbean* films, the team at Industrial Light and Magic successfully implemented on-set motion capture to record the facial and body performances of the actors portraying Davey Jones' crew. This system used patterned markers, a few video cameras rather than the array of fixed cameras flooding a volumetric space, and computer vision algorithms to track the points through space during regular filming. Once back at the studio, the data were analyzed, turned into skeleton data, drove the character rig, and the rendered digital character replaced the performer in the shot. This process was particularly effective for facial animation which can often be cumbersome and inhibit actor performance but in this case appeared to be lower impact to many shoots. This is an oversimplification of the process, but, as we will see later, there is research that takes some of these ideas even further and attempts to remove the markers altogether from the motion capture process.

The placement of the markers is an evolving area of debate and study, but basically markers are placed to capture the performer's skeletal motion, body proportions, and the orientation of the body segments as a whole. Markers are placed at points of articulation in a symmetrical

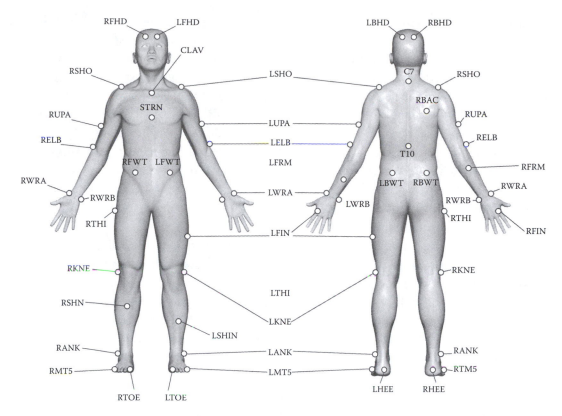

FIGURE 25.2 Sample motion capture marker placement.

layout. In addition, asymmetrical markers are placed to capture performer orientation or some-times just to distinguish between multiple performers (see Figure 25.2). Once captured, marker data are stored as a point cloud, representing each marker's motion over time for each take. This raw motion information usually needs to be cleaned up and then must be integrated into the production pipeline and fit to the rig.

25.2 MOTION CAPTURE DATA CLEANUP

The unfortunate downside of motion capture collection is the amount of noise that must be removed from the collected data in order to make the clip usable. Each type of motion capture apparatus is susceptible to noise and errors. These are as varied as physical marker drop-off, occluded markers, environmental interference, and camera or sensor calibration. Cleanup amounts to the reconstruction of a marker's path through space over time. Markers may have disappeared or become switched with other existing markers. Typically, motion capture systems record at 60 frames-per-second, whereas animation is produced at 30 or 24 frames-per-second. This difference allows the data to be down-sampled so that cleanup occurs at a lower resolution. This smoothing of the data will often help alleviate initial errors in the data.

The data, when it is looked at in its raw form, is a dense curve, keyed at each frame, for each marker in the three transformation dimensions. After a motion has been down-sampled, the curve shape can be reconstructed based on the sparser number of points. Once the motion is preserved and defined by the smaller number of points, an artist can adjust the curve as needed and apply functions to further smooth the curves or split and reattach curves created by markers that have become entangled or switched. When points disappear, and an interpolation does not work, then the point needs to be reconstructed. This is done based on the motion that exists, its relationship to other markers, and the eye of the artist cleaning up the data. Markers that flip positions with each other are endemic to systems where the markers are optical objects with no knowledge of a distinct identification number. This is common for reflective markers and less so for pulsed-LED (light-emitting diode) markers. Reflective marker identities are infered based on an initial setup of the marker set.

During fast occluding motion, marker identities may be switched with each other in the system. This is common for shoulders and hips. These regions are, of course, crucial for correct motion and difficult to untangle. Pulsed-LEDs each have a unique identification. This means that between times of occlusion where the marker becomes invisible to the system and is thus temporarily lost, there is no danger of markers reemerging and being tagged as another marker. When a marker is occluded, the position for that marker may be set to zero and the interpolation for these points has them appear to head back to the origin. This interpolation is usually performed by the motion capture data management software as the recording software will only store the raw data stream. The cleanup process can also involve editing together portions of different takes into one cleaner master take. However, because of the performative nature of motion capture, the overall position and action of the performer may be drastically different numerically between two takes of the same directed action. This may result in clips that cannot be blended together if an overall global transformation to adjust performers position or orientation cannot be manipulated. Motion capture clean-up can be a costly and time-consuming process, so every effort should be made to get the best capture possible using the most noise-free system and environment.

25.3 SKELETAL SOLVERS

Fitting the data collected to a skeleton is when you get to see the motion you have captured applied to your character. Algorithms are applied to reference skeletons to recover motion from the data set. There are a variety of solvers published, each with their own strengths and weaknesses. Many productions develop their own algorithms based on the needs of the pipeline or the production. The basic idea is that the external markers positioned on the performer need to be reconstructed to create the internal skeleton required for animation production. For example, the head is usually represented by at least four markers positioned at the front, back, and sides of the performer's head in 3D space. From these four points, the goal is to reconstruct the correct position and orientation of the single or multiple head joints over time. As the head is a rigid, nondeforming object, the reconstruction of this point is relatively straightforward. Complex regions like the shoulders are more difficult. As every region needs to resolve to form rigid chains of joints. Complicated regions like the clavicle and scapula, for example, are hard to collapse down to a single point. More often this region is defined as two or three points starting from the origin of the clavicle near the medial plane to another point at the top of the lateral end of the clavicle which connects to the upper arm/shoulder point. The spine can be solved as a curve drawn through the points recovered from the hips, mid-spine, and upper-back, or base of the neck. The rigid chain of joints is usually created in advance of the solving, so skeletal solvers have more to do with mapping motion from markers to joint elements. It can be assumed that the lengths between joints are fixed and rigid. As such, dependent markers will need to be moved (through rotation and some translation) to accommodate a "best-fit" solution for all the joints, but not scale the length between the joints in an unrealistic manner to achieve this fit.

Some solvers use an IK chain which solves quickly with stable results, but the high-frequency spacial and temporal information in human motion is often dampened or lost. Often the joint chains for knees, for example, exhibit a popping artifact as they are moved beyond full extension. Other solvers implement a nonlinear minimization algorithm to find the optimal position for all joints in the system as opposed to breaking the problem into individual chains as the IK solution does. The solution fits the skeleton to the markers by maintaining the relationship between the bones and markers defined during initialization. Solvers must deal with the rotation order, degrees of freedom, joint orientation, and preferred angle of bending for each solved joint. They also often include functions for filtering noise and for constraining the motion of joints to each other through the usual constraints related to translation, orientation, and aiming. Aiming is the process of orienting a single axis of a node at another point in space by defining the axis to aim and the up-vector which controls the orientation of the constrained object about the aim vector.

Whatever methods are used, the goal of skeleton solvers is to transform the motion of the markers into the motion of the expected joint structure. This joint structure is defined early in the production and is likely the standard for the studio working with the data. Constraints can be applied to limit the motion of joints within certain ranges or areas. For example, the notion of the floor is often enforced at this point so that joints are limited to moving below the zero unit in the up/down direction (usually y). The "floor" then impacts the other nodes affected by the length-preserving function and moves everything to a reasonable place with regard to the floor. When joints are transformed by non-motion-related solving such as collisions, they often introduce other problems due to the fact that these points do not have a means to represent the volume of the character. As a result, collision response will often put the character into unnatural poses. Some solvers implement rigid-body dynamics where joints can have surfaces parented to them to represent the volumes of the body. Then, as they are solved, collisions can help keep joints from getting too close. This helps the issues inherent with constraining the motion, but of course, increases the time required to solve a single take of motion capture performance. There are often many takes which must be compared before the best one, or part thereof, is selected for production.

25.4 PIPELINES FOR MOTION CAPTURE

While video games have been using motion capture on a much larger and more common scale, films are increasingly incorporating it as a source of character animation. Some of the most successful film animations are those which layer keyframe animation on top of motion capture. The pipeline for motion capture requires passing the data through whatever cleanup is needed, then mapping it to the rig. The motion can either drive the model directly, replacing the rigging process, or more effectively can be an input to the rigging solution as either an alternate rig or an input on the existing controllers. This latter, blended solution is the ideal. A blended rig has input for dense motion capture data and has the ability to layer animator-created performance on top of, or in lieu of, the motion for regions or the whole character at different intervals. The selection of motion for a region should be weighted between the motion capture data and the animation data, allowing an animator to augment, say, 40% of the motion capture for the arm for a sequence of 40 frames and 100% of the animation for 60 frames. This allows the motion capture to act as a base that can be added to by the animator to make the shot work. The setup can be two parallel hierarchies, one for animation and one for motion capture, that are blended into a third hierarchy responsible for deformations. It can be a set of hierarchical nodes that exist in the setup so each node has an input for animation and motion capture data (Figure 25.3).

From an asset management perspective, motion capture data is usually large, requiring a sizable amount of storage as well as the ability to access it quickly. The data should be accessed via a database through a front-end that has descriptive information about the shot and each take, possibly even a low-resolution clip of the motion. Motion capture is accessed at the clip level and, like clip-based animation, can be blended and edited to suit the needs of the shot. The power of an organizational system like this is that animators have the ability to pick and choose

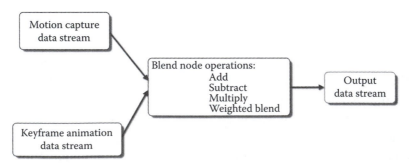

FIGURE 25.3 Blended input on a node.

animation and motion capture as needed. When dealing with many characters on a production, it is imperative to develop conventions that allow for motion to be shared across similar characters. This requires that the rig architecture and naming conventions be compatible. As an example, for humanoid characters you will want to ensure the ability to take a motion capture clip of a performer running then offset it, edit it, and repurpose it to a crowd of characters.

The decision-making tree for choosing motion capture clips is built into gameplay architecture for video games. As a character is directed to move in different directions, perform specific actions, or encounter triggers in the environment, the necessary motion capture clip can be called and performed by the rig. So if a character needs to (1) run to the left, (2) stop, and then (3) lean over to pick something up, each of those discrete actions is pulled from the library and blended to create a reasonable chain of events. The blending between these actions is done on-the-fly and is generally just an overlapping interpolation from the ending state of one action to the beginning state of another.

25.5 MOTION RETARGETING

Motion capture data in its raw form is completely specific to the performer that it was captured from. A performer often does not match the proportions of the character they are portraying in the production. This is the case when the motion collected must be remapped to a control set with different proportions and, less ideally, different joint configurations than it was collected to represent. Scale is a major factor for retargeting both for the overall character and individual limb proportions. Characters might need to have slightly longer arm proportions or the overall scale of a human performer might need to be mapped to a creature with very nonhuman proportions. Because motion capture data are stored as an animated point cloud, once the relationships between markers are established and the skeleton is built, other information can be computed from the data. Most importantly, when rigid chains are created between the joints, their motion can be computed as rotations. These rotations are more portable to characters of other proportions, as rotations can be applied to nodes regardless of position or scale. Constraints can be utilized to proceduralize the control of the data. For example, the feet need to be constrained to the floor when the character makes contact with it, so position-based code can be implemented that will not let the foot slip below the ground plane. If a cycle of motion is captured of a person clapping their hands, one can imagine that the relationship between the hands is dependent of the scale of the character and the length of the arms. This is a case where retargeting is used to make sure that every character in a crowd looks like their hands are making contact no matter the proportion changes applied to create variation amongst individuals. Studios and animation systems have techniques for remapping motion to the required proportions and specifications for the character needed in production.

Motion retargeting is akin to comparative kinematics where biologists will compare the proportions of animal limb lengths, joint orientations, and scale to compare locomotive strategies and adaptations. By exploring the mechanical properties of motion of living animals, inferences can be made about extinct species. For example, because of the inherent morphological similarities between a *Tyrannosaurus rex* and modern terrestrial birds like chickens and turkeys, researchers have made comparisons between them and even tried to remap motion captured turkey locomotion to come up with hypothetical kinematic models of the extinct carnivore. Dr. John Hutchinson of the University of London's Royal Veterinary College captures the motion of extant species such as elephants and other large animals and compares it to information collected from dinosaur anatomy [26]. Of course, we do not have the benefit of using motion capture on dinosaurs but this comparison is done to gage what generalities about large animal stance and gait emerge from comparing these different lineages. Problems with motion retargeting, the transforming of one creature's proportions to those of another, and anatomy prevent a transfer of joint angles from elephants to dinosaurs but the connections gleaned from traditional and emerging biomechanical analysis tools have shed an innovative light on the subject.

25.6 MARKER-LESS MOTION CAPTURE

The limitations of marker-based motion capture and the rise of computer vision and image-based modeling have opened the door for marker-less image-based motion capture. The idea behind marker-less motion capture is that the performer can just walk into the calibrated stage and with little to no proportion registration, their motion can be captured in real time. "Stage™" by Organic Motion™ is an innovative example of this (Figure 25.4). Organic Motion's technique synthesizes the imagery from cameras positioned on the same object from multiple views. These views are compared and incorporated into data which can be used like traditional motion capture data or for volume filling operations. Behind the scenes of such systems is usually a jointed character model which the system fits into the volumes captures by the cameras on each frame. Once the data is collected, it then works just like standard motion capture and can be integrated into the production pipeline identically. The data may be different down the line, as video-based systems have the potential of capturing surfaces with lighting and textures.

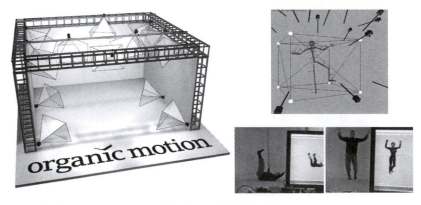

FIGURE 25.4 Markerless motion capture by Organic Motion™.

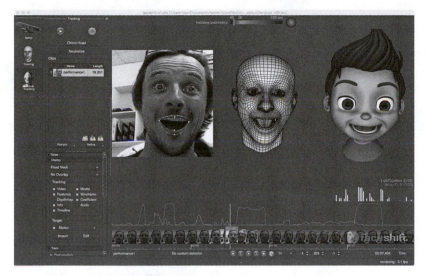

FIGURE 25.5 Faceshift Studio™ capture session.

Companies such as Faceshift use off-the-shelf stereoscopic cameras to analyze the face motions of an actor and capture a mixture of expressions, head orientation, and gaze that are then used to animate virtual characters for use in movie or game production (Figure 25.5). The software analyzes the face motions of an actor and describes them as a mixture of basic expressions. This information is then used to animate virtual characters for use in movie or game production (Figure 25.6). The avatar is created using training expressions and the more training that is done the more stable and accurate the results are. Because it uses video and real

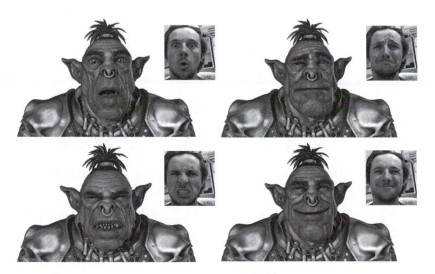

FIGURE 25.6 Facial expressions on an avatar using Faceshift.

3D data as an input, the quality has the potential to be better and potentially more robust than video-only or marker-tracking solutions.

With these markerless systems, motion capture can be brought into the public arena for sports, entertainment, and medical applications for the general public, thanks to the minimal setup and performer calibration required. Applications such as these are very good for capturing the larger motions of the body or face and over time will get better at capturing the more subtle, smaller emotions that are key to a performance. These emerging systems are the future of motion capture and will change the paradigm that we work with today.

25.7 EXERCISE

This exercise is intended to expose you to motion capture data. To start, you will need access to a sample motion capture file. A good source of this data is Carnegie Mellon University's Motion Capture Database (http://mocap.cs.cmu.edu). As motion capture data come in a variety of formats, you will need to find the one most convenient for you to open in your animation software of choice. Autodesk's MotionBuilder is quickly becoming the motion capture workhorse in production.

1. Load the motion capture file into your animation software.

2. Select a single node and look at the translation animation curve associated with it. Notice how dense it is.

3. Attach primitive objects or joints and a simple polygonal mesh to the data points.

4. Use your application's curve editing tools to simplify the curve. Notice how the highfrequency noise disappears as you sparse the curve.

5. Create a simple rig that allows you to replace and/or offset the movement provided by the motion capture for one appendage. This can be done as simply as creating a duplicate arm that rides along with (or hierarchically below) the motion capture arm.

6. Attempt to revise the action of that one appendage.

FURTHER READING

Two good resources for working with motion capture in production:

Liverman, M. 2004. *The Animator's Motion Capture Guide: Organizing, Managing, and Editing*. Charles River Media, Inc., Rockland, MA, USA.

Menache, A. 1999. *Understanding Motion Capture for Computer Animation and Video Games*. Morgan Kaufmann Publishers Inc., San Francisco, CA, USA.

CHAPTER 26

Interview: Brad Clark, Character Technical Director, Consultant

26.1 BIO

Brad Clark has worked on a wide range of projects, from modeling and rigging for television and video games to editing motion capture for Gollum in *The Lord of the Rings: The Two Towers*, while at Weta Digital. His career has taken him around the globe: from Florida to the Philippines, and from Texas to New Zealand. Brad taught animation, character design, and setup classes at Full Sail, trained 2D animators on Softimage in Manila, and headed up internal training on motion capture, character rigging, and scripting for artists while with Acclaim Studios, Austin. During his time at Acclaim, Brad designed an automated scripted character rigging and weapon system with Steev Kelly for *The Red Star* game and helped create a universal animation pipeline for the studio. A previous two-time Autodesk Master Class instructor including coauthoring with Chad Moore, the only class dedicated to custom character rigging with MotionBuilder—The Character Animator Toolkit for MotionBuilder and presented at the Hacking MotionBuilder the GDC 2014 Technical Artist Bootcamp. Brad has twice been a workshop instructor at Conceptart.org and was the lead author of *Inspired 3D Advanced Rigging and Deformations* with John Hood and Joe Harkins. Brad has provided custom training and consulting for EA, Bungie, Disney Junction Point Studios and Reel FX and more on Motionbuilder, Maya, and 3ds Max. During his work with Disney, Brad designed and built the Epic Mickey character rig and evaluated and helped guide the engine animation requirements needed to meet the extreme demands of the design. Brad is currently a Character Art and Technology Consultant actively working with several

Brad Clark, Character Technical Director, Consultant

next-generation rigging and animation software projects, while mentoring and helping run Rigging Dojo.

26.2 Q&A

Q: *The components of character technology are diverse and span the artistic and technical spectrum. How did you get your start in the industry? Based on where you see the field heading what experience/training do you recommend people have?*

A: I started out going to school for film in 1995. When I walked into the SGI lab and saw the animation and media students working I knew I needed to change majors. I was hooked! Like many, when I was younger watching a making-of *Star Wars* and reading articles on Glen Keane working on animation at Disney mixed with my love of art growing up, I had always wanted to do something in animation. Unfortunately, I grew up on ranches far from any source of really learning about animation so I thought I had to be able to draw final frames . . . and I kind of just put the thought of ever doing it to the side. In high school, I learned more but, with lack of internet resources that exist now, I still didn't see how to make that happen so I focused on film and technical theater production—learning lighting, sound design, staging, and set construction. I really enjoyed that so that was where I started my journey.

I started learning on Alias Power Animator and in order to animate, you had to rig. My instructors at the time put us into groups and I found rigging made sense and so I set up the characters for our group animation project. This would later become a pattern: wanted to animate—had to rig—started rigging, enjoyed that, started to animate then want to tweak the rig—then someone saw that I could rig and would ask me to rig something for them, loop. Once people know you can deal with technical work, suddenly everyone comes to you to do technical work, fix problems, design things, evaluate software, test tools, make tools . . . until one day you realize you haven't had time to animate in a long time and you are ok with that.

So, that was my start. There are many ways to become a technical artist and I found my way in but almost every character technical director I know has had their own unique path to get into rigging, though many have had the same epiphany of "I started rigging to animate something, then found it more exciting to rig than to animate."

Over the past 10 years the industry, audience expectations, computer power, and very talented developers have really pushed what is possible to create now, something that wasn't even a wild dream when I started. This means for a character TD to be able to get started and do well they have to have more than just technical talent and more than just artistic talent. The more well rounded as a human that they are the more they can bring to the table. Knowing how to troubleshoot and learn and deal with production problems that are never so neat as a step-by-step tutorial is very important. Thankfully there are many resources both free and paid beyond college that a character TD can learn from: books, videos, private mentoring, full online schools dedicated to teaching character TDs. This is a double-edged sword though because much like learning anything new alone, people don't know what they don't know. I see lots of students come to us at Rigging Dojo to get training and they list all the other previous training they have learned from and unfortunately most of it doesn't help prepare them to understand why something is done or how to deal with production problems and situations.

So now there are lots of resources and lots of skilled people but like animation, the competition is that much more prepared and it is harder to stand out. This comes back then to how well rounded are you as an artist or a programer first then how well can you showcase your skill at understanding how to speak to animators, and how to build tools and rigs that are stable through time, not just in a T pose. Communication with artists, understanding art, anatomy, having a trained eye is just as important as knowing how to write a C++ plugin and being able to build a rig. Showing an understanding of the rest of the pipeline, having animated, having had to do lighting or mocap or modeling creates a TD that is always in demand because they get the job done, they make animation happy and they keep the project on time and most importantly within the budget. Specializing early and deep with out the rest of the wider education runs the risk of being a early mistake that you have to deal with at some point.

Q: *Creating compelling digital characters is part art and part science. What is the greatest challenge you encounter on a daily basis? What aspect of character technology keeps you up thinking at night?*

A: Fast—how to make things fast and easier to use while still hitting all the complex requirements of the art style, animator requests, time constraints and the biggest is expectations.

Second is stable software for character animation and rigging. Of all the disciplines working to create a great digital character, rigging and to some extent animation is still stuck in 1995 dark ages of old IK solvers, hacks, tricks and tools that are aging out. Where is our rigging ZBrush? Where are the rigging tool equivalent of HDR physical based realtime lighting and shading environments? Fabric engine is the closest thing but it isn't ubiquitous yet and we are several project cycles away from the industry upgrade even to the current versions of the existing software.

What keeps me up at night is dealing with the fact that rigging has been left as good enough, we as character TDs were good at making workarounds and hacking together systems that got the work done we held back our own progress.

For me, I work in both training and remote freelancing for many clients so I don't get the same options and ability to work with a team of developers for months on end to create a new tech like an in-house studio TD. I have to take existing assets, pipelines, tool choices and work with outsource managers that may or may not be technical and make it work. Rigging and technical arts are equivalent to 2D principles of animation of solid drawing, appeal, and squash and stretch with a bit of the pencil thrown in and without a good rig we know there would be no animation to watch. I am ready for rigging to catch up to the modeling side of things and have a toolset for rigging that is as modern and powerful as Zbrush.

Q: *What are the ingredients for a successful digital character?*

A: Making a character successful takes the right mix of all the disciplines of art from plausibility of design, anatomy to rigging, animation, and texturing. One of the foundations for getting a character right through has to be in where the joints are placed and how that is translated to the final deformations of the character. Often I can feel or when it is really bad, see, motion happening from the wrong place in a character. My view is anatomy and joint location must be accurate first so that once the skeleton is animated the movement will feel correct. This is also extremely important when working with motion capture. For example, making sure the captured motion first looks right on a matching digital double of the capture subject, then mapping that motion onto the final digital character creates a much better result. I think most recently Digital Domain used a similar idea on the face capture for the fairy godmother in *Maleficent*. Students and more inexperienced character TDs miss the understanding of anatomy beyond just muscle placement, they haven't looked at anatomy in motion, the movement of pivots over time. I love the concept at Pixar on *Cars*, "truth to materials" was the mandate that the characters couldn't deform or animate in a way that what they were made out of couldn't do. This is another area where you can see the detail or attention missed in many demo reels, a metal plate or a leather belt deforming an odd way and it pulls me out of the suspension of disbelief. While we are mostly talking about the creation of the digital character, the final part of this comes into play with animation. The animation based on real world timing and physics, Sony Pictures Imageworks got this right on *The Amazing Spider-Man 2*, where they created a nice gravity tool to help animators understand how the center of gravity of Spider-Man should move respecting gravity and inertia of the web swings. We had tools in the motion edit department for doing similar things for helping with editing captured characters falling off of tall ladders or buildings.

Q: *While the industry is competitive, it is ultimately respectful of great work. Outside of the work you have been personally involved in the production of, what animated characters have you been impressed or inspired by? What is the historical high-bar?*

A: From an animation standpoint what I enjoyed most as a kid was Chuck Jones and the wild Warner Brothers cartoons and for me personally films like *Hotel Transylvania* and *Cloudy with a Chance of Meatballs* hit that sweet spot of classic animation, super flexible cartoony characters and rigs.

I also have been a fan of Glen Keane since I learned what an "animator" was. His work *Tangled* has been the most successful of taking classic Disney animation and forcing the rigs, the tools and the animators to push beyond the limits of what was acceptable and good at the time in 99% of CG animated films. It showed how far away that was from where it could be with a strong artistic force driving it.

VFX wise, Smaug created by WETA Digital for *The Hobbit: The Desolation of Smaug* and the latest Incredible Hulk character in *The Avengers* are just awe inspiring for the detail, believability and consistency of that quality, being so high, I don't know how they could have done it better.

Games characters are harder due to legacy issues and game play. While many characters look better and the deformations and rigging are better, game play issues around animation and a disconnect between game design and art still feels like it shows up often. That said, I think the biggest inspiration right now in games is the animation technical work that Wolfire Games (David Rosen at Wolfire) is working on and showing on his twitter feed. I saw his work presented at GDC and the collective gasp, mine included of what he showed off was amazing. Rigging wise *Ryse: Son of Rome*, I think was top notch and there are several other games that push the limits of the hardware visually in different ways from EA, Ubisoft, Insomniac, and Epic. It is always inspiring to see great feeling characters rigged up within extreme limits that game engines and design create for artists to work in but there is still much room for improvement going back to the believability of characters once they start moving.

I feel like the historical high-bar moves every month with another movie release but I think the benchmark that set a new standard and pushed everyone else was the work on Gollum in *The Lord of the Rings* trilogy and improved even more for *The Hobbit*. There have been other characters that are more complex or more difficult to manage, like the Davey Jones from ILM or even the apes in *Dawn of the Planet of the Apes*. The reason I single out the Gollum work is because of the characters, I feel he is the closet to a human feeling character that has had some incredible range of emotion and close up, long detailed shots right along side live actors and held up. He also set in motion the advancement of FACS, onset motion capture, more and more complex face work that brought us all the amazing work that came after the success of Gollum.

Q: *Where do you see digital characters in 10 years? Where are animated characters for film and games heading?*

A: Ten years in the future is always dangerous to try and predict even one year away let alone 10. If we look back from now 10 years to see if there are hints that visual FX would be this far along, holding their own as photo real along side human actors we can see the signs that amazing talented teams were getting things right and laying the foundation but wasn't anywhere close to what has hit now. Animation was still feeling floaty and inconsistent and characters, they looked amazing but still didn't integrate as well as they could have. The big change that happened I feel is the speed of iteration. Software got faster, more parts of what makes a CG character feel believable were figured out (lighting, grime, shaders, high detail geometry, physical based rendering . . . the list goes on).

What was happening 10 years ago was the best that was possible with the time available. Games and animated films and VFX blockbusters all have improved to the point that more often than not, now and I will risk a "in 10 years" from now, the problems for character artists and everyone in the pipeline for that matter, won't be in figuring out if or how it can be done, instead it will be the "Paradox of Choice" where decision making and self imposed constraint will be required. Even now, the fantasy that everything is possible and changeable down the end as the movie gets streamed to the theater and shows as bad choices the audience can feel. This also seems to be the driving force putting studios and game houses out of business . . . lack of clear decision making forced by technology limits. The illusion of "computers do it" and it is easy to change something forever is going to be beyond terrible. Art needs constraints and 10 years from now fur, skin, muscle, water, lighting, rigs will all be so common and standard near final-render quality at 60FPS in view, what you see is what you get in HD, 3D interactive immersive creative software to do what WETA and ILM and IMAGEWORKS are doing now with hundreds of people will be directly achievable by handfuls of people and a director with a clear vision and guts to stick with it.

The game characters keep catching up, eventually the animation systems and all the other details will be able to be done for a few games but time, budgets, team size, and legacy pipelines, I think will continue to hold games back from what they could really do. Film digital characters on the other hand have, as I mentioned, improved immensely with every new film. While true digital human actors have yet to fully conquer the creepy feeling of unease that they need to be truly convincing, with a few more years of improvements, I have no doubt they will get past that. We will have digital humans that feel and look and move and act as if they were a live actor being filmed. This improvement will not, of course, make the script better or cover up poor choices from the director, instead it will magnify the problems of choice for all but a few the really good directors.

CHAPTER 27

Procedural Animation

P ROCEDURAL ANIMATION IS THE application of algorithms to create or modify motion. Examples range from the motion of a simulated character tail to a hair system where the curves react to the character motion and forces applied to them, to a leg system that walks on its own avoiding obstacles and traversing uneven terrain. These algorithms can be intelligent manipulation of the character based on rules and constraints or the implementation of a physics engine to drive the character based on simulated forces in relation to the environment it exists in. The combination of intelligence and physics is the direction that game engines and intelligent animation systems are headed. By combining smart procedural motion with the weight and reality created by a physics engine, highy believable results can be achieved for large groups of characters.

27.1 FUNCTIONS TO CONTROL MOVEMENT

The use of mathematical functions for controlling the motion of objects is a typical means of controlling movement. This method uses mathematical (e.g., trigonometric) functions to inform the motion of objects based on the position or orientation of other objects. Many animation systems refer to this type of code as "expressions." When simple functions are used, this motion has a tendency to look mechanical which is why expression-based motion is very suitable for inorganic motion. With a little work, however, function-based motion can complement keyframed curves by adding secondary motion to objects that are already animated. Elements such as the tail of a dog, the trunk of an elephant, the feather in a cap, or even the tentacles of an octopus can be controlled through procedural functions. Expressions can be as simple as a direct relationship between multiple objects with an offset so that as, for example, a character's hips rotate, its tail moves in the opposite direction as counter motion. Sinusoidal motion can be attached to objects so that they oscillate along a curve function (Figure 27.1). These wave functions are useful as they are inherently arcing curves that easily add appealing

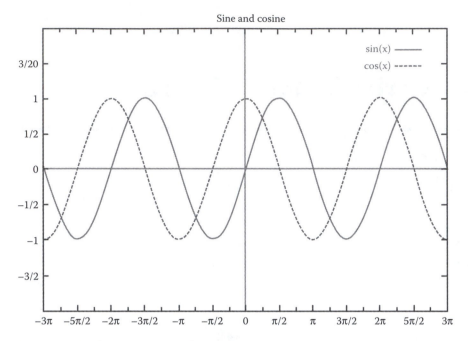

FIGURE 27.1 A graph of sine and cosine functions.

visual motion to objects. When described as a function of time (t):

$$y(t) = A \cdot \sin(wt + \theta)$$

where A is the amplitude, w the radians per second, and θ the phase.

Basic procedural animation in games typically involves head and eye tracking to allow characters to look at the appropriate object in the scene and IK for hands and feet to be placed in the right position based on goals.

27.2 SCRIPTED ANIMATION AND PROCEDURAL ACTORS

Taken a step further, using expression-based transformations, entire motions can be procedurally scripted and incorporated into the animation system. These discrete motions can be built up modularly so that motion elements can be moved from character to character and mixed and matched as needed or combined with function-based motion. The movement can also be animated cycles that are called upon at the right moment from a database of actions which are then strung together by an animator or by a procedural system. With scripted motion, we delve into the notion that, in these scenarios, the animator acts like a director of a live-action film telling characters how to act out a series of motions. "Walk into the room, drop your bag on the floor, and open the window." The individual scripted motions can be thought of as actions in a database which have specific in and out points, but that must be blended into each other. This blending is a difficult prospect, as the motions on each end of the blend may be drastically different from each other. Situations such as this may require hand-animated blend segments in order to look correct.

Character motion is difficult to distill down to discrete procedural motion, but researchers such as Dr. Ken Perlin at New York University are leading the way in the creation of fully procedural characters. By offsetting and blending trigonometric curve functions, such as sine and cosine, with noise, Dr. Perlin has been able to achieve body and facial motion which is both pleasing to view and completely interactive. This work can be seen in the software "Actor Machine" that Dr. Perlin is helping to develop. On the simplest level, a character controlled by the "Actor Machine" software can be directed to walk across a room and everything regarding the animation is taken care of. The feet hit their marks on the floor based on the pace of the walk and the arms, and torso move appropriately based on some basic tunable parameters. The user, who in this case is acting like the director of the shot, has access to many types of "emotional dials" that they might choose to use. For example, they could turn up or down how tired, sad, happy, or arrogant a character is and all the combinations in between. Similarly, the user can direct the level and type of emotional relationships in a scene between the characters such as their respective mutual interest, love, or fear of each other. Moods and relationships can be changed over time within a scene to reflect the "inner thoughts" of the digital actors. As emotional curves, these high-level directives can affect a suite of underlying parameters over time (Figure 27.2).

These directions would affect the body language, glancing motions, hand gestures, facial expressions, or other appropriate expressions which physically describe the directions conveyed. Unlike blended animation, all motion is procedurally generated, so the engine never produces the repetitiveness seen in game engines that call the same mocap clips over and over. The small amount of performance randomness gives the character more of a sense of being alive, in that the same action will be performed differently every time. Social interactions, meaning expressive interactions between two or more characters, are a challenge to procedural actors as characters need to have a sense of history with their social partner and also must be able to see into the future of the scene to avoid any emotional latency that may arise from actions needing to be processed by the counterpart. Many of these issues are solved by the notion of a procedural actor script. Like a live actor's script, a procedural actor's script will have their

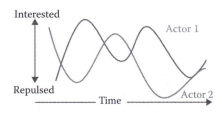

Emotive "Dial" over performance

FIGURE 27.2 Emotional curves for a procedural system by ActorMachine™.

dialog and information about their emotional state and the setting in which the scenario occurs. A procedural actor's script might contain more detailed information about a character's relationship to the other characters in the scene. These details would set the appropriate attributes, allowing the script to be baked into the inner workings of that character. The following actions for that character would build upon those settings and modify them as needed.

The emotions applied to the character act like surface shaders. Shaders in computer graphics rendering are programs that define the visual properties of a surface with regard to color, texture, how light reacts to it, and how it appears to the camera and ultimately the renderer. Shaders have inputs and outputs to connect them to the results of other operations and can be layered together to create more visually complex results. In the same way, emotional shaders can be strung together and layered atop each other to replicate complex behaviors and emotional states. One can imagine a situation where a character is scared, but putting on a brave face, as a scenario where you would apply a "scared" shader with a layer of "bravery" with partial opacity on top of it. In this case, the animation input has a semantic quality with regard to mood, emotion, and intent that is resolved by the procedural animation subsystem. For example, the game's AI system and/or game cinematographers will be able to have the engine communicate to the emotion-based system with tokens like "set tired to 80%" and the actor engine will be translated into an appropriate animation. This is as opposed to telling it which exact clips to blend in.

The ActorMachine™ software (Figure 27.3) is an evolution of the "Improv" project that Dr. Perlin helped develop in the late 1990s [27]. "Improv" dealt with the understanding and

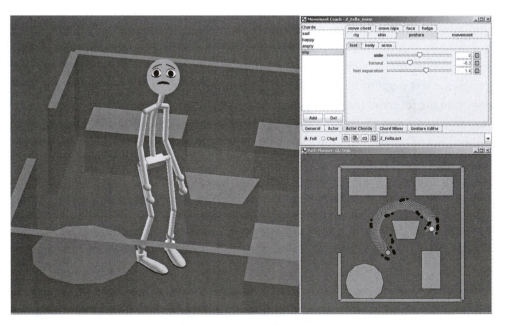

FIGURE 27.3 A prototype procedural character engine by ActorMachine™.

recreation of motion from the perspective of algorithmic functions. Part of this is the analysis of motion created by animators and through motion capture. Once these performances are captured, the expression and animation curves associated with the performance are analyzed in an attempt to distill them down into procedures. This work attempts to convert motion into procedural functions that can be reused by the character or mapped to others. In many ways, the data produced by procedural systems looks remarkably like motion capture as it ends up being absolute matrix positions for character nodes per-frame. As such, the integration of motion capture data into a procedural system is another way to teach a digital character how to move. The "proceduralization" or replacement of motion capture data with procedural motion, is also a form of compression. As stated in the motion capture section, the data captured and needed to be maintained is voluminous. Once established, the amount of data required to create a procedural performance is negligible as it is only animated parameters to a system and not the raw per-control, per-frame positions that swells mocap data. This paradigm shifting mode of motion production is like mocap-in-a-box and stands to be a valuable tool for previsualization, background characters for film, and machinima, to name some initial applications.

27.3 USING PHYSICS TO CONTROL MOVEMENT

Rigid body or "ragdoll" physics is being increasingly implemented for both film and game characters and is usually combined with motion capture data. The combination of these techniques requires the use of simulation to solve a scenario. Rigid bodies are defined as nondeforming objects whose position is defined by linear and angular vectors representing position and orientation. The rigid body is ascribed a mass value as a scalar and its angular mass, or moment of inertia, is calculated by its size. The moment of inertia of an object about a given axis describes how difficult it is to rotate about that axis. A simulation is an imitation of a real event, system state, or evolving process and involves the algorithmic representation of the characteristics or behaviors of physical or abstract systems. Objects in a simulated scenario may start as animated entities or exist as purely simulated entities. The motion of animated objects is controlled by keyframes or motion capture data, whereas the simulated objects depend on the representation of physical processes, to drive motion such as forces and collisions in the environment. All of this needs to be controlled by a physical dynamics engine that calculates the position of each of the elements in the character on a per-frame basis with regard to the forces in the world and the collision objects in the environment. As the object is affected by the forces in the world and reacts to collisions, its linear and angular velocity and acceleration are calculated and used to place the object from frame to frame. Velocity is the rate of change of position defined by speed and direction from frame to frame and acceleration is the rate of change of velocity.

For example, a character can be defined and then attached to a piece of motion capture data to have it walk then run. A low obstacle can be placed in the middle of its running path. Depending on the shape and size of that object, the character will collide with it as the chain of rigid objects that connect to match the proportions of a human. Limits and constraints can be placed on all the character joints so that the impact and subsequent reaction of the character will happen within the limits of human motion. These rotational limits are a range of values with the extremes softened so that high-velocity motion can push a joint towards extreme motion, but be dampened as it reaches the extreme limits. Simulated characters need to be represented by polygonal surfaces which are representative of the character volume so that collisions and interactions with objects in the world can be calculated with the lowest amount of surface resolution possible. These surfaces also have mass properties so that forces such as gravity produce predictable results. Characters in dynamic systems are never solved in their highest resolution state, so characters in these systems are representations of the production character. Once the system has solved the position of all the rigid links from frame to frame, this data can be written to disk and stored as a cache of the simulation. This acts like dense keyframes for the character preserving the results of the simulation, but now playable in real time without the need to solve it again. Now that the simulated motion is stored as essentially animation data, characters can be blended into or out of existing animation as needed as described previously (Figure 23.2). This combination of keyframed animation, motion capture, and procedural motion allows an animator to mix and match motion sources to create the final performance in that shot.

27.4 BEHAVIORAL ANIMATION

Behavioral animation is a form of procedural animation whereby an autonomous character determines its own actions based on a set of rules. As an example, flocking is one of the most widely explored behavioral animation systems. In this system, a layer of rules is added on top of a group of agents which gives them a framework with which to behave in relation to one another. Craig Reynolds [14] described flocking with regard to computer graphics by outlining the behaviors, on what he called "boids," that needed to be implemented to recreate the phenomenon. The basic flocking model consists of three simple steering behaviors to describe how an individual member of the flock should maneuver based on the positions and velocities of its flock neighbors:

1. Separation: Steer to avoid crowding local flockmates.

2. Alignment: Steer toward the average heading of local flockmates.

3. Cohesion: Steer to move toward the average position of local flockmates.

This model of simple rules that, when combined, create the possibility for emergent behavior is the foundation for behavioral animation. Emergence is the scenario where complex global behavior arises from the interaction of simple local rules. On top of this, an individual's understanding of the world around them through means of virtual sensing opens up even more complex behavior. Virtual sensing is the application of senses, such as sight, proprioception (the sense of where ones limbs are in space), or even bounding-box-based, positional collision detection to nodes in a scene. Once enabled with these abilities, they can avoid other characters and objects in their environment. Similarly, action-on objects are functions used to perform a specific action upon a certain object. This could be actions related to what a character is to do when it encounters a door. As characters interact within complex scenes and navigate within a dynamic environment, the requirements for collision detection, collision response, and on-the-fly decision-making increase. Once obstacles are included in a scene, characters must be able to anticipate their path in order to avoid them. This notion of path-finding, sometimes referred to as path-planning, is critical to crowd simulation which will be introduced subsequently.

Historically, algorithms such as A* (pronounced A-star) have been the default path-finding implementation (Figure 27.4). A* is a best-first graph search algorithm that finds the most economical path from an initial position to a goal node. Best-first search algorithms traverse a graph of choices by exploring the most promising node chosen according to a defined rule.

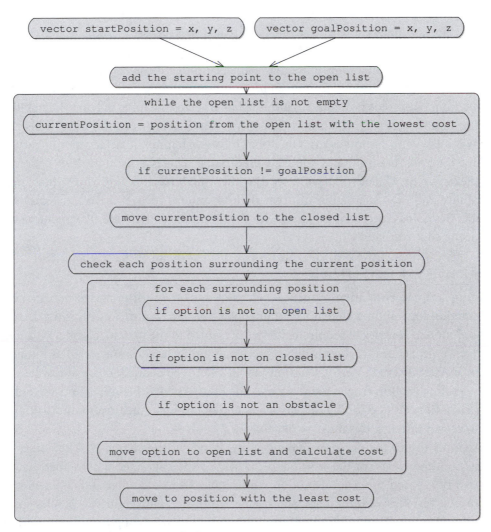

FIGURE 27.4 A method for A* path-finding.

A* iteratively searches all possible routes leading from the starting point until it finds the shortest path to a goal. Like all informed search algorithms, it searches first the routes that appear to be most likely to lead towards the goal. There are usually secondary functions that deal with terrain constraining and obstacle avoidance but these too can be incorporated into A*. The cost of each tile in a two-dimensional grid is calculated as the cost of getting there from the starting location (in unit steps) plus an estimate of the cost of getting from the tile in question to the goal.

Path-finding is a form of iterative two- or three-dimensional searches over time. Other algorithms like A* have been developed, as have the notion of heat dispersion maps which flood a volume with values and attempt to map the most efficient, or coolest, path through them. While real-time methods have been implemented into game engines, off-line pathfinding used for films requires longer computation time and is ultimately more accurate, while at the same time, opens the door for many more characters. Non-real-time processing also allows for collisions and avoidance of arbitrarily shaped obstacles and higher-resolution terrain processing.

While behavioral animation is more than path-planning, this is a major consideration. The goal of behavioral animation is to imbue characters with enough rules to build up emergent life-like actions. Reynolds has stated that this behavior takes the form of "unpredictability over moderate time scales" [28]. It is impossible to predict which direction boids in his flocking system will be moving 5 minutes from the time you are watching them. On the contrary, within short time intervals, the motion is relatively predictable. This is a distinguishing characteristic of complex systems. Chaotic behavior, on the other hand, have neither short- nor long-term predictability and the observation of many natural systems reveals them to be on the verge of chaotic. Reynolds cites Chris Langton with the observation that "life-like phenomena exist poised at the edge of chaos" [28].

27.5 ARTIFICIAL INTELLIGENCE

Combining scripted animation sequences with notions of algorithmic decision making lays the foundation for building an artificially intelligent system that makes decisions based on a rule-based model. A series of requirements are presented to the system, along with a database of motions or procedural motion events. Once goals and behaviors are added as inputs to the system, the AI is allowed to make decisions about where the characters are and what they are doing by pulling motion from a database of some kind. As Matt Elson [11] postulated, this is a major evolutionary step for digital characters and opens up a huge realm of possibility with regard to crowd systems. It is the core of behavioral animation.

AI attempts to put the decision-making in the hands of the character. The ability to reason based on knowledge of the world and the system the character is contained within is a step above rule-based procedural motion. Techniques for AI for digital characters typically comes in two varieties: deterministic and nondeterministic. Deterministic is behavior which is defined and generally predictable. Basic chasing algorithms are a good example, where the behavior is clear from the beginning and the result is evident from the behavior. A character moves toward a goal. The character does not need to have any knowledge of where it has been. Nondeterministic behavior, on the contrary, is unpredictable and its results uncertain. This is due to the notion of behavior adaptation whereby the character's behavior is enhanced by learning the user/player's tactics or evolving new strategies. This makes the results unpredictable and gives rise to emergent behavior which develops without specific instruction. Nondeterministic behavior is essentially simulation, motion, and actions based on a solver that is generating motion based on all available data in the scene. Most game engines incorporate some notion of deterministic AI, whereas nondeterministic AI is usually implemented as a module created by a third-party engine developer. As a subset of AI research, intelligent agents are defined by their ability to adapt and learn. Within a crowd system in animation production, they are the node-based embodiment of nondeterministic AI on a per-character level within a scene. At times, "agent" merely implies an individual character in a crowd but we will reserve the term for an autonomous adaptive entity. Adaptation implies sensing the environment and reconfiguring behavior in response. This can be achieved through the choice of alternative problem-solving rules or algorithms, or through the discovery of problem-solving strategies. Learning may proceed through trial and error, implying a capability for analysis of behavior and success. Alternatively, learning may proceed by example and generalization. In this case, it implies a capacity to abstract and generalize the information presented (see Reference 29 as an example).

AI is often ascribed to nodes which act as agents in a system. This guides the agents based on functions related to environmental awareness and animatable attributes. The entities are given goals and then interact with each other as members of a real crowd would. Agents are the base unit character in a multicharacter environment usually termed a crowd system.

27.6 CROWDS AND VARIATION SYSTEMS

Once artists were able to produce one digital character well, the impetus was to create many, and before long many turned into full crowds. Crowd systems have, at their core, frameworks for creating character variations and applying animation to them at a group behavior level. "MASSIVE™" developed by Massive Software is the best known commercial software for producing crowds and was developed in parallel with the production of *The Lord of the Rings* trilogy. The motion of crowd individuals is typically either particle-based or agent-based. When controlled by a particle system, characters are driven via simulation and by establishing forces, attractors, goals, and defining obstacles for the characters to avoid. Most animation systems have these functions built-in, so the creation of a particle-based crowd is fast to implement and does not require specialized software. In fact, there are a number of lightweight crowd systems that small studios have developed that rely on these tools and provide good results. Regardless of the software used to create and steer crowds of characters, as with all simulations, this method is extremely difficult to art direct and the actions of a single individual's motion is almost impossible to control. Agent-based systems utilize AI to drive motion and, while more

Crowd System Execution Steps

1. Define environment topology and boundaries

2. Define number of agents and initial positions

3. Define agent properties: Motion library, relationships, and variations

4. Define agent goals and obstacles

5. Simulate: Pathfinding, character steering, and AI

6. Output agent data to animation system or renderer

FIGURE 27.5   A basic crowd system.

expensive to compute and often requiring specialized software, provides much more accurate results and more compelling and life-like character behavior.

Crowd systems are usually computed using generic representations of the final characters. These are stand-in rigs that are computationally lightweight and representative of the final group. Because crowd systems implement many of the techniques we have discussed thus far, it is no surprise that they are complex systems that require a large amount of planning to integrate into the production pipeline. All aspects of rigging, deformations, animation, motion capture, procedural motion, and behavioral animation are tied up into the processing of these systems. Therefore, they are computationally optimized to process large amounts of data per-frame and can run the simulations at multiple levels of resolutions for fast iterations. Most important is the choreography of group character motion. A simplified walk-through of the inner workings of a crowd system is described in Figure 27.5 (see Reference 30 for a more complete overview).

Building on the AI we discussed earlier, crowd systems synchronize multiple actors by applying principles similar to flocking to implement group behavior. The AI involved with crowds is in many ways far less complex than that which is associated with the single individual, the pair, or the small group. Crowd behavior is ultimately not very complex and due to the large-scale number of characters, the problem is as much a graphics problem as it is an AI problem. Once agents and goals are defined, even if goals are just to mill about in a specified area, character path-finding is implemented so that the characters build an internal map to their goal. This is a dynamic process because although environmental obstacles are static, other characters are not and therefore path-planning needs to be executed as one of the first processes. Iterations of the character path-planning are run until a functional solution is found. Character steering, which is the planning and execution of body positioning related to the results of path-finding, is the second step. From this point, character collisions trigger responses based on character attributes. Often times, it is these character interactions that define the action required of the scene, such as the warring crowds in *The Lord of the Rings* trilogy. It is these moments of interactions or character collision that become action-on scenarios which trigger a sequence

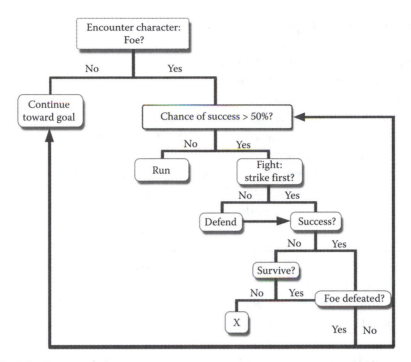

FIGURE 27.6   A basic decision tree for a crowd character engaging in a fight sequence.

of events, and subsequently calling clips from the motion library, to carry out hand-to-hand combat. This is all based on a decision tree (Figure 27.6) where probabilities are assigned to actions, and the outcomes of actions trigger other responses, all building up to the point where one character perseveres against another. All of these actions can have an overarching weighted curve associated with them that shifts the balance of the action toward one outcome or another.

Variation systems are those which allow an artist to create a series of characters based on a core model or character database. Variations can be as simple as a change of clothing or as complex as an entirely different species. Variation systems are basically high-level controls for switching attributes on a character. For a small number of minor variations, the attributes to select different variations on a character may just control the visibility of different objects. A good example of this is a character who may or may not wear a hat. This basic variation of the main character is essentially a binary switch, but the principle can be applied to crowd characters that may have a multitude of minor variations.

The distance from the camera has direct impact on digital characters as well. A character that is at a substantial distance from the camera will not need the same amount of resolution as a character that is in the foreground of a shot. Model resolution, texture resolution, density of hair, and quality-of-cloth simulation are all issues related to the notion of distance-based level of detail (LOD). LOD is essentially an optimization step that attempts to minimize the weight of the scene and the length of rendering. It is particularly important in game engines where processing power is at a premium. Many of these decisions reside in the character setup as switches that can be automated based on the character's distance from the camera. This is especially important when it comes to crowd scenes where a large number of digital characters will fill the screen. Automated LOD allows those characters to be optimized both with regard to screen presence and computational execution.

For more complex variations, we get into the realm of procedurally built characters which are created on-the-fly when the scene is loaded. These systems can take many forms. One configuration is that a file is associated with the scene that contains all the variation details for the specific characters in the scene. When that scene is loaded for simulation, each character is loaded and the variation file tells the system what variations are associated with it. The creation of this file of selections is manual, but the art director has specific control over the amount of character variation in the scene. Crowd builders can be more automated, whereby the system is loaded with all the possible variation choices and allowed to build the characters at random. There can be internal logic associated with these variations so that the system can make accurate decisions related to the fit between variations. For example, certain body types may not fit with certain clothing variations or certain hair styles must be associated with certain hats. By being able to include exceptions for certain variations, the user can minimize the number of simulations that need to be rerun later to eliminate incorrectly assembled characters. Variations can also encompass body types which have an impact on the locomotion of the character, particularly body height modifications which change limb lengths. If a piece of raw motion capture data is applied to a character whose legs are longer than the captured character, the stride will not look appropriate for that character. If there is no possibility of using a procedural motion solution, then the system must scale the mocap data to fit the character. If the data has been attached to constraints like IK, then the position of the feet are controlled by two points which can be scaled to offset the base position and look correct for this new taller or shorter character. This is akin to retargeting which was discussed in Chapter 25.

27.7 HAIR AND CLOTHING

This chapter has focused primarily on the overall motion of the character but it is also worth noting that the simulated motion of hair and clothing that a character wears and interacts with is a common procedural system that the character rig often needs to include. These setups are often included with the character rig to provide overall silhouette feedback to animation but sometimes all that is installed is a fast solving proxy of the final result. This allows the animator to get a sense of the hair and clothing without sacrificing the interactive speed of the character by waiting on a high-resolution simulation. Another reason only proxy hair and cloth is installed in a character rig is that often the simulation of those assets is dependent on the environmental factors that are desired in the shot. Is there wind blowing through the character's hair? Are the clothes wet? These forces and parameters will impact the look and feel of the simulation, so this work is handled on a shot-by-shot basis. This shot-based work is usually handled by a technical animator and is often not started until animation performance of the character has been approved so that it can be completed on stable motion and not something that is in progress.

27.8 EXERCISE

In this exercise, we go through the conceptual process of designing a decision tree for a group of procedural characters. Split into groups of two or more. Split evenly between programmers and art/animation directors. Follow the steps below.

1. Sketch out an environment for the character to exist in along with a descriptive goal that they are trying to reach or accomplish.

2. Based on the spec, develop the relationships between the characters. Are they enemies that must battle? Are they allies that must cooperate to succeed?

3. Implemented on a digital grid or on paper, run characters step by step to their respective goals.

4. When a character comes in contact with another character, obstacle, or the goal, diagram out the decisions that they must make for those scenarios. Be as detailed as possible, as procedural systems must deal with these situations by making many microdecisions as opposed to one complex over-arching decision.

5. Does the decision tree work for all situations? Can you break it down further to be as generic as possible? Have others step through the tree. Does it make sense to them? Exchange it with another group. Do your rules make sense for their scenario? Does theirs work for yours?

6. Maintain this review/fix feedback loop until satisfied.

FURTHER READING

A good introduction to AI for programmers and nonprogrammers alike:

Bourg, D. M. and Seemann, G. 2004. *AI for Game Developers*. O'Reilly Media, Inc., Sebastopol, CA.

Perlin noise as it relates to textures and to characters:

Perlin, K. 1985. An Image Synthesizer. *Computer Graphics* 19(3):287–296.

Perlin, K. and Goldberg, A. 1996. Improv: A system for scripting interactive actors in virtual worlds. In *SIGGRAPH'96: Proceedings of the 23rd Annual Conference on Computer Graphics and Interactive Techniques*, New York, NY, ACM, pp. 205–216.

http://www.actormachine.com/.

Craig Reynolds' seminal paper on flocking and the introduction of his "boids":

> Reynolds, C. W. 1987. Flocks, herds, and schools: A distributed behavioral model. *Computer Graphics* 21(4):25–34.

Crowds as implemented for various media platforms from Massive Software:

http://www.massivesoftware.com/.

The game *Spore* from Will Wright revolutionized people's thinking about procedural characters and procedural character animation:

http://www.spore.com.

Interview: Terran Boylan, Lead Character Technical Director, DreamWorks Animation

28.1 BIO

Terran Boylan started at PDI/Dreamworks in 2000. He worked for a year as an F/X developer before moving to the Character TD department, where has been ever since. So far, Terran has worked on 12 Dreamworks animated features: *Shrek* (2001), *Shrek 2* (2004), *Madagascar* (2005), *Over the Hedge* (2006), *Shrek the Third* (2007), *Bee Movie* (2007), *Monsters Vs. Aliens*

Terran Boylan, Lead Character Technical Director, DreamWorks Animation

(2009), *Kung Fu Panda 2* (2011), *The Croods* (2013), *Mr. Peabody & Sherman* (2014), and the upcoming *Kung Fu Panda 3* and *Boss Baby*. As of this writing, his films have grossed $5.3 billion in worldwide box office. His greatest professional "claim to fame" was his work on the amorphic B.O.B. rig for *Monsters Vs. Aliens*. Outside of work, his hobbies include self-publication and writing about himself in the third person.

28.2 Q&A

Q: *The components of character technology are diverse and span the artistic and technical spectrum. How did you get your start in the industry? Based on where you see the field heading what experience/training do you recommend people have?*

A: Before working at PDI/Dreamworks, I worked for 10 years at a technology startup creating our in-house animation software and supervising projects ranging from a tour of the interior of the human body for a herpes medicine to Barbie's Magic Hair Styler, but my real interest was CG character animation. Back in the ancient past when I went to college, the state of the art in computer graphics was laughably primitive by today's standards. For example, I worked on Tektronix vector graphic terminals where you had to press a button to clear the screen! In those days, there were only a few colleges in the United States where you could specialize in computer graphics, with Ohio State University being the best known. And you could forget about any home use: Both the hardware and software were prohibitively expensive, costing as much as a house! Nowadays, powerful graphics computers are cheap and ubiquitous and software like Autodesk Maya is widely available.

As for my advice to anyone starting out, I would strongly suggest covering both academic and practical/experiential bases: (1) Pursue a professional degree of some sort, like the Masters program at Texas A&M, as an example. (2) Balance the theoretical with your own personal projects, and not just those assigned in class. I cannot understate how much I learned writing code on my own time, intended for my own late-night experimental animations. Remember, there is no substitute for genuine, fire-in-your-belly passion.

Q: *Creating compelling digital characters is part art and part science. What is the greatest challenge you encounter on a daily basis? What aspect of character technology keeps you up thinking at night?*

A: One of the great things about the studio where I work is that its proprietary rigging processes and software components have evolved significantly and continually over the years. The downside of that has been having to relearn how to do my job every three or four years.

As for the technology itself: I have a programming background coupled with what I like to think is a strong understanding of core concepts, and so I'm well-equipped for keeping up with the technical dimension of our tools. Having said that, I have often wished our workflow was simpler, more consistent and more elegant. Recently we've made tremendous steps toward all of those goals, and I'm super excited about that.

Q: *What are the ingredients for a successful digital character?*

A: Success can be measured in many different ways, but here's what I believe to be a good recipe for a top-notch CG character: An appealing design, a rig that's easy to use for the animators and equally easy to maintain, aesthetic and technical consistency across both its show and the studio as a whole . . . plus magic.

Q: *While the industry is competitive, it is ultimately respectful of great work. Outside of the work you have been personally involved in the production of, what animated characters have you been impressed or inspired by? What is the historical high-bar?*

A: I know it's more than 10 years ago now, and I haven't watched it in many years, but I vividly remember sitting in the theater and being blown away by Gollum in *The Lord of the Rings: The Two Towers* (2002). The painstaking work the riggers and animators did to pull off the subtlety of emotion was amazing. On the other end of the stylization spectrum, lately I've been impressed by how Disney has been able to take their traditional "princess" aesthetic and execute it successfully in 3D in *Tangled* (2010) and *Frozen* (2013).

Q: *Where do you see digital characters in 10 years? Where are animated characters for film and games heading?*

A: Over the past five or so years I've watched with great interest as more people are doing incredibly impressive character design and rigging as a hobby. I believe this to be driven in part by the availability of 3D printers and software like Pixologic's ZBrush.

As deformation technologies continue to coalesce, I would love to see a greater encapsulation of characters in the form of a unified rigging standard format, with widespread support across software platforms. Following that—and recognizing this currently exists on a crude level— I would love to see hundreds or thousands of feature film quality rigs sold as downloadable products, licensed for commercial and/or home use.

CHAPTER 29

Case Studies in Character Interactivity

M UCH OF WHAT WE HAVE BEEN discussing fits neatly into the realm of digital characters for animation and video games. That being said, the implementation of AI in the system allows for more advanced interaction and opens a field of research and design in character interactivity. There is currently much promise for practical "virtual interviewers" and other avatars who interact with us to serve various functions and to be a familiar life-like interface for interacting with digital systems. There is another possibility in the form of gallery-based work that demonstrates research, aesthetics, or tools for filmmaking for a new medium. This is a direct descendent of work in video games, but with a focus more fixed on user interaction for artistic expression and social relationships between characters for research. It is worth making the distinction between animation created for linear animation and that which is produced for interactive products. While there are many similarities between these two outputs, there are also distinct differences. Both linear and interactive animations share a common goal which is the creation of an engaging experience for the viewer/player. Table 29.1, from UC Irvine's Bill Tomlinson's paper [31] entitled, "From linear to interactive animation: How autonomous characters change the process and product of animating," outlines the major differences between linear and interactive animation. The brief descriptions below are generalizations. There are exceptions to each of these topics and active research is on-going in all of these areas.

When it comes to intelligence in linear animation, the behavioral modeling of the character happens in the mind of the artist. Animators, writers, and directors define and execute the behavior that the characters should undertake. In interactive animation, the modeling of character intelligence that will be seen by an audience happens instead inside the animation system itself. The creative team designs the behavior and this interactive system acts as an intermediary between the artists and the audience. During an interactive animation production process, like

TABLE 29.1   A Summary of Five Major Differences between Linear and Interactive Animation

Topic	Linear Animation	Interactive Animation
Intelligence	The intelligence and behavior of characters are determined by screenwriters, storyboarders, and animators prior to the audience experiencing the work	The intelligence and behavior of characters are generated by a computer program in real time
Emotional expressiveness	The animator controls emotional state exhibited by characters in each shot. Each action a character takes is inextricably tied to an emotion	The animator creates dynamic emotional ranges explored during game play based on a range factors. Emotions may be layered on top of actions and controlled independently
Navigation collision avoidance	Characters only run into things when the animator wants them to	Characters may accidentally collide with others and with objects in their world. Characters need a mechanism for avoiding collisions dynamically and coping if they occur
Transitions	Since the sequence of events is fixed, transitions between small chunks of animation are controlled by the animator, and may be long or short	Since the sequence of events is variable, cycles must be kept short or they cause a character to take too long to switch to a different action (if this is solved by animations not running to completion, characters may exhibit discontinuous motion)
Multicharacter interaction	Two characters may be animated simultaneously	Enabling two characters to robustly engage in expressive close contact (fighting, affection, etc.) is an unsolved problem

those we have discussed for procedural animation, animators and programmers produce the raw material for believable behaviors and the rules for connecting them, while linear animators produce the behaviors themselves. This distinction can be frustrating to a linear animator and often requires that they only produce "cycles" or discrete motions. It is also more difficult to document the work that has been done by a single artist. It can be an interesting new undertaking to think through a character in sufficient depth to determine all possible actions and reactions that the character could take, but this is a very different prospect than working through a complete performance by a character over the course of a moment in a film.

Another frustration for animators transitioning from linear production to interactive work is that when animating for interactive products, it is not possible to see the final form that the animation will take in every possible situation. The animator can play-test the game and get a broad sense for the way an animation will look when it is finally rendered and make revisions based on that process. For linear animation, animators typically animate "to the camera," meaning that the camera is placed first and then the character is posed for the shot. The position, orientation, size, and other features of on-screen elements, including character components, may be adjusted (also know as "cheated") to the camera to make a scene look better. Often, when viewed from other angles, the character looks totally broken and off-camera elements may not even be animated. Digital characters for 3D interactive work must read in-the-round at all times and due to the broad range of potential interactions among interactive characters and their environment, there can be no final round of hand-tweaking by the animator to make sure that every element of the scene works together.

In interactive animation, main characters often face away from the camera, so that players are able to see where the characters are going rather than seeing the character's face. This de-emphasizes facial complexity in interactive systems, leaving cinematics and cut-scenes to use a different facial rig to emote through the narrative elements of the game. To create a variety of motion and to ensure that the motion is not repetitive, multiple animations are often created for each action to provide variations of actions. Rather than having just one animation for a given behavior, a character may have several subtly different alternating variants. Procedural noise, in particular, Perlin noise (which is deterministic and repeatable), may also be added to the actions to give them a more life-like quality and to give the viewer/player the sense that the motion is unique at every instant, even while being controllable since it is not completely random. The process of interactive animation and the design of interactive systems requires animators to more fully understand their character's behavior than compared with linear formats. In an animated film, if a character wanted to show disgust at a situation, the animator would just animate them reacting at the right moment with the facial and body cues that communicate the feeling of being disgusted. However, in an interactive system, the animator might create a similar disgusted animation clip, but the conditions that should cause the behavior would have to be defined in the system.

The quality differences that exist lie in the fact that animation created for interactive systems is more difficult than animation created for linear applications such as film. Linear animation has an established set of conventions and techniques on which to draw, with numerous examples of well-developed and compelling characters, whereas computer games and other interactive media are still working out many core questions on how to present believable and engaging characters in an interactive format. For example, in a traditional linear animation, making a character that can smile requires a few strokes of a pencil, but is a complex pursuit in an interactive domain.

In areas where linear animation has laid groundwork, interactive animation should be able to draw on the established forms of its linear predecessor but nothing can be taken for granted.

Take for example, the point Tomlinson [31] makes about comedy. He notes that in linear animation, comedic timing is relatively easy to manipulate, while in interactive animation it is much more challenging. Linear animation can be easily re-timed to achieve the desired effect. Any comedian will tell you how difficult comedic timing is. The same rules and ability to make something funny apply to animators—there is no software that has the ability to encapsulate comedic timing. However, in interactive animation, where users may impact the timing of events, certain kinds of comedy become very difficult. We can animate a character to tell a prerecorded joke or pratfall, but this is simply a prerecorded dialog or action and without the controlled timing of linear animation, these often fall flat. Comedy is a staple of linear animation and while most animation, from *Loony Tunes* to *South Park*, has traditionally been based on humor, it is not nearly as prevalent in interactive animation. As John Lasseter, director of *Toy Story* and other Pixar films, offered in describing an early computer animation he had created, "It was not the software that gave life to the characters, it was these principles of animation, these tricks of the trade that animators had developed over 50 years ago" [25]. The similarities between linear and interactive animation could lie in the principles of the traditional animation formulated by Walt Disney Studios. An understanding of the differences between linear and interactive animation may help interactive animations exhibit the same appeal that has made traditional linear animation so successful to such a broad audience for its long history.

Three projects are introduced below that demonstrate interactive character technology outside of the conventional context of computer games. These projects provide a unique perspective on digital characters and lead us to speculations on the future of research and development on the subject.

29.1 *ALPHAWOLF* (2001) BY THE SYNTHETIC CHARACTERS GROUP AT THE MIT MEDIA LAB

AlphaWolf is an interactive installation in which people play the role of wolf pups in a pack of autonomous and semiautonomous gray wolves (*Canis lupus*). Presented at SIGGRAPH 2001, *AlphaWolf* allowed users to howl, growl, whine, or bark into a microphone. In turn, the vocal cues influenced how the participant's pup interacted with the other members of the pack. The focus of the project was on social learning, allowing the digital wolf pups to benefit from context-preservation as they interacted in their environment (Figure 29.1). As such, in each successive intercharacter interaction, individuals were able to bring their interaction history to bear on their decision-making process. The computational model captured a subset of the social behavior of wild wolves underscored by two lines of inquiry: the relationship between social learning and emotion, and development as it relates to social learning. The combination of these threads, as applied to digital characters, advanced the idea of character learning and the ramification of historical lessons on current behavior and reactions to stimulus. The applications of a project such as this are numerous, especially with regard to group dynamics. Just as individual animals provide good models for creating individual agents, populations of

FIGURE 29.1 *AlphaWolf* by the Synthetic Characters Group at the MIT Media Lab.

animals can inspire mechanisms by which those individual agents will interact. Social learning has huge ramifications for groups of agents both virtually, in animated crowd systems, or physically, in swarms or small groups of robots. Long-term applications such as computer interfaces that can interact more appropriately with humans by utilizing human social abilities are also possible.

The initial sketch was based primarily on the notion of dominance and submission between puppies. The intelligence is basic, everyday common sense that animals exhibit including the ability to find food, know who they like, and to build simple emotional relations with each other. The procedural wolves used blended animation clips to produce smart collections of behaviors, but in many ways the motion of the characters was outweighed by the notion of learning and development in a digital character. The ramifications for this are tremendous and form the beginnings of a computational scaffolding for intelligent digital characters that can learn. These autonomous and semiautonomous wolves interacted with each other much as real wolves do.

AlphaWolf offers initial steps toward computational systems with social behavior, in hope of making interactions with them more functional and more inherently rewarding. The notion of character memory is monumental. This, coupled with the idea that memory of behavior dictates current behavior, is a level of character adaptation that has benefits to crowds that need to be able to share knowledge about their environment. The work is a stepping stone for character intelligence in the realms of interactive character research and associated industries.

29.2 *TARTARUS* (2006) BY ALAN PRICE

Tartarus is a real-time 3D simulation in which the viewer interacts with a digital character. Traversing an infinite interior structure of dark rooms and dilapidated staircases, the "absurd man," as Price calls him, is destined to carry a wooden chair throughout the space, guided by the viewer's prompts. It is an exploration of an exercise in futility. As the viewer moves the character through the space, the perpetual replication of his environment is discovered. Iterations of the chair begin to accumulate, eventually building up to an impasse. At this critical point, the obstacles fade and the cycle repeats. The absurd man becomes a celebration of his fate as we rationalize the tormented plight of the individual in this world.

Tartarus incorporates real-time 3D graphics and game engine technology (Figure 29.2). Facial expressions are procedurally driven and respond to the location and prompting of the viewer's position in the scene. The virtual camera is in constant motion, programmed to follow the character and navigate within the confines of the architectural space. Over two dozen animation sequences are randomly accessed and blended to control the character in response to the viewer's interaction and to the geometry of the environment. High level shading language pixel shaders were utilized to render high-definition surface features on the character's skin and clothing. Open dynamics engine (ODE) was implemented for dynamic interaction with the chairs that accumulate in the scene.

FIGURE 29.2 *Tartarus* by Alan Price.

The real-time simulation involved the visitor engaging in an exercise in futility at the expense of a digital character. The viewer used a touchscreen to guide a virtual figure carrying his burden in the form of a wooden chair through dilapidated staircases and dark rooms. Over the course of the installation, replications of the chair began to accumulate, eventually building an impasse within the space. At this critical point, the obstacles fade and the cycle repeats. Real-time 3D graphics and game engine technology put the viewer in control of this representation of the individuals daily burden. *Tartarus* won the Prix Ars Electronica, Honorary Mention Interactive Art, at Ars Electronica in Linz, Austria in 2006. The write-up by the curators of the exhibition was as follows:

> Alan Price's *Tartarus* utilizes real-time graphics and game engine technology to create the unlikely virtual character of an emotional old man in a nihilistic and absurd environment. The user accompanies the old man whose burden is a single chair. As you adventure through this world of naked stairways and unwelcome rooms, more and more chairs begin to accumulate in a metaphoric homage to the Sisyphean task of being an individual.

Price followed-up *Tartarus*, with a series called *Empire of Sleep* (2009) which includes similar touchscreen technology for user interaction, but follows a group of characters (Figure 29.3). *Empire of Sleep* is an experiment in the application of the traditional narrative and temporal structure of cinema to the medium of real-time rendered graphics and user interaction. A touchscreen installation displays interactive real-time 3D renderings of surreal landscapes depicting events haunted by calamity on massive scales, and a protagonist's attempts at evading the impending consequences. By incorporating the immediacy, immersive, and non-linear characteristics of real-time rendering with temporal and narrative structure of traditional cinema, this work explores the combination of real-time and traditional animation. The intent is to find a balance between these modes of representation, attempting to make the viewer aware of the issues being examined while engaging in a narrative sequence that simultaneously depicts the perspectives and fates of the digital characters as they strive to comprehend their own relationship to their simulated environment.

The Conspirators (in progress) is the latest work by Price. It is a game in which players clandestinely enter a small town in order to observe its inhabitants. The people in the town are

FIGURE 29.3 *Empire of Sleep* by Alan Price.

FIGURE 29.4 *The Conspirators* by Alan Price.

autonomously driven characters. Although the visual design of the characters was not the primary focus, the design of the game is more about the emergent behavior of groups. According to Price, "The concept for the game is loosely inspired by overt and covert practices of governments caught up in the confusion of terms like peace-keeping and nation-building to justify meddling in unfamiliar cultures" (Figure 29.4).

29.3 *MOVIESANDBOX* (ON GOING) BY FRIEDRICH KIRSCHNER

Friedrich Kirschner develops tools to support creating films using game engines. His 2004 film *The Journey* (Figure 29.5), was screened at film festivals and available as self-playing modification, often just called a "mod," for the popular game Unreal Tournament 2004. Mods are customizations of existing games ranging in scale from custom characters or elements, to brand new games developed within the framework of the game.

With the creation of this film and others following the same *machinima* paradigm, Kirschner began developing an authoring tool for others to create films within game engines. The current incarnation of this toolkit is *MovieSandbox* (Figure 29.6). *MovieSandbox* is a graphical scripting tool that enables users to script their own gameplay elements. *MovieSandbox* does not use a linear timeline but rather is designed to string together actions in a procedural node network where you can create relationships between nodes and trigger actions and commands. It allows you to easily create your own characters, sets, and poses, and direct them in a quick and modifiable manner.

While the initial implementation of Kirschner's *MovieSandbox* was created as a toolkit within Unreal Tournament, it is now being conceived as a stand-alone application. It is an

FIGURE 29.5 *The Journey* by Friedrich Kirschner.

evolving toolkit that strives to put unique creative control in the hands of film-makers who want to work in an interactive context. By incorporating do-it-yourself instructions for building a simple 3D scanner, fast tools for rigging models, and intuitive controls for puppeteering motion, the system opens the door to creative people who need an entry point into the great potential of machinima. The puppeteering controls often utilize physical interfaces, giving the artist a tactile response which has a shallow learning curve by limiting the controls. Kirschner utilizes the puppeteering analogy because most people have probably played with a marionette or other form of puppet at some point in their life. As such, it is quickly evident that even though the initial mechanical construction might seem complicated, the act of pulling a string and seeing the puppet react to it in a physically comprehensive way is comforting and demystifying of the process. This is in sharp contrast to typical digital animation where complicated rigs and animator controls often do not have a direct relationship.

The toolkit also attempts to transition the aesthetics of game engines from vertex-based computer games to a more artistic and organic style based on particle-based pointillism. Kirschner believes that today's computer game engines have all the technical prerequisites to offer a wide variety of art directions and visual styles, but they are too often utilized in a very traditional way. A performance entitled *Puppet Play*, created using an early version of *MovieSandbox*, moved away from the traditional computer game look and feel, demonstrating alternatives not only to the naturalistic trend in computer game graphics, but also showing new usage scenarios for computer game engines that are closer to animated film-making and

FIGURE 29.6 *MovieSandbox* by Friedrich Kirschner.

puppetry. By advancing this new art form, *MovieSandbox* gets the technology out of the way of the artistry and is a stepping stone into a new realm of aesthetics for the interactive industry.

FURTHER READING

For more information on *AlphaWolf* and Bill Tomlinson's more recent work, refer to his website:

http://www.ics.uci.edu/wmt/

His article on the difference between animating characters for films and interactive applications is very insightful:

Tomlinson, B. 2005. From linear to interactive animation: How autonomous characters change the process and product of animating. In: *ACM Computers in Entertainment*, Vol. 3, No. 1, ACM, New York, NY.

More information on Alan Price's *Tartarus* and his recent work can be found on his website: http://accad.osu.edu/~aprice/

Information and the latest news on Friedrich Kirschner's *MovieSandbox* can be found on the project website: http://moviesandbox.com/. More information about Kirschner's films and other projects can be found on his personal website: http://www.zeitbrand.net

CHAPTER 30

Interview: David Hunt-Bosch, Rigging Tech Art Lead, Bungie

30.1 BIO

David Hunt-Bosch is the Rigging Tech Art Lead at Bungie. He contributed to Bungie's recent release Destiny and was part of the team that made *Halo 3*, *Halo ODST*, and *Halo Reach*. Prior to joining Bungie, David worked as an animator, combat designer, and cinematics artist at game studios in the Seattle area. David earned his BA in Interdisciplinary Visual Art at the University of Washington in 2000. David has a passion for teaching and has been a visiting lecturer in the Animation Capstone program in the Computer Science and Engineering Department of UW since 2007. David presented an Autodesk Masterclass tour in 2008 and a lecture at the Game

David Hunt-Bosch, Rigging Tech Art Lead, Bungie

Developers Conference in 2009 on the subject of Modular Procedural Rigging. David currently resides in the Seattle area with his wife Beata and kids Ellena, William, and Faith. In his spare time, David enjoys science, reading, cycling, playing music, and devising new and different ways of creating animation.

30.2 Q&A

Q: *The components of character technology are diverse and span the artistic and technical spectrum. How did you get your start in the industry? Based on where you see the field heading what experience/training do you recommend people have?*

A: Stop-motion animation is how I got my start in the industry. In 1997, I was an art student with dreams of making live action films, but I had few available resources other than my knack for tinkering and my determination to tell stories. I found that stop-motion was an optimal way for me to realize my ideas. I was able to assemble whole imaginary worlds of my own within my small apartment, bringing them to life in animation one frame at a time. I fell in love with the seemingly unlimited creative potential offered by this medium and I got hooked on the constant learning and problem solving required to make it happen. I was inspired by the talented folks at Digital Domain's miniature model shop where I got to spend a summer as an intern helping with special effects for the film Titanic. After completing my stop-motion project it was a natural next step to learn digital 3D animation, which added even more powerful storytelling tools to my creative arsenal.

In sharp contrast to my small independent stop-motion production, the animation industry of today has grown to formidable proportions. Big games and films are produced by huge teams of highly specialized workers. I feel there is a danger in artists becoming too specialized and losing sight of how their part fits into the larger project goals. So the training and experience I would recommend to people getting started in the industry is to always work on small personal animation projects. Making your own short game or film is a great way to learn the skills necessary to break in and it's also the best way to stay sharp and diversified throughout the lifespan of your career. Today's technology provides more opportunities than ever before for individuals or small teams to make successful animation projects of smaller scope. And there is nothing more satisfying than seeing your own ideas come to life in animation.

Q: *Creating compelling digital characters is part art and part science. What is the greatest challenge you encounter on a daily basis? What aspect of character technology keeps you up thinking at night?*

A: Production agility is the greatest challenge I encounter on a daily basis. Creating compelling digital characters in a full scale production is highly complex work that involves the collaboration of many different specialists over long spans of time. In the early stages we do our best to previsualize the final result, but inevitably once we see it fully animated in the final context we only then gain realistic insight into how it could be better. I believe that great studios are the ones who stay agile and can do the final polish changes that make the work truly excellent. As a Rigger and Tech Artist it's my job to make the impossible easy. My team and I do a lot of tool development in Python and C# to enable artists to make these kind of late stage changes. It is a big challenge to simultaneously improve efficiency and flexibility, but this is a challenge that I'm passionate about. Although it does keep me up at night, I'm convinced this is what I would be doing anyway for my own projects.

Q: *What are the ingredients for a successful digital character?*

A: A successful digital character is one that viewers can empathize with. It is not just that the viewer understands what the character is feeling. I'm convinced that it goes deeper than that. When the digital character emotes, the viewer involuntarily feels the same emotion personally. Any imperfection or flaw in the visual appearance breaks the illusion that the character is real and destroys the viewer's sense of empathy. Therefore, the most important ingredients are the details that contribute to emotional empathy.

When developing digital characters it is critical to consider and plan how they relate to the Uncanny Valley. That decision sheds light on what type of details should be included or omitted. Stylized cartoon characters are capable of achieving a high degree of believability and emotional empathy even though they may represent less overall detail. Stylized characters have an advantage here because the details that relate to their personality are exaggerated. It can be even more difficult to achieve empathy with a photorealistic character because so many more details need to be present. With each detail that is included there are more chances for imperfections that can prevent empathy from being achieved. So it is wise to use all available resources such as lighting, shading, camera, and animation in addition to the model and rig itself to emphasize the intended performance and emotional result of a digital character. Wherever possible, it is good to remove details that do not contribute to empathy so that the ones that do can be more effective.

Q: *While the industry is competitive, it is ultimately respectful of great work. Outside of the work you have been personally involved in the production of, what animated characters have you been impressed or inspired by? What is the historical high-bar?*

A: The historical high-bar for animated characters is the work of Frank Thomas and Ollie Johnston who, along with their collaborators at early Disney, pioneered the fundamental principles of animation. Their traditional 2D character animation is truly timeless and continues to amaze and entertain young kids and seasoned professionals alike all across the world. And as the tools and media have evolved, the principles they defined remain every bit as relevant and inspirational to the work we do in the industry today.

Two recent examples of great work in animation stand out in my mind, one from film and one from games. As a former stop-motion animator I was blown away by the quality of animation in Laika's film, *The Boxtrolls*. Stop-motion animation usually achieves success by embracing the little imperfections, which can be ascribed to quaint charm, at least that's how my short films got by! But the character motion in this film is on par with the highest quality CG animation with all of its squash and stretch and exaggeration that usually can only be done in purely digital media. Amazingly, this film was made and photographed in the real physical world. The facial animation was especially expressive and believable. While I watched the film I couldn't stop thinking to myself what an impossibly large amount of skilled work it must have taken. I am glad that studios like Laika are keeping stop-motion alive and pushing the envelope of what is possible with animation in the real 3D world.

Interactive characters are grounded in the same fundamentals of animation, but they face additional challenges in forming a connection between the player and the game world. In my opinion, the current high-bar for games is the character Fetch from *Infamous First Light*, PS4 by Sucker Punch. Fetch's animations strike a great balance between looking good visually and feeling responsive to the player. They also told a great story in the game's cinematics. It is very challenging to achieve this balance with a playable character. Readability and physicality of body mechanics (mainly found in the animation fundamentals such as anticipation and follow-through) are in direct competition with responsiveness to player input. The artists and programmers at Sucker Punch pulled it off by authoring great looking movement animations and allowing them to be canceled appropriately when new commands are input from the player. The effects work is also an important part of Fetch's success because of how they exaggerate her motion and tie in her superhuman abilities to the environment. The final result feels intuitive, satisfying and amazing to watch. When I am playing *Infamous First Light* I often get sidetracked from missions by just wanting to run around the map and see where I can go with Fetch and her awesome neon powers. I feel like that is one of the true signs of a successful game character.

Q: *Where do you see digital characters in 10 years? Where are animated characters for film and games heading?*

A: Digital character avatars play an important role as one of the most powerful interfaces between humans and machines. It seems there is a new form of empathy emerging in digital characters that serve as avatars. This is the empathy that forms when a person bonds with an avatar such that they feel it extends their own identity. Some avatar systems strive to replicate verisimilitude, while others delve into fantasy and nonphotorealistic styles. Both have their place, but I believe it is in the latter where the greatest potential for this new kind of empathy exists. Avatars may represent character traits that the person feels are part of their true self that would be impossible in the physical world. Over the next 10 years we will see many more applications for digital avatars. Sophisticated tools such as 3D scanning are already becoming commonplace and they will continue to become more available for nontechnical people to make avatars look like themselves. A further step would be to build tools to enable anyone to create highly customized avatars from their own imagination that embellish their ideal or fantastical identity. There is a slippery slope here where the so-called real world identity alone can feel incomplete without its digital counterpart. Sometimes I feel this way about my blue robot space wizard in the game I helped create, *Destiny*. This trend will only continue to evolve and blur the lines between humans and machines over the coming years as technology advances and our artistic mastery of it matures.

IV

Conclusions

CHAPTER 31

The Frontiers of Digital Character Development

IN EXPLORING THE THEORY AND PRACTICE of digital character technology, we are constantly reminded of the many advances that have been achieved, but also the many challenges ahead. Most productions need to innovate to make the process more efficient and to overcome the seemingly impossible expectation of bringing the unimaginable to life under the constraint of shrinking budgets and timelines. It is this need for innovation that drives not only the art and technology of digital characters, but also the character technical directors that create them. Although we have achieved near realism in film characters and responsive interaction in game characters, the ability to merge these two hallmarks is the challenge faced by future artists.

The practical challenges in the near future for digital characters fall mainly in the realm of rig interactivity with regard to the manipulation speed and efficiency while processing complicated constraints and deformations. Performance capture, as a means for artists to breathe life into digital characters, is another challenge. While character animation is consistently successful in bringing characters to life, we still have many hurdles when it comes to translating a motion capture performance into something where the actor inhabits the character on screen. Many solutions to these concerns are at hand and under active development, but there are always long-term issues to think about. In this section, we briefly discuss some current character technology research threads and the potential impact of this work on the future of the field.

Innovation, within the many disciplines contained by computer graphics comes from multiple sources. Research from the academic world has established the core ideas relating to the theory and technology behind our understanding and techniques for creating digital characters. These core ideas range from computer graphics concepts related to more stable joint rotations, to new ways of deforming surfaces, to the psychology of using digital characters as interviewers and avatars in our daily lives. Studios engaged in the production of animation and video games often take these ideas and implement them directly into their production pipelines. The innovation in studios often comes from the optimization of, and interface for, techniques gleaned directly from academic research, but much original research also comes directly from the production of projects at studios. It is at this stage that studios are engaged with finding answers to the questions that the upcoming production poses. With regard to character technology, this will involve defining the conventions of character setup for the project and the general character pipeline, as well as solving character-specific issues such as simulated elements and unique deformation situations. Whole new techniques are often developed during this preproduction phase that may end up being global to every character, such as a new technique for hair simulation, or discreetly specific to the intricacies of a single character. While academic work is often published in journals and at conferences, studio research (often carried out by research and development staff with advanced academic degrees) may also be presented at conferences and published in journals, but finds its home in the output of the project either in consumer's homes or in the movie theater. While the goal of academic research is to publish and document new knowledge, studio research often remains proprietary to that studio and controlled by patents. In most cases, however, there is a lot of overlap between academia and production with artists with studio experience teaching the next generation of artists in the university setting and academic researchers acting as consultants on production challenges.

Character technology advances exponentially from year to year and production to production. Starting at the base level of a digital character, for example, with motion systems, there is a lot of development around "auto-rigging." When a studio develops a rig that is production tested, animator approved and satisfies the production requirements, it is often turned into a system that can be used to generate instances of that rig for characters of any proportion. This is most common for humanoid characters. These systems are usually procedural where the rig is built via code based on interactive input parameters. For example, limb lengths are defined based on specified points of articulation and variable options such as the number of joints define a character's spine. The rig can also be built with a smart architecture that can be refitted to a character of any proportion without the use of code. Either way, systems such as these are critical for creating multiple rigs and these instantiated rigs result in characters that have the same functionality and naming conventions; every character has the same rig so that maintenance and upgrading is simple and standardized.

Along these lines, and because many characters are not strictly humanoid in configuration, studios will often develop a modularized rigging system that allows a character setup artist to build the character in scriptable, or proportionally malleable, pieces that are then connected together to form the full character rig. This building-block approach infuses company knowledge into the modules so that no matter what the character is, the approved arm rig (for example), with all its functionality and naming conventions, is in place. If a unique element must be built, say a mermaid's tail, then that module can be built in a way that it can become part of the character module library and reused by other artists. Thinking this way and creating tools such as these make the tedious tasks easier and allow character setup artists to focus on the innovative technical challenges that do not fit neatly into an existing tool set. These also allow a single artist to set up many more characters which fit with the trend of crowd and variation systems. Automation of repetitive tasks minimizes user error as well. This then minimizes character fixes which is a tremendous part of the character setup artist's job. In the near future, one can imagine simpler and more intuitive character rigs, so that an arm is a single chain of joints and only a couple of controllers are used without the need for blending between IK and FK using a multitude of nodes.

Since the purpose of the motion system is to define the architecture of the character and to provide an interface for animators, one can imagine that these two functions will become abstracted from each other. Character architecture is one of the most complicated pieces of character development and the intention of animator interface is to be intuitive and simple. Placing both of these responsibilities on the same system, in fact, makes it more difficult to achieve both of them to a high degree. The animator interface should be a layer above all this, as a whole other system that plugs into the motion system and can be tailored to the animator's preference. This way, animators define the interface in the way they prefer and all of the characters on the project follow those conventions. A system that does this and interacts with whatever motion system it is manipulating will create happy animators and free character setup artists from needing to be user interface designers as well.

As we have discussed throughout this book, the influence of anatomy has greatly advanced the art of character rigging. For motion systems, there is still a need for intuitive tools to build anatomically accurate rig elements and systems. Much of this knowledge remains in the minds of experts and is difficult to port from project to project. Character setup artists, working under the advisement of anatomists and experts in locomotion, are well poised to develop such tools for artists seeking to develop anatomically complex characters.

The trend in deformation systems lies primarily in computationally expensive simulated layers of surfaces. As such, there are a number of existing techniques that cannot be performed interactively by the artist in real time and must be run as a postprocess with the skin solving after animation is complete. Solutions which cause muscle jiggle across the character in response to motion are typically simulated after the fact. Simulated solutions produce good results but are notoriously difficult to art-direct. While the paradigm for simulation often involves computational knowledge of the state of the system in the past and thus caching large amounts of data, we can expect advances in computing power to make this intense operation faster. Physics research will likely also develop faster ways of computing dynamically deforming surfaces. A rethinking of character deformation from the algorithmic level can also be expected. Drawing on biological models for muscle contraction and skin deformations, much research is going into the elasticity of modeled surfaces and systems of implementation. In a hypothetical world, a truly biological model could be developed that takes animation direction and triggers the correct muscles to carry that out, which in turn would manipulate the motion system to move the character element into the correct position per frame. We have a long way to go before naturalistic functioning such as this enters our workflow, but it is interesting to consider.

In the nearer future, we can expect smart algorithms that produce better deformation results with less manual labor. Building layered deformations or painting weights is an incredibly time-consuming task. The desired end result for a deformation system is visually pleasing surface deformations based on the aesthetics and technical limitations of the project. Although additive techniques such as skinning, blendshapes, and surface layers allow an artist to get to that point, the time and investment is large and often the character mobility is still limited. What artists crave is a single technique that gets the combined results of these techniques but is fast to set up and easy to maintain. By creating relationships between the vertices of a polygonal mesh, tension and relaxation methods can be implemented to move the vertices based on a surface-derived method and not based on direct response to the underlying driver. Generating a local co-ordinate system and a knowledge of a base pose will allow the surface to react to deformations but the surface will attempt to maintain the original per-vertex relationships to stay "on model." This drives the surface to maintain its original proportions and prevent common issues with loss of volume and collapsing regions. Combined with simple collision functionality to add underlying surfaces, a system such as this could maximize the results of skinning without the need to manually paint weights or define pose-space fixes. This notion of surface relaxation, although not always available in commercial software without a plugin, is becoming more commonplace. While there is no substitute for true multilayered anatomically derived deformations for creating the sense of surfaces moving over each other, this system, combined with underlying colliding surfaces, could produce anatomically convincing digital characters with little overhead.

Being able to create something that looks and seems real requires that we develop a deep understanding of the world around us and create novel techniques for creating it digitally. Scientists at Disney Research Zurich are doing just that for our understanding of the human eye [32]. The researchers developed a technique, which uses multiple cameras and varied lighting, to capture the shape and texture of the white sclera, the shape and refraction of the transparent cornea, and the shape and coloring of the iris. This also included capturing how the iris deforms as the pupil narrows and widens. All of this allows them to create very realistic 3D models of the human eye (Figure 31.1) which will be used to inform the modeling and animation of the eyes of digital characters in the future. This kind of innovation will have an impact for years and on productions to come.

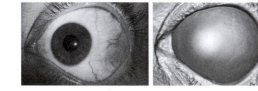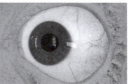

FIGURE 31.1 Eye-scanning technique from Disney Research Zurich. (Image created by Disney Research, © Disney).

Innovation may also come from rethinking how we build characters and the way we collaborate in doing the work. The modular work flow we have described for character technology development has simplified the back and forth that often happens when one person sets up a character motion system, another the deformation system, and yet another the face. These are all complicated, interconnected systems that influence each other during development and in running the character. Since the task is huge and the details voluminous, working collaboratively with experts in each system simultaneously is often a necessity.

One can imagine technology that integrates all of these systems more seamlessly and procedualizes the work to integrate them. This will likely fall into methods of abstracting the relationships and dependencies between systems so that the deformation system can be tuned regardless of changes to the motion system and vice versa. By defining the systems as a series of inputs and outputs, small bits of code can be defined to handle the changes between layers to keep them updated. At first, this would happen within strict limits of robustness, but over time one can foresee that this "sewing" process could be smarter and able to deal with larger modifications between stages. For example, consider the motion system step as a single procedure where its input is the collection of joints, controls, and constraints, and its output is simply the position of a subset of joints by which the deformation system is dependent. If these joints are procedurally placed and relatively transparent to the motion system developer, and the deformation system is defined to accept a collection of joints and output a deformed model, then ideally the work done at this step is abstracted and isolated from the other stages in a modular and insulated manner. This also allows artists to work on systems relatively concurrently. If the stages are relatively automated as well, then a change to the input data to a system can be procedurally handled and pave the way for any manual artistic decisions that may be needed. The point of all these steps is to get the technology out of the way of the artist so that they can get to their desired esthetic result faster without worrying about the process.

If we were to follow Matt Elson's [11] thoughts on the subject, the future of digital characters is autonomy. Without a doubt, this is on the horizon for digital characters. Expressiveness is in the hands of the skilled animator but the challenge that remains is procedural emotion. This, coupled with autonomy, will produce some interesting results. Autonomy puts decision-making in the hands of the digital character at runtime. Once the system starts, the character does what it wants. This will have a lot more relevance to interactive and real-time systems over prerendered animation projects. Film directors and animators producing shorts would likely be less interested in characters that did what they wanted in lieu of what was required of them for the scene. Even with live actors, directors give them limits and performance direction. While we have discussed procedural actors that work within those limits to create unique performances, an autonomous digital character with a "mind of its own" may be difficult to get the desired performance.

Autonomy really comes down to spontaneity and giving a character the ability to create impromptu performances based on their desires and knowledge of the world around them. Autonomy requires more than smartly triggering canned motions but actually generating those motions as needed based on a complex AI. This entails a higher level of sensing the world than we have seen thus far, possibly including variations on the human senses such as sight, touch, and hearing (maybe even taste and smell in the future), but even more basic functionality such as proprioception. Again, proprioception is the sense of the position of parts of the body. This provides feedback to the body internally and gives the organism a sense of where their limbs are in space and in relation to each other. As one would expect, spiders have a very keen internal system for proprioception. To illustrate the use of this sense, law enforcement officers often tests the functioning of one's proprioception to test sobriety. If a driver is unable to accurately touch their fingers to their nose while their eyes are closed, they are suffering from an impaired sense of proprioception and are more than likely intoxicated. The introduction of the proprioceptive system to digital characters implies that by giving characters a system that controls the relationship between their limbs, they can then make smart decisions as to where those limbs are at any moment with regard to balance, locomotion, and performance.

This local motion knowledge could be very powerful when applied to large numbers of characters. At the high level, crowd system agents often need to be "dumbed down" so that they behave heroically and not as a normal person would when confronted with and impossible situation or certain death. For films, local autonomy might be more appropriate where characters can make small decisions in an autonomous manner based on the direction of the system. Video games would be a completely different experience if the developers had no idea what the nonplayer characters (NPC) would do after they released the game. This is where innovation in this realm would radically transform digital characters from puppets that we animate, to entities that we need to contend with. What if a digital character in your system became better at building new games than the original designer. What games would digital characters build? What characters would a digital character design? This all, of course, gets fuzzy and intangible, sounding in many ways like cyberpunk fiction. One would like to think that we get to see these questions unfold over time.

As psychologists unravel more about emotion and how the human mind operates, we may start to see models which can be implemented into our autonomous character systems. While AI often deals with the notion of thinking, when we discuss emotion we are strictly dealing with feeling. While thinking can often be distilled down into logical blocks that can be envisioned by a programmer, feeling resides very much in the illogical and is intrinsically wrapped up with personality. These are difficult notions to implement into the logical structure of programming and why AI research is often tied to ideas of machine learning and large databases of questions and answers that a system can "learn." Modeling AI and autonomous characters as a replica of how the human mind works may not be the answer, especially when our knowledge of that subject is still evolving. So far, the best means we have to give emotion to a digital character is to put an actor, in the form of an animator, in its shoes. It is hard to top these results. As such, the development of autonomous characters has to be informed by animators and actors. For digital characters to be truly autonomous, they need to have the mind of an actor, and for stylization, the eye of an animator. This is a tough challenge. As we have mentioned, this is all runtime behavior that is dictated by the state of the system in which the character exists. What about a system that never starts or stops? As computing systems make their way into every aspect of our lives and network communication moves our data from a local hard drive to some easily accessible centralized network space, digital characters have the ability to exist on multiple platforms at once. This is a question that leads us into the notion of digital character ubiquity.

In parallel with improvements in character rigging and motion will be the growing ubiquity of digital characters in our lives. Digital characters will find their way into our homes. In the same way that voice-enabled driving direction systems have been implemented in cars, familiar avatars will assist us with the set up of new electronics, act as home messaging systems, and answer our questions. Would advertising agencies jump on the chance to send you product endorsements through a life-like system? Could movie trailers come to life in your living room? Have we scratched the surface of the notion of immersion in games? We have already seen attempts at personalizing help systems both in fictional films and books and research into human–computer interaction. Pop culture has given us a number of visions of how something like this could look. Is it a realistic projection that appears life-like in our homes? A high-end version of the little paperclip in Microsoft Office products? A hologram straight out of the world of *Star Wars* emerging from our mobile device or coffee table? Likely it is something completely novel. It is unclear as to whether a human face is an effective front-end for a ubiquitous information system, but there is little doubt that we will be seeing digital characters more often and in more places.

As we move from the future back to the present, we are obliged to recall the past and to remember the analog precursors of digital characters and the lessons that they still have to teach us.

FURTHER READING

It is interesting to think how the future of digital characters overlaps and relates to puppeteering, particularly the work of late Hollywood special effects wizard Stan Winston and his studio. Cynthia Breazeal, Director of MIT's Personal Robots Group collaborated with Winston in the creation of Leonardo, a compelling animatronic character which was used as a test bed for state-of-the-art research in autonomy and socially intelligent robots.

http://web.media.mit.edu/cynthiab/

Similarly, Hanson Robotics partnered with Massive Software (mentioned in the previous section) and use their crowd simulation software MASSIVE™ as part of the brain for their robot, Zeno. Using Massive, Zeno was able to analyze a 3D image of his environment to determine and control physical action and reactions. Massive Software's vision and decision-making components gave Zeno the ability to navigate, make facial expressions, and move his body based on what he saw in the physical environment. The video feed coming in from Zeno's eye camera is fed into the MASSIVE™ part of his brain so that he can move appropriately and respond emotionally to what is going on around him.

http://www.hansonrobotics.com/

Some interesting work from MotionPortrait creates 3D avatars for use on various platforms from a single photograph:

http://www.motionportrait.com/

Interview: Ken Perlin, Professor, Media Research Laboratory, Courant Institute of Mathematical Sciences, New York University

32.1 BIO

Ken Perlin, a professor in the Department of Computer Science at New York University, directs the NYU Games for Learning Institute, and a participating faculty member in the NYU Media and Games Network (MAGNET). He was also the founding director of the Media Research Laboratory and director of the NYU Center for Advanced Technology. His research interests include graphics, animation, augmented and mixed reality, user interfaces, science education, and multimedia. He received an Academy Award for Technical Achievement from the Academy of Motion Picture Arts and Sciences for his noise and turbulence procedural texturing techniques, which are widely used in feature films and television, as well as the 2008 ACM/SIGGRAPH Computer Graphics Achievement Award, the TrapCode award for achievement in computer graphics research, the NYC Mayor's award for excellence in Science and Technology and the Sokol award for outstanding Science faculty at NYU, and a Presidential Young Investigator Award from the National Science Foundation. Dr. Perlin currently serves on the program committee of the AAAS. He was general chair of the UIST2010 conference and has been a featured artist at the Whitney Museum of American Art.

Ken Perlin, Professor, Media Research Laboratory,
Courant Institute of Mathematical Sciences, New York University

Dr. Perlin received his PhD in Computer Science from New York University and a BA in theoretical mathematics from Harvard University. Before working at NYU, he was Head of Software Development at R/GREENBERG Associates in New York, NY. Prior to that he was the System Architect for computer-generated animation at Mathematical Applications Group, Inc. He serves on the Advisory Board for the Centre for Digital Media at GNWC and has served on the Board of Directors of both the New York chapter of ACM/SIGGRAPH and the New York Software Industry Association.

32.2 Q&A

Q: *The components of character technology are diverse and span the artistic and technical spectrum. How did you get your start in the industry? Based on where you see the field heading what experience/training do you recommend people have?*

A: I was lucky enough to start out in the industry working for a company, MAGI, that shortly thereafter ended up doing most of the animation for the original *TRON*. It was wonderful training. If that experience is any guide, I recommend finding and joining a small and exciting team of innovators, and then working very, very hard. ☺

Q: *Creating compelling digital characters is part art and part science. What is the greatest challenge you encounter on a daily basis? What aspect of character technology keeps you up thinking at night?*

A: Technology is easy, people are hard. Yes, you need to be completely immersed and in love with the technology—forward and inverse kinematics, dynamics, procedural rigging and skinning, A.I. methods, etc.—and be comfortable with the underlying math, but you need to be driven by the burning desire to bring characters to life.

Q: *What are the ingredients for a successful digital character?*

A: The character needs to be psychologically believable—not necessarily real, but believable. Think of animated characters you may have known and loved: maybe Bugs Bunny, Woody the Cowboy, Chihiro Ogino, Shrek, depending on your tastes, and then think of what their motivations were, why you were drawn to them, what made them interesting and complex? These are the elements that make for a great character, whatever the medium.

Q: *While the industry is competitive, it is ultimately respectful of great work. Outside of the work you have been personally involved in the production of, what animated characters have you been impressed or inspired by? What is the historical high-bar?*

A: To me the historical high bar in character animation is consistently set by the work of Studio Ghibli. I think the key is that they make stories involving deep and compelling characters, not stories and characters that have been dumbed down for some hypothetical attention-challenged audience. In my experience, both children and adults greatly appreciate being respected in this way. If digital animated characters could be more like Totoro and less like the standard hyper-kinetic and unrealistic American animated character, the industry will have a brighter and more interesting future.

Q: *Where do you see digital characters in 10 years? Where are animated characters for film and games heading?*

A: As the set of production tools—and therefore the great animation talent—shifts steadily toward procedural methods, digital characters will become less and less like traditional animation (where everything needs to be done frame by frame) and more like directable "smart puppets." Filmmaking and games will begin to merge, as these "actors," already having been infused with body language and emotional nuance by their creators, can be directed in real time with psychologically compelling results. This in turn will enable new and exciting forms of character and story creation and interaction, especially as augmented and virtual reality media become the norm for content delivery.

CHAPTER 33

Conclusions

A S WE HAVE TRAVERSED through the concepts and code that bring digital characters to life, we are reminded by how quickly this has all come together. Moore's Law stipulates that the transistor density of semiconductor chips would double roughly every 18 months, meaning that the chip complexity would also be proportional to this rate. While digital characters and their interactive potential is somewhat tied to the speed of the underlying system, the rate at which this technology advances is expected to improve the performance and potential expressiveness of digital characters not only related to the core functioning of the character, but also with regard to all the accessory aspects, such as real-time hair and clothing. Production has conquered anatomy; realistic characters can be created, animated, and rendered to be almost indistinguishable from their live counterparts. What remains, as we discussed previously, is the spirit and heart of the character.

When the original *King Kong* (1933) was released, it was a monumental event in cinema that ushered in a new era of film-making and audience expectation. At the same time, it was the first big monster on the screen as well as the first film in which the title character in the film was animated (Figure 33.1). This required that the character rise to the challenge of being viewed center stage and the creators knew that Kong would need to have an emotional impact on the audience. They wanted him to be fierce and sensitive at the same time. They wanted, at times, to convey humor. They wanted the audience to be terrified of him in the beginning and sobbing at his demise at the end. They achieved these benchmarks. We feel sympathy for Kong, and he has stood the test of time as a film icon. This legacy was founded heavily in the technology developed to produce the film and the planning and care taken with the animation of Kong himself. After the grueling manual process of animating the Kong puppets (a few rigs were produced), the character transcended the 18-inch metal frame, the foam and rubber padding and skin, and the rabbit fur exterior to become a living, breathing character that the audience could relate to. The design and construction was deeply informed by anatomy. When director

FIGURE 33.1 *King Kong* (1933). (© Hulton Archive/Getty Images.)

Merian C. Cooper saw effects artist Willis O'Brien's first and second concepts for Kong, he was greatly disappointed. He felt it looked too much like a cross between a man and a monkey. Cooper wired New York's American Museum of Natural History for the correct gorilla specifications and had O'Brien base his next concepts on them. The construction of the mechanical armature that Kong is animated with is very reminiscent of gorilla skeletal anatomy and much emphasis was placed on making sure the proportions, anatomy, and motion was entirely based on a real gorilla.

All the techniques that pioneering special effects artist O'Brien developed for the production ushered in the concepts that are still in place for visual effects today, including optics, composites, and miniatures. We live and work with modern analogies today, much of which are digital replacements of O'Brien's sophisticated analog solutions. Kong's creation, like that of most stop motion puppets, has many analogies to digital character development. The manipulatable metal armature provides the points of articulation and the limits of rotation of all the joints. This metal structure is ostensibly the motion system. Wrapped over this was a filling of foam covered with rubber that created the skin of the character which was deformed, with muscles even seeming to bulge, by the motion of the armature as the animators posed it. This is akin to the deformation system. Atop the rubber skin was a short trimmed layer of rabbit fur. While the modern analogy here would be character effects like fur, hair, or dynamic clothing, our computer-driven modern equivalents lacked the one thing that Kong's fur had: fingerprints. As the animators posed Kong from frame to frame they had no choice but to affect the fur as they touched it. Studio executives initially saw this as sloppy work until reviews of the film discussed the fur appearing to be blowing in the wind. The executives then decided they loved it.

The production of *King Kong* was kept a secret. The intention was to preserve the magic so that audiences would have no choice but to believe it was real. O'Brien was no stranger to magic. The dinosaurs he created and animated for Arthur Conan Doyle's *The Lost World* (1925) were presented by Doyle at a meeting of the Society of American Magicians in 1922. Magicians in the audience, including the great Harry Houdini and even the press, were astonished and tricked into believing that what they had seen at the meeting was real footage of live dinosaurs. Doyle explained the trick the next day and the "magic" of Willis O'Brien gained appreciation from an elite group.

Through the use of technology and character performance, O'Brien had tricked the professional illusionists and skeptics alike. While modern filmgoers have seen the impossible on a regular basis in the theaters, we continue to strive to astonish them with modern digital characters. The classic quote from the author Arthur C. Clarke states that, "Any sufficiently advanced technology is indistinguishable from magic." With regard to digital characters, the technology behind it is increasingly magical, but the true magic comes from the performance and the life breathed into characters by talented artists.

FURTHER READING

There are many books and video documentaries with accounts of the creation of the original *King Kong* but a good article by Tom Huntington for *American Heritage: Invention and Technology* is a great overview of the technology behind the production:

Huntington, T. 2006. King Kong: How the greatest special-effects movie was made with the simplest technology. *American Heritage: Invention and Technology* 21:3 (Winter).

References

1. Tim McLaughlin. Taxonomy of digital creatures: Interpreting character designs as computer graphics techniques. In *SIGGRAPH'05: ACM SIGGRAPH 2005 Courses*, ACM Press, New York, NY, 2005. p. 1.
2. Scott McCloud. *Understanding Comics: The Invisible Art*. HarperCollins Publishers, New York, NY, 1994.
3. Masahiro Mori. Bukimi no tani (the Uncanny Valley). *Energy* 7(4):33–35, 1970.
4. Roger Ebert. Final fantasy: The spirits within. *Chicago Sun Times*, July 11, 2001.
5. James C. Lester, Charles B. Callaway, Joël P. Grégoire, Gary D. Stelling, Stuart G. Towns, and Luke S. Zettlemoyer. Animated pedagogical agents in knowledge-based learning environments, In: *Smart Machines in Education*, Kenneth D. Forbus and Paul J. Feltovich (Eds.). MIT Press, Cambridge, MA, 2001, pp. 269–298.
6. James C. Lester, Sharolyn A. Converse, Susan E. Kahler, S. Todd Barlow, Brian A. Stone, and Ravinder S. Bhogal. The persona effect: Affective impact of animated pedagogical agents. In *CHI'97: Proceedings of the SIGCHI Conference on Human Factors in Computing Systems*, ACM Press, New York, NY, 1997. pp. 359–366.
7. Winslow Burleson. Affective learning companions: Strategies for empathetic agents with real-time multimodal affective sensing to foster meta-cognitive and meta-affective approaches to learning, motivation, and perseverance. PhD thesis, Adviser-Rosalind W. Picard, Cambridge, MA, 2006.
8. Frederick G. Conrad and Michael F. Schober. *Envisioning the Survey Interview of the Future (Wiley Series in Survey Methodology)*. Wiley-Interscience, Hoboken, NJ, 2007.
9. Frederick G. Conrad. Animated agents and user performance in interactive systems (research description). http://www.psc.isr.umich.edu/research/project-detail.html?ID=33983.
10. Katherine Isbister. *Better Game Characters by Design: A Psychological Approach (The Morgan Kaufmann Series in Interactive 3D Technology)*. Morgan Kaufmann Publishers Inc., San Francisco, CA, 2006.
11. Matt Elson. The evolution of digital characters. *Computer Graphics World* (September), 1999.
12. Isaac V. Kerlow. *The Art of 3D Computer Animation and Effects*, 3rd Edition. John Wiley & Sons, Hoboken, NJ, 2004.
13. Alvy Ray Smith. The making of Andre & Wally B. http://alvyray.com/Art/Andre&WallyB_The MakingOf.pdf, 1984.
14. Craig W. Reynolds. Flocks, herds, and schools: A distributed behavioral model. *Comput. Graph.* 21(4):25–34, 1987.
15. *Vanity Fair*, February, 1999.
16. Linden Labs. Second life. http://secondlife.com.
17. Guido van Rossum. Python. http://python.org.

18. Karim Biri Kiaran Ritchie, Jake Callery. *The Art of Rigging*, Vol. I. CG Toolkit, San Rafael, CA, 2005.

19. Karim Biri Kiaran Ritchie, Oleg Alexander. *The Art of Rigging*, Vol. II. CG Toolkit, San Rafael, CA, 2005.

20. Karim Biri Kiaran Ritchie, Oleg Alexander. *The Art of Rigging*, Vol. III. CG Toolkit, San Rafael, CA, 2006.

21. William T. Reeves. Inbetweening for computer animation utilizing moving point constraints. In *SIGGRAPH'81: Proceedings of the 8th Annual Conference on Computer Graphics and Interactive Techniques*, ACM Press, New York, NY, 1981. pp. 263–269.

22. Judy Foreman. A conversation with: Paul Ekman: The 43 facial muscles that reveal even the most fleeting emotions. *New York Times*, August 5, 2003.

23. Yi Lin. 3D character animation synthesis from 2D sketches. In *GRAPHITE'06: Proceedings of the 4th International Conference on Computer Graphics and Interactive Techniques in Australasia and Southeast Asia*, ACM Press, New York, NY, 2006. pp. 93–96.

24. Frank Thomas and Ollie Johnston. *The Illusion of Life: Disney Animation*. Disney Editions; Rev Sub edition (October 5, 1995), New York, NY, 1981.

25. John Lasseter. Principles of traditional animation applied to 3D computer animation. In *SIGGRAPH'87: Proceedings of the 14th Annual Conference on Computer Graphics and Interactive Techniques*, ACM Press, New York, NY, 1987. pp. 35–44.

26. John R. Hutchinson and Mariano Garcia. Tyrannosaurus was not a fast runner. *Nature* 415(6875):1018–1021, 2002.

27. Ken Perlin and Athomas Goldberg. Improv: A system for scripting interactive actors in virtual worlds. In *SIGGRAPH'96: Proceedings of the 23rd Annual Conference on Computer Graphics and Interactive Techniques*, ACM Press, New York, NY, 1996. pp. 205–216.

28. Boids (flocks, herds, and schools: A distributed behavioral model). View-source: http://www.red3d.com/cwr/boids/. Accessed on January 22, 2015.

29. Toni Conde and Daniel Thalmann. Autonomous virtual agents learning a cognitive model and evolving, In: *Lecture Notes in Computer Science, Themis Panayiotopoulos*, Jonathan Gratch, Ruth Aylett, Daniel Ballin, Patrick Olivier, and Thomas Rist (Eds.). Springer-Verlag, London, UK, 2005, pp. 88–98.

30. Daniel Thalmann, Christophe Hery, Seth Lippman, Hiromi Ono, Stephen Regelous, and Douglas Sutton. Crowd and group animation. In *GRAPH'04: Proceedings of the Conference on SIGGRAPH 2004 Course Notes*, ACM Press, New York, NY, 2004. p. 34.

31. Bill Tomlinson. From linear to interactive animation: How autonomous characters change the process and product of animating. *Comput. Entertain.* 3(1):5–5, 2005.

32. Pascal Bérard, Derek Bradley, Maurizio Nitti, Thabo Beeler, and Markus Gross. High-quality capture of eyes. *ACM Trans. Graph.* 33(6):223:1–223:12, 2014.

FURTHER READING

Irene Albrecht, Jörg Haber, and Hans-Peter Seidel. Construction and animation of anatomically based human hand models. In *SCA'03: Proceedings of the 2003 ACM SIGGRAPH/Eurographics Symposium on Computer Animation*, Aire-la-Ville, Switzerland, Switzerland, 2003. Eurographics Association, pp. 98–109.

Jennifer Greene Andrew Stellman. *Applied Software Project Management*. O'Reilly Media, Inc., Cambridge, MA, 2005.

Jim Bloom. Tippett studio muscle system and skin solver on *Hellboy*. In *SIGGRAPH'04: ACM SIGGRAPH 2004 Computer Animation Festival*, ACM, New York, NY, 2004. p. 250.

David M. Bourg. *Physics for Game Developers*. O'Reilly Media, Inc., Cambridge, MA. 2001.

David M. Bourg and Glenn Seemann. *AI for Game Developers*. O'Reilly Media, Inc., Cambridge, MA, 2004.

N. Burtnyk and M. Wein. Interactive skeleton techniques for enhancing motion dynamics in key frame animation. *Commun. ACM* 19(10):564–569, 1976.

Steve Capell, Matthew Burkhart, Brian Curless, Tom Duchamp, and Zoran Popoví. Physically based rigging for deformable characters. In *SCA'05: Proceedings of the 2005 ACM SIGGRAPH/Eurographics Symposium on Computer Animation*, ACM Press, New York, NY, 2005. pp. 301–310.

Thierry Chaminade, Jessica K. Hodgins, Joe Letteri, and Karl F. MacDorman. The uncanny valley of eeriness. In *SIGGRAPH'07: ACM SIGGRAPH 2007 Panels*, New York, NY, 2007. ACM Press, p. 1.

Edwin Chang and Odest Chadwicke Jenkins. Sketching articulation and pose for facial animation. In *SCA'06: Proceedings of the 2006 ACM SIGGRAPH/Eurographics Symposium on Computer Animation*, Aire-la-Ville, Switzerland, 2006. Eurographics Association, Geneve, Switzerland. pp. 271–280.

David S. Ebert, F. Kenton Musgrave, Darwyn Peachey, Ken Perlin, and Steven Worley. *Texturing and Modeling: A Procedural Approach*. Morgan Kaufmann Publishers Inc., San Francisco, CA, 2002.

Paul Ekman. An argument for basic emotions. In: *Basic Emotions*, N. L. a. O. Stein, K., (Ed.) Lawrence Erlbaum, Hove, UK, 1992. pp. 169–200.

Kenneth D. Forbus and Paul J. Feltovich, editors. *Smart Machines in Education: The Coming Revolution in Educational Technology*. MIT Press, Cambridge, MA, 2001.

David Gould. *Complete Maya Programming: An Extensive Guide to MEL and the C++ API (Morgan Kaufmann Series in Computer Graphics and Geometric Modeling)*. Morgan Kaufmann Publishers Inc., San Francisco, CA, 2003.

David Gould. *Complete Maya Programming. Vol. II: An In-depth Guide to 3D Fundamentals, Geometry, and Modeling (Morgan Kaufmann Series in Computer Graphics and Geometric Modeling)*. Morgan Kaufmann Publishers Inc., San Francisco, CA, 2005.

Yoram Gutfreund, Tamar Flash, Yosef Yarom, Graziano Fiorito, Idan Segev, and Binyamin Hochner. Organization of octopus arm movements: A model system for studying the control of flexible arms. *J. Neurosci.* 16(22):7297–7307, 1996.

Ed Hooks. *Acting for Animators*. Heinemann Publishing, Portsmouth, NH, 2001.

Tom Huntington. King Kong: How the greatest special-effects movie was made with the simplest technology. *American Heritage: Invention and Technology* 21, Winter 2006.

David Jacka, Ashley Reid, Bruce Merry, and James Gain. A comparison of linear skinning techniques for character animation. In *AFRIGRAPH'07: Proceedings of the 5th International Conference on Computer Graphics, Virtual reality, Visualisation and Interaction in Africa*, ACM Press, New York, NY, 2007. pp. 177–186.

Angie Jones and Jamie Oliff. *Thinking Animation: Bridging the Gap Between 2D and CG*. Course Technology PTR, Boston, MA. 2006.

Kenneth Kardong. *Vertebrates: Comparative Anatomy, Function, Evolution*, 4th Edition. McGraw-Hill Science, New York, NY, 2005.

Eric Keller. *Introducing ZBrush*. SYBEX Inc., Alameda, CA, 2008.

Vladislav Krayevoy and Alla Sheffer. Boneless motion reconstruction. In *SIGGRAPH'05: ACM SIGGRAPH 2005 Sketches*, ACM Press, New York, NY, 2005. p. 122.

J. P. Lewis, Matt Cordner, and Nickson Fong. Pose space deformations: A unified approach to shape interpolation and skeleton-driven deformation. In Kurt Akeley, editor, *Siggraph 2000, Computer Graphics Proceedings*. ACM Press/ACM SIGGRAPH/Addison Wesley Longman, New York, NY. 2000.

Matthew Liverman. *The Animator's Motion Capture Guide: Organizing, Managing, and Editing*. Charles River Media, Inc., Rockland, MA, 2004.

Mark Lutz. *Learning Python*, 3rd Edition. O'Reilly & Associates, Inc., Cambridge, MA, 2007.

Terrance Masson. *CG 101: A Computer Graphics Industry Reference*, 2nd Edition. Digital Fauxtography, Williamstown, MA, 2007.

Tim McLaughlin and Stuart S. Sumida. The morphology of digital creatures. In *SIGGRAPH'07: ACM SIGGRAPH 2007 Courses*, ACM Press, New York, NY, 2007. p. 1.

Albert Mehrabian and James A. Russell. *An Approach to Environmental Psychology*. MIT Press, Cambridge, MA, 1974.

Alberto Menache. *Understanding Motion Capture for Computer Animation and Video Games*. Morgan Kaufmann Publishers Inc., San Francisco, CA, 1999.

Alberto Menache and Alberto Manache. *Understanding Motion Capture for Computer Animation and Video Games*. Morgan Kaufmann Publishers Inc., San Francisco, CA, 1999.

Fiorenzo Morini, Barbara Yersin, Jonathan Maym, and Daniel Thalmann. Real-time scalable motion planning for crowds. In *CW'07: Proceedings of the 2007 International Conference on Cyberworlds*, Washington, DC, 2007. IEEE Computer Society, Alamitos, CA. pp. 144–151.

L. P. Nedel and D. Thalmann. Real time muscle deformations using mass-spring systems. In *CGI'98: Proceedings of the Computer Graphics International 1998*, Washington, DC, 1998. IEEE Computer Society, Alamitos, CA. p. 156.

Michael O'Rourke. *Principles of Three-Dimensional Computer Animation: Modeling, Rendering, and Animating with 3D Computer Graphics*. W. W. Norton & Co., Inc., New York, NY, 1998.

Jason Osipa. *Stop Staring: Facial Modeling and Animation Done Right*. SYBEX Inc., Alameda, CA, 2007.

Rick Parent. *Computer Animation, 2nd Edition: Algorithms and Techniques (The Morgan Kaufmann Series in Computer Graphics)*. Morgan Kaufmann Publishers Inc., San Francisco, CA, 2007.

Ken Perlin. An image synthesizer. *SIGGRAPH Comput. Graph.* 19(3):287–296, 1985.

Jason Patnode. *Character Modeling With Maya And ZBrush*. Focal Press, San Francisco, CA, 2008.

Michael Pratscher, Patrick Coleman, Joe Laszlo, and Karan Singh. Outside-in anatomy based character rigging. In *SCA'05: Proceedings of the 2005 ACM SIGGRAPH/Eurographics Symposium on Computer Animation*, ACM Press, New York, NY, 2005. pp. 329–338.

James A. Russell. Reading emotions from and into faces: Resurrecting a dimensional-contextual perspective. In *The Psychology of Facial Expression*, Russell, J. and Fernandez-Dols, J. (Eds.), Cambridge University Press, Cambridge, UK, 1997, pp. 295–320.

Mario Russo. *Polygonal Modeling: Basic and Advanced Techniques (Worldwide Game and Graphics Library)*. Wordware Publishing Inc., Plano, TX, 2005.

Ferdi Scheepers, Richard E. Parent, Wayne E. Carlson, and Stephen F. May. Anatomy-based modeling of the human musculature. In *SIGGRAPH'97: Proceedings of the 24th Annual Conference on Computer Graphics and Interactive Techniques*, ACM Press/Addison-Wesley Publishing Co., New York, NY, 1997. pp. 163–172.

Thomas W. Sederberg and Scott R. Parry. Free-form deformation of solid geometric models. In *SIGGRAPH'86: Proceedings of the 13th Annual Conference on Computer Graphics and Interactive Techniques*, ACM Press, New York, NY, 1986. pp. 151–160.

Francisco J. Seron, Rafael Rodriguez, Eva Cerezo, and Alfredo Pina. Adding support for high-level skeletal animation. *IEEE Trans. Vis. Comput. Graph.*, 8(4):360–372, 2002.

Alla Sheffer and Vladislav Kraevoy. Pyramid coordinates for morphing and deformation. In *3DPVT'04: Proceedings of the 3D Data Processing, Visualization, and Transmission, 2nd International Symposium*, Washington, DC, 2004. IEEE Computer Society, Alamitos, CA. pp. 68–75.

Susan Standring. *Gray's Anatomy: The Anatomical Basis of Clinical Practice*. Churchill Livingstone, New York, NY, 2004.

Nadia Magnenat Thalmann and Daniel Thalmann. Computer animation. *ACM Comput. Surv.* 28(1):161–163, 1996.

Bill Tomlinson and Bruce Blumberg. Synthetic social relationships in animated virtual characters. In *ICSAB: Proceedings of the Seventh International Conference on Simulation of Adaptive Behavior on From Animals to Animats*, MIT Press, Cambridge, MA, 2002. pp. 401–402.

James Van Verth and Lars Bishop. *Essential Mathematics for Games and Interactive Applications: A Programmer's Guide*. Morgan Kaufmann Publishers Inc., San Francisco, CA, 2004.

Tim D. White. *Human Osteology*. Academic Press, New York, NY, 2000.

Mark R. Wilkins and Chris Kazmier. *MEL Scripting for Maya Animators, 2nd Edition (The Morgan Kaufmann Series in Computer Graphics)*. Morgan Kaufmann Publishers Inc., San Francisco, CA, 2005.

Richard Williams. *The Animator's Survival Kit*. Faber & Faber, London, 2001.

Yoram Yekutieli, Roni Sagiv-Zohar, Ranit Aharonov, Yaakov Engel, Binyamin Hochner, and Tamar Flash. Dynamic model of the octopus arm. I. Biomechanics of the octopus reaching movement. *J. Neurophysiol.*, 94(2):1443–1458, 2005.

John M. Zelle. *Python Programming: An Introduction to Computer Science*. Franklin Beedle & Associates, Wilsonville, OR, 2003.

Victor Brian Zordan, Bhrigu Celly, Bill Chiu, and Paul C. DiLorenzo. Breathe easy: Model and control of simulated respiration for animation. In *SCA'04: Proceedings of the 2004 ACM SIG-GRAPH/Eurographics Symposium on Computer Animation*, Aire-la-Ville, Switzerland, 2004. Eurographics Association, New York, NY. pp. 29–37.

Index